The Good
and the Realm of Values

The Good
and the Realm of Values

DONALD WALHOUT

UNIVERSITY OF NOTRE DAME PRESS
NOTRE DAME ∾ LONDON

Library of Congress Cataloging in Publication Data

Walhout, Donald.
　The good and the realm of values

　Includes bibliographical references.
　1. Values. 2. Good and evil. 3. Perfection
(Philosophy) I. Title.
BD232.W27　　　121'.8　　　　77-89757
ISBN 0-268-00997-X

Manufactured in the United States of America

To
Paul Weiss
and in memory of
Theodore M. Greene,
former teachers at Yale

Contents

Preface

In this book I endeavor to formulate a coherent and applicable theory of value based on the classical notion of perfection but with important revisions drawn from contemporary modes of thought. The chief classical contributor to the theory is Aristotle, or at least what has come to be called the Aristotelian tradition. This is simply a general identification, however, since my purpose is a systematic argument and not a historical exposition. In any case, the approach is greatly modified in these pages by the influence of theistic metaphysics, modern psychological developments, and contemporary phenomenological, existential, ethical, and linguistic interests in philosophy. The term "perfectivism" is chosen as a technical label for the theory; but more widely the theory belongs within the overall metaphysical and valuational orientation of theistic and personalistic realism.

Two other points of general orientation should be mentioned. One is that my approach moves neither within the empirical inquiry into value phenomena nor within the isolated analysis of value words, important and prominent as these movements have been in twentieth-century philosophy. Rather my concern is with normative philosophy of value as this has been traditionally considered an adjunct to, or even a part of, philosophical ethics. The other point is that I have not tried to dissociate metaphysical considerations completely from philosophy of value. Obviously man has relationships to the rest of reality, and it would seem unduly restrictive, if not misleading, to avoid reflection upon them in our efforts to understand the good.

The central argument of the book may be said to run, in briefer form, through chapters 1, 5, 6, and 9 and 10, which deal, respectively, with the good in general, the right, human values,

and the idea of nonhuman good. These are, I suppose, the perennial topics in the philosophy of value, regardless of the orientation or methodology adopted to investigate them. From this
standpoint, the other chapters deal with special questions related
to the main topics. Some readers might wish to proceed in this
order.

The larger organization of the book, however, proceeds in
three stages: first, a general statement of the perfection theory
of the good; second, a normative account of various questions regarding human value; and third, speculation and analysis on the
topic of good beyond the human realm. A concluding chapter
then seeks to answer assorted types of criticism that have been
made, or might be made, against the sort of theory elaborated
and defended throughout the book.

In the general statement of the first chapter I attempt to re-
formulate the classical Aristotelian idea of perfection or excellence or fulfillment of being as the key to the nature of the good.
I do not think that in the end we can define the good apart from
reference to conscious experience or some relation to conscious
experience. Thus one stock criticism of the perfection theory,
namely, that it misreads valuation by denying this relation to
consciousness, is inapplicable here. But within this general framework much room for interpretation is possible, and we need to
ask what precisely is it in conscious experience or the relation to
conscious experience that constitutes the good. Later chapters
explore this problem in detail, as well as comment on other approaches.

Part 2, on human values, deals with three sorts of topics. First,
in chapter 2 I discuss the subjective origin of valuation and propose a classification of modes of valuation based on the subject's
various relationships to the actual world. Some cultural embodiments of these modes of valuation are also suggested to illustrate their character. Second, I discuss several traditional philosophical questions about human value, namely, what is the nature
of human value, what is the norm or ground of value judgments,
and how can human values be classified and related to choice. These
questions are taken up, respectively, in chapters 3, 4, and 6.

The nature of value is held to be best explained through reference to man's needs and capacities. The norm of value judgments
is claimed to be the ideal of harmonious perfecting. The classification of human values is based upon the four modes of valuation—
theocentric, natural, moral, and intellectual—discussed in chapter 2,
and, following this, various principles for choosing among values are

proposed. Third, three important traditional values—moral, esthetic, and religious values—are selected for particular treatment. Obviously many other values, such as political or intellectual values, could be singled out for this same purpose; but I have limited this phase of the discussion to these three.

One alteration in order of chapters from the above outline should be mentioned. The chapter on moral value or ethics, chapter 5, has been placed before the chapter on kinds of value because of a judgment that the sort of ethical theory with which the classification of values is associated in the entire account would be relevant first. I should also add that I have chosen to handle the chapter on ethics through a critical study of A. C. Garnett's ethical theory, rather than independently, because of several crucial insights of Garnett which I believe are very helpful to the perfectivist value theory. These include the concept of perfection of voluntary conduct as a norm, the proposal purporting to overcome the conflict between naturalism and nonnaturalism in ethics, and the skillful combining of classical notions and current analysis. I discuss esthetic and religious value in the same chapter, chapter 7, because the challenge to compare and contrast them is inviting.

In part 3 I attempt to extend the relational, perfective conception of good, discussed in part 2, to the nonhuman realm. In chapter 8 I first collect a large number of testimonials to the good that people have felt characterize natural things and the world as a whole. I do not look on them as evidence or proof of intrinsic nonhuman good but simply as good reasons for taking such a claim seriously. Then in chapters 9 and 10 I give a more systematic and more speculative account of how the perfective notion of good might be interpreted in the case of nonhuman things. In this context the idea of instrumental good can be formulated without reference to consciousness; but to say the nonhuman is intrinsically good does require, I shall maintain, a relation to consciousness and ultimately a theistic orientation in metaphysics. Chapter 11 deals with the special case of the term "good" when applied to God and also completes the discussion of good in the cosmic order. This entire part adds a speculative emphasis to the previous normative emphasis.

The answers to objections in chapter 12, as well as elsewhere in the book, add a critical emphasis to the previous two emphases. Thus the entire work may be said to be at once normative, speculative, and critical.

To speak of the applicability of a normative theory of value is to speak of it as a guide for practical life. This means mainly the articulation of those values and value priorities which it is reasonable to embody and foster in a rational plan of life. We need to clarify what things to aim at in order to act intelligently. This is the function of all normative value theories as an adjunct to practical ethics. In addition, a perfection theory of value will focus on the needs and capacities inherent in man's nature which ought to be discovered and fulfilled; on the ideal of self-fulfillment for every person; on the wider aim of harmonious perfecting in the community of persons; on the worth of created beings other than man; and on the relationships between self and world within which man must live and move in order to have his being more abundantly. The best guidance of course depends on what is true or at least reasonable or plausible.

Besides this perennial connection between theory and practice, there are specific policy questions that confront each age. We need only mention the concern with value education and the rise of ecology to realize the importance of value clarification for our own time. We can hardly underscore values in education without inquiring into what we want to underscore, and we may not be able to solve environmental problems without a revised attitude toward the good in nature. Our own discussion remains at the theoretical level, for such practical questions belong properly to a further study. But there must be normative thinking for practical acting.

Several portions of the book are adaptations of previously published articles of mine. Chapter 1 is an expansion of "A Perfection Theory of Good," in *Philosophy*. The last section of chapter 4 is from "Why Should I Be Moral?—A Reconsideration," in *The Review of Metaphysics*. Chapter 5 is an expansion of "Garnett's New Analysis of Ethical Concepts," in *Ethics*. Chapter 9 is a revision of "Nonhuman Value," in *The Journal of Religion*. Grateful acknowledgment is here made to these journals for permission to adapt this material.

I wish to thank collectively all those authors, teachers, and students who through the years have provoked my thought on these matters. I also wish to thank, for different kinds of support, my family, Rockford College, and the editorial staff of the University of Notre Dame Press.

Donald Walhout
Rockford, Illinois

PART ONE

Preliminary Statement of Theory

1: A Perfection Theory of the Good

In this chapter I wish to set forth in a preliminary way the main concept in a theory of the good which seems to me more plausible than any of those now current. The perfection theory of the good can claim weighty historical roots, especially in Plato and Aristotle; but I shall proceed systematically rather than historically. The exposition of the theory will be presented in three parts: first, a statement of a generic definition of perfection; second, an attempt to give a more specific content to the definition; and third, an indication of my reasons for upholding the truth of the theory. I shall add, in conclusion, some terminological considerations that will be helpful in employing this notion of perfection in the discussions of value to follow.

I am using the word "good" as a noncommittal term at first, simply to mark off the subject matter under discussion. Precisely because of its many meanings, the word can be used in this way, for it is not likely to convey anything too specific. Nevertheless, "good" has so many human connotations that I need to make one assumption explicit at the outset. This assumption is that it is meaningful to say that "good," both in the instrumental and in the intrinsic sense, might refer to nonhuman and perhaps even to nonconscious beings as well as to human beings. I shall not argue here that such a doctrine of the universal extent of good is a true doctrine but will only assume that it is a doctrine worth considering. I do not wish the term "good," therefore, initially to preclude this possibility. I shall repeat this point at the end, within the context then available.

3

The Definition of Perfection

It will seem at first that to define the good as perfection is simply to replace one vague term by another and to raise the same question of meaning with different words. Consequently, we must proceed directly to an understanding of the nature of perfection, which will justify us in using "perfection" as more than an empty synonym for "good" and as actually designating instead a meaningful and possibly true theory of the good. We can then say that the good is something discovered by experience and that the perfection theory seems to be the most adequate conception of what that good essentially is.

There is a fruitful suggestion for our definition in a discussion of perfection by Charles Hartshorne. Interestingly enough, the suggestion comes from a meaning of perfection which Hartshorne himself considers unimportant and therefore confines to an appendix.[1] Hartshorne begins by defining perfection in its broadest sense as unsurpassability. This definition seems clear and simple enough; a thing is perfect if it cannot be surpassed in whatever characteristics or attainments are peculiar to it. Hartshorne then distinguishes two kinds of perfection, absolute and relative.[2] A being is said to be *absolutely* perfect if it cannot be surpassed in any respect by any being whatsoever, even by itself. On the other hand, a being is said to be *relatively* perfect if it cannot be surpassed in any respect by any other being besides itself, but may surpass itself in some respect. This distinction is employed by Hartshorne to differentiate the God of Scholastic theism from the God of many modern forms of theism. In the discussion of this theological issue, he deliberately leaves out of account two other logical possibilities concerning surpassability and unsurpassability which he recognizes. These other two possibilities are, first, the possibility that a being cannot be surpassed by itself but might be surpassed by other beings and, second, the possibility that a being is surpassable both by others and by itself. A logically exhaustive classification of possibilities is stated by Hartshorne as follows:

> The four modes of surpassability are: surpassability (1) by both self and others, B; (2) by self only (unsurpassability "relative" to others), R; (3) by others only, O; (4) by neither self nor others ("absolute" unsurpassability), A.[3]

Mr. Hartshorne rightly confines himself in his particular inquiry to modes 2 and 4, R and A, as being the only possibilities relevant to the idea of God; for no one would describe God as surpassable by other beings. I think we may also say that these possibilities are relevant exclusively to God, or whatever is taken as supreme. They would in any case have no wide application, since most beings seem to be surpassable by others, quite apart from reference to deity. Again, mode 1, B, is really a definition of imperfection and hence not useful for our purpose either. But in mode 3, O, we find precisely the meaning which will give us the most universally applicable and therefore the most satisfactory generic definition of perfection. According to this conception, anything is perfect when it has fulfilled the limits of its capacities, although it might be surpassed by some other being. This definition describes the perfection of any being except the highest or supreme.

The elaboration which the definition requires must be given briefly. We may begin with the unobjectionable statement that everything which exists is distinguished by certain characteristics, powers, and potentialities. To be a being at all is to be characterized by distinguishing traits and tendencies. Furthermore, it seems equally reasonable to suppose that such potentialities and traits have, for any given being, finite limits. What these limits are may be impossible to determine in a given case; but that there are definite bounds would appear to be ingredient in the very meaning of being an individual entity. The conclusion in this sequence of thought is then the inference that the perfection of anything means the attainment in actual fact of the possibilities latent in that creature. When a being has reached the supreme limit of its potentiality—when, in other words, it is unsurpassable by itself any further (although, of course, it might still be surpassed by some other being)—then it has achieved perfection. The agency by which this perfection is reached need not detain us. The agency might come from within the being itself, or it might come from the outside; or both types might be involved. Nor need we be detained by the fact that many beings seem to have no potentiality for development; momentary or enduring, they are what they are, once and for all, without increasing toward perfection. The main point is that all beings, including these, have the common characteristic that however and whenever they reach their self-surpassable limit, that is their perfection.

Such, then, is the meaning of perfection—the unsurpassability of a being relative to itself. My contention is that this is what is essentially meant by the notion of intrinsic good.

Perfection in Existence

The definition of perfection just given is straightforward enough but general. We must therefore attempt to capture something of the specific content of perfection, something of what it involves in the actual world of existing individuals. Incidentally, I think it is evident that a perfection theory of this sort presupposes a world of real individuals. It does not seem to be compatible with a doctrine which denies the ultimacy of individuals and resolves them into the universal. Furthermore, it appears equally evident to me that our world is the type presupposed. This is a strenuous metaphysical question which would have to be argued at more length in another connection, but which cannot be so pursued here. We will confine ourselves to the claim that the denial of the ultimacy of individuals can never overcome the existential absurdity which such a denial makes of both our everyday experience in the world of things and our experience of ourselves as persons. With this presupposition, then, the endeavor to grasp something of the individual context of perfection becomes meaningful. Let us make this endeavor by noting three significant contrasts and emphasizing the third. These contrasts are those of the actual and the ideal, individuality and form, and structure and function. They are relevant to every instance of perfection (except the highest, as always understood here).

We may approach the first contrast by taking notice, first of all, of a principle of existence which Spinoza enunciated in a way that has become classic. Every entity, according to him, tends toward the preservation of its own being. If we add to this principle a normative connotation, we may say that every being tends toward its essential being, toward what it can ideally become. In living creatures this tendency takes the form of an active striving, a striving to actualize or attain those characteristics and potentialities which will make the creature more fully itself, or, rather, more fully what it can become. It may be thought anthropomorphic to impute a similar striving to inanimate things; so I hasten to add that the tendency in question need not be thought of as homogeneous in the same sense throughout nature. In some areas it might mean no more than the persistency of identity. On the other hand, it can be plausibly maintained that there is no sufficient warrant for supposing that there is a real break in nature between the living and the nonliving, between entities which have some sort of internal directional activity and entities which do not. For our purpose, this possible difference may be waived, for our theory of the good does not rest upon the solution of that issue; it will be the same on either alternative.

Now the mention of a tendency to exemplify, or a striving to realize, inherent possibilities immediately reminds us of the extreme disparity, which is so frequent, between the present state of an entity and its possibility for becoming. This disparity is most obvious in ourselves, since our own failings, which detract from the fulfillment of ourselves and of others, are in most cases only too painfully vivid to us. But it is also true that the creatures of nature are often less than they might be; and the same may be said of artificial creations. The actual is but a faint imitation of the ideal. Now it is this very disparity between the actual and the ideal, between the present stalemate and the beckoning possibility, that yields perhaps the most illuminating impression of what the doctrine of the good as perfection refers to in the world of existence. Here am I; yonder is my real self.

At this point it would be well to clarify the use of the term "real self" or "essential self," which is a key concept and one that will be employed in several places later in the book. It is common to recognize two meanings of the term "essential self": (1) what constitutes the self as it is and (2) what comprises the self as it ought to be. These meanings may be called the ontological essence and the moral essence. The ontological essence connotes those characteristics, such as consciousness, bodily relatedness, personality, rationality, and moral capacity, which are required in order to be a human person at all.[4] The moral essence connotes those virtues and attainments which the self ought to cultivate, allowing for the fact that the self might do otherwise and still be a self in the ontological sense, that is, a morally bad self but still retaining the ontological essence of selfhood. Now the way I shall be using the term "essential self" does not correspond exactly to either of these meanings taken by themselves. Let us call this third meaning the valuational essence. It includes, of course, the ontological essence, for otherwise there would be no human person at all. It also includes the moral essence as its focus of emphasis. That is, it designates what the self ought to be, morally. But what I want to stress in addition is that this moral essence is somehow more native, more natural, to the human person than is its opposite. It is more native in the sense that this is the self that *would develop*, normally and progressively, if there were not the inner and outer obstacles to the self's fulfillment that there in fact are. It is the realization that *would be* the culmination of the ontological essence if it were not for deflection and perversion. The valuational essence is therefore more ontologically rooted in the self than is the "morally bad self." The essential self in this valuational sense is indeed the self that should be striven for morally; but there is more to it than just a set of independent good qualities that are obligatory: there is an ontological mooring involved as well as a moral demand. Thus every self can remain a self, ontologically, whether good or bad, morally; but only the realization of the essential self in the valuational sense will put the self in its most characteristic, most "normal," state.

This usage of terms can be effectively compared with Karen Horney's distinction between the actual self, the idealized self, and the real self.[5] The real self, in her usage, is not just a moral demand; it is the self that really would eventuate from a person's growth if it were not for neurotic tendencies and drawbacks. Dr. Horney is writing as a psychologist, of course, whereas I wish to assert an ontological point, and there is not an exact correlation among the distinctions made. But there is an interesting analogy in usage here with respect to the essential self.

The metaphysical anchorage of this concept of the valuational essence will differ according to different systems. A Platonic model would place essential selfhood among the eternal forms of things. An Aristotelian outlook would find it in the natural teleology inherent in the universe. A theistic metaphysics would locate it in the purpose willed for every self as well as in the natural directiveness of created selves. Meanwhile, apart from the metaphysical system involved, I think the experiential evidence of man's career supports such a notion.

Unless otherwise specified, then, we shall have this valuational essence in mind when we speak of the essential self. It is the moral essence conceived of as having ontological priority, because it is rooted in the very tendencies and longings of the ontological self.

All of these meanings are different from what is today called, in the possible-world semantics of modal logic, the individual essence.[6] The question there is whether an individual has any identical properties in all possible worlds in which it exists, which properties constitute its unique individuality, quite apart from any general essences that involve other individuals. This metaphysical question is beyond our compass here, since we shall be concerned for the most part with the actual world.

This is one way, then, of clarifying our definition of perfection, namely, by focusing upon the contrast between the actual and the ideal. For a being to overcome this disparity, to achieve the ideal, to realize the utmost promise inherent within it: these are so many ways of describing what constitutes the highest perfection or excellence within that limited realm of possibility. The ideal is reached at the point of unsurpassability in attainment, the limit beyond which the creature cannot go, although it might be surpassed in any given respect by some other being with greater potentiality. This ideal attainment is the intrinsic good of the being in question, and whatever conduces to it is instrumentally good for it.

Another contrast which is fundamental is that between individuality and form. Every being has features of potentiality and goal which it shares with other creatures of its kind. This is its generic essence or form. But it also has such features which are unique to itself; otherwise there would be no real individuals. These unique features give it its particular existence or individuality. The Greek doctrine of perfection referred only to the form; individuality was ignored. The Scholastic doctrine included an emphasis upon the individuality of personal selves but not of other beings. But if individuals are in any sense ultimate, it seems to me that it would be metaphysically more consistent to maintain that a perfection of individuality, as well as of form, is universally possible. If we are to take individuality seriously, there must be a perfection of individually unique qualities as well as of formal characteristics. An ontological corollary would be the belief in individual essences besides generic ones, as in Plotinus. Thus a being might (or might not) be perfect in its generic essence, and it might (or might not) be perfect in its individual characters.

Our third clarificatory contrast may be regarded as giving a more specific definition of the concept of perfection. This contrast is that of structure and function, that is, what a being is and what it does. I think we may say that the intrinsic nature of anything can be exhaustively comprehended under these two aspects: the aspect of composition, organization, or structure, on the one hand, and the aspect of purpose, directional activity, or function, on the other. And if the nature of a being is comprised in these two aspects, then the perfection of that being will consist in the perfection of these aspects. This is why they yield a more specific definition of perfection. Before we consider the criteria by which the perfection of structure and of function are to be judged, however, two parenthetical remarks need to be inserted.

One remark is in response to the objection that the function of inanimate things, especially artificial creations, is definable only by reference to human purposes, that is, that their function is not intrinsic. I think it is appropriate to say that, even if it is true that there are some entities with no function natural to them, no internal directional activity (a proposition which, however, as already pointed out, is by no means self-evident to all [for example, Whitehead in his philosophy of organism]), the function of such an entity, even though derivative from some purposer or willer, is still an intrinsic part of what it means to be that entity. We can still speak of the defining function peculiar to that entity.

The other remark is that the factors of individuality and form, previously mentioned, apply to both structure and function. A being has a formal and an individualized character in its structure or composition, and it may have a generic and an existentially unique side in its function or purpose.

Now concerning the criteria for judging the perfection of structure and function, let us consider structure first. Three criteria seem to be most prominent in our judgments on this head. I shall call them purity, harmony, and richness.[7] In the first place, a structurally perfect entity will have parts which are well developed and free from defect. Secondly, the parts will be effectively interrelated; the composition, organization, or arrangement of parts will be harmoniously integrated. Finally, it will have as rich a variety of content, as wide a scope, as its nature permits. These three criteria may not be equally significant in every case, but together they appear to constitute the substance of our notion of structural perfection.

In describing the perfection of structure in this way, we may be led to think primarily of inanimate objects, such as landscapes or jewels. This is partly a fault of language. Our language (especially such words as "structure" and "parts") is simply not adapted to convey the vitality and dynamic character of living organisms and human beings. Nevertheless, I think the criteria mentioned are useful categories for characterization in these latter realms as well. I believe it is instructive to describe the structural perfection of plants and animals as consisting in these three factors: effective development of parts, harmonious interaction of parts, and breadth of resources. And certainly the ideal of human selfhood includes (1) the undeteriorated manifestation of those faculties and qualities which are distinctive of man and of the individual person, (2) the unity and integration of personality, and (3) variety and depth of experience. All of these examples are different instances of what we have for brevity called purity, harmony, and richness of composition.

On the functional side, the two criteria which appear most central are proficiency and economy. The first thing we want to know about the performance of anything is whether or not it is successful, whether or not the purpose has been fully accomplished. Has the function or aim actually been achieved? But we also judge perfection here by the extent to which the result has been achieved economically, with minimum deterioration or dissipation of the being in question. A person may achieve proficiency in functioning, but at great cost to the personality. Hence the dual criterion is relevant. The criteria of functional perfection also find ready illustration in the inanimate, the living, and the human realms. The determination of what the function of a given being is may be impossible or at best disputable; and it generally involves a nonempirical value judgment. But this would be a question of specialized application and does not affect the suggested criteria for evaluating functional perfection in general.

In summary, we may say that the perfection of an individual being, meaning the unsurpassability of that being relative to itself, comprises purity, harmony, and richness of structural composition, and proficiency and economy of functional achievement. With this brief discussion we conclude our endeavor to make the perfection theory of good more specific. There remains the problem of validation.

The Rationale of the Theory

In lieu of a proof for the theory of good just explained, whatever that might involve in a philosophical context, I would like simply to identify some of the dialectical considerations which lead me to believe that the perfection theory illuminates our understanding of the good more adequately than do alternative theories. I shall confine myself here to the human good, even though my previous descriptions have been arranged to include nonhuman good as well, should that be regarded as a plausible line of inquiry.

In the human realm we shall be referring, of course, to the perfection of the self, or, more simply, to self-fulfillment, as the intrinsic good. It will first be necessary to turn aside some misunderstandings which often occur at this point. To begin with, self-fulfillment, as the good, does not mean that any and every expression of the self is justified, that every outrageous and pernicious action now becomes good. Self-fulfillment refers to the attainment of the essential self. Without this distinction between the essential self and the present self, I do not think we can make sense out of the experience of the actual and the ideal alluded to earlier, nor, indeed, out of the import of responsibility. Another misunderstanding is that self-fulfillment, being the intrinsic good of an individual, must be thought of as good from every viewpoint, so that a person now has the right to drive to his own self-realization no matter what. Ideally this may be so, because ideally one's perfection is not attainable apart from all others'. But in our world it is not so. What may seem to be the intrinsic good of one person may have to be curtailed for a higher end, either voluntarily or forcefully. Moral choices are often choices between different intrinsic goods. But in this respect the perfection theory is no different from other theories. Every theory must face the issue of moral choices between different intrinsic goods, not all attainable.

Turning to more positive considerations, I submit, in the first place, that alternative theories of the good tend to be too limited in their scope. I think we may fairly classify the many theories of human good according to whether they claim the good to consist in some form of right knowing, right willing, right enjoyment, or self-fulfillment. The alternatives to the perfection theory tend to magnify one of these functions of the self and to discount other important functions, or at least to subordinate their distinctiveness. The distinctive values of intellect and moral will can hardly be reduced to enjoyment: hedonism has been refuted a thousand times. Likewise, the other possible subsumptions are awkwardly managed. All of these goods, however, so far as they are good, are comprehended in the meaning of self-fulfillment. They are various aspects in the good of perfection. The view of certain latter-day utilitarians, who hold that there are a number of intrinsic goods besides happiness, such as knowledge, virtue, beauty, etc., a synthesis of which constitutes the highest good, seems to me merely a splintered, more abstract and inadequate version of the doctrine of good as self-fulfillment.

In the second place, I think that philosophical speculation about the good of the individual should learn more from those human activities which are directly concerned, in an existential way, with securing the good of the individual. Most prominent among these activities are those relating to psychology, social work, and religion, which are all concerned with the "cure of the soul." It seems to me that self-fulfillment is increasingly recognized in these fields as the standard for judging the good of the individual. They may differ widely as to the exact nature of this ideal self and as to the types of relationship through which the ideal is reached, but they tend to agree that the discovery and perfection of those potentialities which are most basic to the self comprise the intrinsic human good. Eric Fromm, for instance, basing his views upon his clinical work, makes this goal his primary emphasis.[8] Similarly, I think it is safe to say that responsible workers in religion and social work find concepts like "self-discovery," "being one's true self," and the like more meaningful than concepts like "balance of pleasures" or "synthesis of goods." Such practical relevance lends weighty evidence to the self-fulfillment theory of good.

As a third consideration, I would suggest that the perfection theory is best able to reconcile the absolute and the relative characteristics which are generally recognized to qualify the good. All theories which hold that judgments of good can be true as well as emotive maintain, on the one hand, that there is an ultimate nature of the good which is relevant to everyone and to which everyone's judgments must conform in order to be true. On the other hand, they recognize the good to be exemplified only in individuals, to be peculiarly one's own, to be relative to a particular person. There is at once a common meaning and an indefinite variety in the good. It seems to me that the self-fulfillment theory is ready-made to express this double character of the good, absoluteness and relativity, whereas other theories are too prone to ignore one pole. Hedonism, for instance, finds great difficulty in allowing variety of pleasure. The theory of right willing tends to suggest universal commands and to minimize the individual character of obligation. The good, regarded as a synthesis of various intrinsic goods, tends to lose sight of the particular individual altogether. The perfection theory, on the contrary, maintains unambiguously that there is a meaning and standard of good applicable to everyone, but that the content of the good in concrete existence varies with every individual according to his unique capacities, so that while there may be many common aspects in the good, it may also be radically diverse.

Finally, I would like to recur to the assumption that was made in the beginning: that it is meaningful to regard the doctrine of

the universal extent of good (that is, the coextensiveness of goodness and being) as a possible view. I believe that the perfection
theory of good just sketched has the advantage of allowing this
doctrine to be meaningful, whereas most other theories do not.
Of course this advantage does not prove the perfection theory
true; but it is a fruitful adjunct. And perhaps the two doctrines
are reciprocal, mutually supporting each other. In any case, most
theories choke off the discussion of this question, before it can
meaningfully begin, by too narrow a conception of the good. If
the very subject matter of the good is human consciousness, then
there is an end to the matter.

I think there are only two theories of the good which allow
the universal extent of good to be meaningful: the theory that
good consists in some sort of feeling in a very broad sense, and
the perfection theory. The feeling theory, in order to uphold
the doctrine in question, requires, of course, the additional theory
that feeling or internal response is present throughout all of nature and existence. The perfection theory does not require this
panpsychist belief, although it is compatible with it. The perfection theory is likely to maintain in any case, however, that the
good, in its universal extent, does not exist independently, apart
from all consciousness whatsoever, albeit the consciousness in
question may not be limited to human consciousness. My own
theory maintains this involvement of good with consciousness,
and accordingly we differ more in emphasis than in substance
with William Frankena's insistence that "some kind of satisfac-
toriness is a necessary condition for something's being intrinsically
good,"[9] and that excellence is an additional good-making feature
in many cases. Our theory is that perfection is fundamental to
the good in some way and that conscious experience is an indispensable relatum. The connection between perfection and consciousness needs to be investigated more fully, for there is room
for difference of interpretation even if the relation of good to
consciousness be granted. But my only point here is that it
seems to me important to keep the question open regarding
the possible universal extent of good. I think it is a significant
advantage of a theory if it is fruitful for further inquiry.

Some Terminological Considerations

This preliminary statement of position will conclude with some
clarifications and innovations of terms that will be used in the following chapters.

The concept of good that we have just discussed, and have defined by the notion of perfection, is the concept of intrinsic good: that which is good by virtue of its constituent properties and their composition. And since, in keeping with the Aristotelian and Scholastic tradition, we have allowed that the good might pertain to any realm of being and not just the human, this concept might also be called the metaphysical good. Better yet, we may refer to it as the *intrinsic good metaphysically considered*. In contrast, the "instrumental good" is whatever contributes to the intrinsic good of anything without being a constituent component of that good.

There is a wider linguistic use of "good" that will be discussed in chapter 5. It is the most general sense of "good" and covers all other senses, including that of "intrinsic good." This general meaning may be given as "that in anything which is reasonably favored.[10] This meaning is not itself a normative ethical or valuational concept, or any kind of answer to ethical and valuational questions. It is simply the widest linguistic usage that marks off the common ground of the term "good" in all its senses from the meaning of other terms. Normally this meaning is automatically understood in the other uses of "good" without special mention. It is also generally assumed that this meaning of "good" has reference to the human context; but we shall suggest that, by analogy, it can be extended with profit beyond the human dimension.[11]

The intrinsic good of man, or the perfection of man, may be called the *total human good* or the *summum bonum*. The "moral good" may be thought of as part of the total human good, namely, the perfection of his voluntary conduct wherein his actions and attitudes are in accord with the moral standard. The "social good" is the total human good realized throughout an entire community.

There are other senses and shades of senses of the term "good" that can be distinguished were it our purpose to draw up an abbreviated dictionary. The above meanings are the main ones that will concern us. We note only that "good" in the sense of "good of its kind" is sometimes used as a synonym for "perfection" or "partial perfection." We are employing "perfection" for this meaning, and we have argued, and will continue to develop the argument, that this is a fundamental meaning in the valuational senses of "good."

Although we have allowed for the possibility of intrinsic good having a nonhuman reference, it is customary for many writers to

think of such terms as "good" and "value" as totally devoid of
meaning apart from human persons, or at least conscious states.
Our concession to this belief will be to reserve the term "value"
to indicate the good in consciousness. Thus values, that is, intrinsic values, will be considered to be certain sorts of conscious
states, though instrumental values may well be nonconscious in
character. Moreover, for our purposes "value" will normally
mean "human value," although the human is not the only realm
of consciousness. For convenience, "value" and "good" may be
used interchangeably when the context is clearly the human
good. The idea of perfection affords us a key for the interpretation of value as well as the good in general.

Three other terms will be introduced at this point to help
clarify the general structure of the value situation and of the
good in general as conceived in the present theory. The term
perficiendum will designate any entity that is capable of perfection. It is analogous to the term *definiendum* and, correspondingly, indicates the entity being perfected, to be perfected, or
already perfected. The term *perficiens* will designate any entity
which contributes to the fulfillment or perfection of another entity, that is, which helps, as we say, to perfect it. It is analogous
to the term *definiens* and, correspondingly, indicates that which
perfects or enhances the *perficiendum*. The term *perfectio* will
designate the supreme point of perfectability for a given entity,
that is, the point of its unsurpassability relative to itself. This
term is analogous to "maximum" or "optimum" and in like
manner indicates an upper limit, a supreme degree.

The good or value is thus to be interpreted as a triadic situation involving *perficiendum, perficiens,* and *perfectio.* The good
occurs when some *perficiens* brings some *perficiendum* toward
its *perfectio.* The term "perfection" will generally be used to
designate the complex of these three factors. Perfection, or the
supreme good, occurs when an entity (*perficiendum*) reaches its
point of unsurpassability (*perfectio*) in relation to its multifold
perfectors (*perficientia*). Most common in existence is the partial
realization of perfection; and so we may say that the good, as
usually intended, means partial perfection. In the human context
we may say quite simply, but as defined in the technical sense,
that human values are partial perfections.

Exceptions to this terminology may readily suggest themselves.
It might be thought, for example, that the terminology is not
applicable to entities which are generally regarded as not having

a capacity for perfectibility, beings that just are what they are throughout their career. Such entities may, however, be viewed as abbreviated instances of the triadic structure. The actual entity is already what it can become; so there is no factor of *perfectio* that is different from the *perficiendum*. There is still a relationship, however, between *perficiendum* and *perficiens*.

Another qualification in the terminology might be suggested by the classical conception of God. The modern Whiteheadian type of theism would require no qualification at all, since God is conceived as a being in process of perfection through internal relations to the world as his *perficiens*. In the classical conception God as *perficiendum* is eternally what his *perfectio* is, and so any external *perficiens* fulfills his being not through essential contribution to, but as creative expression of, his perfection. Thus God would be a special instance in which *perficiendum, perfectio,* and *perficiens* coalesce in a single perfection of all perfections—a notion we may call *perfectissimum*.

But these are substantive matters to be dealt with in due time. They will occupy us chiefy in part 3, while in part 2 we shall deal with the more familiar territory of value theory.

I conclude part 1 with an outline of the principal senses of "good" that will appear throughout this book.

1. Most general meaning of "good": that which is reasonably favored

   A. Submeanings referring to either human or nonhuman contexts:

      2. Intrinsic good, good by virtue of constituent components (sometimes just "the good")

      3. Instrumental good; good because contributory to, though not constitutive of, intrinsic good

      4. Good of the type or of individualized being (perfection)

   B. Submeanings referring to the human context alone:

      5. Moral good or goodness

      6. Total human good or *summum bonum* (intrinsic human good; sometimes just "the good")

      7. Principal goods or values (constituents or components of total human good)

      8. The highest good or value, i.e., the supreme value among all the intrinsic human values or goods

      9. Social good, the total human good conceived collectively

C. Submeaning referring to God alone:
   10. Divine good, the goodness of a supreme, holy, loving
   deity

PART TWO

Human Value

2: Piety, Value, and Culture

Amid all the contributions and errors that have been alleged to come down to us from Immanuel Kant there is one of his his teachings which we may, without commenting on the rest of the philosopher's thought, accept as a lasting insight and as a starting point for our present inquiry. This teaching is that there is, in Kant's use of the term, a "transcendental" factor in human experience. Our particular concern is to consider this factor in the case of value experience.

The term "transcendental" should not be interpreted to mean "mysterious" or "speculatively remote from life." It merely indicates the presence in valuation of a presupposed dimension of awareness in addition to what can be disclosed by behavioristic reports, analysis of mental dispositions, and descriptive phenomenology of empirical elements. When these latter descriptive techniques have been exhausted there always remains, and must remain, the question of whence springs the very ability to prize, to appraise, to like, to enjoy, to discriminate, to judge behavior, to initiate preferred empirical states, to live for causes—in short, to carry out the many sorts of things comprised under the heading of value activity. In answer to this question it is never enough to point out that we are born with physical desires, that we are subject to unconscious urges, that we are trained in particular cultures, and so forth. The fact that we can value and evaluate the results of these forces rationally and can organize personal and social life cannot be explained, without circularity, by returning to those genetic materials of valuation themselves. The various sorts of value activity, particularly at the judgmental level, could only be possible if there is a primordial capacity for such activity in man as man, or rather the self as self. This capacity cannot be found by listing, compiling, compounding, or abstracting from the various value activities, for these latter presuppose this capacity. That is our basic reason for affirming a transcendental element in human value experience. It is disclosed rationally by attending to the presuppositions of value analysis, and subjectively by attending to the adumbrated depths of value experience.

The Experience of Piety

It is our intention to call this transcendental component, this awareness deriving from the self's primordial capacity for valuation, by the popular and somewhat vague term "piety." This word is thus assigned a more specific reference than is customary for it. At the same time the character of that reference makes the word more difficult to define with any exactness. Certainly it cannot be defined *per genus et differentia*—for we interpret the relation of piety to particular modes of valuation to be analogous to the relation of being to the modes of being, namely, as the widest genus without *differentiae*. Nevertheless, some words can be offered to adumbrate our use of "piety" as the most general term for valuational experience.

An analogy with Rudolf Otto's use of the word "numinous" is relevant. Without remarking on Otto's technical distinction between "the numinous" and "the holy," we may note that for Otto the numinous sense is man's deepest, most pervasive awareness of numinous objects, that is, of the holy. In like manner, we shall interpret piety as man's deepest, most pervasive awareness of value objects, that is, of the good. Piety is man's sense of the good, just as numinous feeling is man's sense of the holy.

Piety is thus identified as the inward, personal, felt awareness or response in the value experience of the self. It never occurs, however, *in vacuo*, without an object. It is always an awareness of that which is taken to be good. The act of valuation is a synthesis of piety and its object, the good.

Reflection on the experience of piety suggests that valuation is first an act of discovery before it is an act of creation in the realm of values. For this reason the somewhat passive-sounding word "piety" is more fitting for our initial response to value than such active-sounding words as "creating," "inventing," "making," "endowing," and the like, which might be taken as the key words in a more pragmatic or naturalistic approach to values. There is no implication in this that man ought to be a passive being in his quest for the realization of values. The life of value is always an active adventure, an activity, of the self. We want merely to indicate that an apprehension of objective good is at the root of value experience and forms a prelude to man's activity, individual or social, in regard to value. This remark should be sufficient to offset any charge that the term "piety" is ill suited to characterize man, the activist, striving to realize personal and social values. We do not deny the activist contention; we *do* insist that apprehension precedes action, vision precedes reform, awareness precedes application. We insist that in the self there is a grasp before the surge, a transcendental intimation behind the surface deed; we insist that piety is parent to performance.

It is not our ambition here to undertake, as Otto did in the case of the numinous, a full-scale phenomenological investigation of the category of piety—a study that would be, like Otto's, at once psychological, anthropological, historical and cultural, ethical and theological. Our interest is axiological and therefore lies with the resultant concrete patterns of piety, that is, with the modes of value and with the nature of the good. The wider investigation is in any case beyond our capacity at the present juncture. Our reference to it in what follows will be in the guise of allusions mainly. It is hoped that even these will do something to set a fruitful path for inquiry in the theory of value. We support, of course, the idea of piecemeal value studies in psychology, piecemeal value-word analyses in analytic philosophy, clarion calls to value consciousness, and so forth; but we also hold that there is a need today, perhaps more than ever, for the classical concern with the nature of man, to whose life these piecemeal studies have reference. The wider investigation suggested would be of man in his totality as valuer, of man viewed as *homo pius.*

Objects of Piety

Since the human sense of value has intentionality, that is, is directed toward what is taken as valuable, we confront the question of identifying the value objects in human experience.

This question may be understood as referring to the widest *genera* of value objects, or to the *infimae species,* or to anything between, or even to the individual objects of value. Aiming, as we are, at a comprehensive account, we shall focus on the widest *genera* or categories under which all valuations may be subsumed. We are concerned, in short, with nothing less than the relation of piety to reality, and in particular with the subdivisions of that relation whose distinction will be illuminating for further study.

Reflection on actual human culture and on metaphysical distinctions suggests a classification of four relationships that have captured the interest of man as valuer, and four resultant piety orientations. The four aspects of reality which are the objects of value in these relationships are God, man, the natural cosmos other than man, and the relations among them cognizable as truths. For brevity we shall refer to these objects as God, man, the cosmos, and truth, and to the resultant piety orientations as theocentric piety, cosmic piety, moral piety, and noetic piety. Different cultures, subcultures, and individuals generally emphasize one of these modes of piety as central and bring the others into perspective under this dominant orientation. Generally also, all four modes in some form are present together in the life of value, though with some frequency the theocentric and cosmic modes have been dismissed altogether or radically reinterpreted. We shall presently note some cultural illustrations of the varying emphases; but first some remarks suggesting a further breakdown of the classification will be in order.

In theocentric piety God is the ultimate object of value and is usually regarded as a personal creator, though attempts have been made to circumvent this description while keeping the idea. The value activities or responses which the apprehension of God's goodness evokes are, on the one hand, appropriate praise, gratitude, and submission and, on the other hand, faithful acts toward men and things which are viewed as deriving their value from the primary source. There are thus two principal forms of theocentric piety: the piety of adoration and the piety of acts. Both seek to worship God and further his value ends.

In cosmic piety we respond to what is commonly called the world of nature. Most immediately this involves our individual interaction with natural things, needed for a sense of physical health, vigor, and adventure. This in turn is part of the need of man collectively to adjust ecologically, to fit in harmoniously and preserve the recycling balance of nature. More detachedly, perhaps there is the simple appreciation felt by plain folk, and sophisticates alike, of the flowers, birds, clouds, rocks, and other natural phenomena all around us. So inherent is this response in man's sense of value that it has acquired a long-standing name, natural piety. But there are more subtle modes of response also. One of these is the manner in which the poet responds, expressively, seeing more than others see. And let us not limit this mode to the poet alone among artists, nor to representational expression. Regardless of one's theory of art, the artist must be seen as interacting with the materials of the natural cosmos in his esthetic endeavors. Then we should mention that form of cosmic piety in which one embraces the cosmos as a whole in one's vision of the good, perhaps identifying oneself with it in a rapturous feeling, but in any case encompassing it emotionally as a work of wonder and mystery. We shall refer to these principal forms of cosmic piety as physical interaction, natural piety, esthetic emotion, and mystical awe.

In moral piety the object of value is man himself, that is, individual persons and their experiences.[1] The value contentions here are, first, that there are certain human experiences that are worth having for their own sake and, further, that it is good that there be existing persons to have such experiences. This realm of value is readily divisible according to the range or scope of moral obligation. First there is the concern for one's own well-being, which is called self-affirmation or prudence. The extension of like-minded concern to other individuals, especially family and friends, has been given the name of filial piety. Devotedness to wider groups and associations of people we shall call community loyalty. Finally there is impartial good will toward the entire human race without discrimination, and this we may call democratic feeling.

Noetic piety differs from the other modes in not being directed toward existing beings and their goodness. There is, however, as with the others, an object in the sense of real, independent correlates of the valuing capacity. These correlates are the objective relationships among entities which, when apprehended by mind, become components in truth relationships. The quest for these relationships, or, in a word, for knowledge, is a significant incentive in man's life and deserves to be singled out as a distinct pattern of piety. Sometimes the pursuit is for knowledge in itself as a good and sometimes for its derivative uses. And so we may speak of contemplative and practical forms of noetic piety.

The four modes of piety and their principal forms may now be shown as follows:

Theocentric Piety
    Piety of adoration
    Piety of acts
Cosmic Piety
    Physical interaction
    Natural piety
    Esthetic emotion
    Mystical awe

Moral Piety
    Self-affirmation
    Filial piety
    Community loyalty
    Democratic feeling
Noetic Piety
    Theoretical contemplation
    Practical inquiry

It will now be relevant to our overall perspective to survey, from the vantage point of this classification, some familiar cultural ground. This will help to accent the scope of the valuational venture. Although we cannot use cultural forms, which are themselves changing, as indices to the objectivity of value judgments—a thesis we wish to uphold—we can nevertheless be reminded thereby that there are wider dimensions of valuation to be contemplated and analyzed than merely private objects of passing interest.

Theocentric Piety

In our culture, theocentric piety is the heartbeat of the Hebrew-Christian religious tradition. The aspiration of theocentric piety in this tradition is to address all that one is and does to God out of love of God and an acknowledgment of his infinite goodness. When genuinely achieved, the two forms of such piety, adoration and acts or, alternatively, praise and obedience, are but two aspects of a single orientation.

Jewish and Christian literature is filled with expressions of both forms of piety. As examples of adoration we need only cite the literature of praise and thanksgiving in the Old Testament, notably the Psalms, and the expressions of glorification and devotion in such Christian writings as the Gospel of John, the *Confessions* of St. Augustine, and the recorded sayings of St. Francis. As examples of the emphasis on worship through acts we may mention the great prophetic calls of the Old Testament, for example, by Amos, Isaiah, and Jeremiah, and the admonitions to Christian living contained in such New Testament letters as Romans, 1 Corinthians, and 1 John. These two dimensions of piety have been the subject of prophetic appeals throughout our religious history: continually there are calls for the renewal of the spirit and for renovated life in the world.

If we ask about the difference between the Jewish and Christian forms of theocentric piety, we may say that Judaism stresses the goodness of God as immediately knowable through his relation to the world and man, whereas Christianity sees the kind of relation which God has to the world and man disclosed and demonstrated in the life of Christ. Thus the emphasis in Jewish piety is, in the words of one interpreter, upon "the sanctification of the everyday,"[2] and the emphasis in Christian piety is, in the words of Thomas à Kempis, upon "the imitation of Christ." The spirit of Jewish piety is communicated remarkably, I believe, in the following passage:

> To speak of the hallowing of life in Judaism is to refer to its conviction that all life down to its smallest element can, if rightly approached, be seen as a reflection of the infinite source of holiness which is God himself. The name for this right approach to life and the world is piety, carefully distinguished from its counterfeit, piosity. In Judaism, piety prepares the way for the coming of God's kingdom on earth: the time when everything will be redeemed and sanctified and the holiness of all God's creation will be fully evident.
>
> The secret of piety consists in seeing the whole world as belonging to God and reflecting his glory. To rise in the morning on seeing the light of a new day, to eat a simple meal, to see a stream running between the mossy stones, to watch the day slowly turning into evening—even small things like these can brim with meaning when seen as illusive of God's majesty.[3]

The meaning of Christian piety is illustrated brilliantly in St. Bonaventure's summary of how such piety suffused the life of St. Francis:

> That true godliness which, according unto the apostle, is profitable unto all things, had so filled the heart of Francis and entered into his inmost parts as that it seemed to have established its sway absolutely over the man of God. It was this piety that, through devotion, uplifted him toward God; through compassion, transformed him into the likeness of Christ; through condescension, inclined him unto his neigh-

bor, and, through his all-embracing love for every creature, set forth a new picture of man's estate before the Fall.[4]

Though there is nothing geographical about theocentric piety itself, and though in practice geographical classifications of philosophy and religion are fortunately becoming less frequent, some references of this kind are nevertheless unavoidable. Thus we must say that when we turn to non-Western cultures we find theocentric piety predominantly in the Islamic tradition. The emphasis upon the infinite goodness of God is similar and the particular stress is upon worshiping God through the moral precepts and devotional practices announced by Muhammed. Other manifestations of theocentric piety are to be found in Sikhism, in the Dvaita or theistic form of Hinduism, and in Ba'hai.

The above are the uncompromising monotheistic patterns of piety in culture. There are other, quasi-monotheistic and polytheistic versions of theocentric piety that might be noted; but they are better interpreted, I believe, as attenuated leanings toward monotheism, or in some cases as symbolic addenda to moral or cosmic piety.

Noetic Piety

To speak of the Greek component in our culture has virtually come to be synonymous with speaking of reason and rationality, the love of truth and wisdom. This is certainly an oversimplification if the reference is to Greek culture as a whole, as if the Greeks had no traffic in mystery cults, in notions of irrational fate and chance, in sophistry and skepticism. But the judgment appears true if we limit our reference to the mainstream of late Greek intellectual culture, where we find both forms of noetic piety in equally celebrated models. Plato and Aristotle have become archtypes of that form of philosophy which sees the culmination of life in theoretical understanding and contemplation. Socrates is the hero of existential inquiry, seeking knowledge, especially self-knowledge, as part of the process of becoming an authentic individual. These forms need not exclude each other, and in Greek philosophy they do not, so that we are dealing with matters of emphasis only. In modern times, with our Hegels and Bradleys on the one side and our pragmatists and existentialists on the other, the split has become severe.

We may formulate the two emphases in a manner that will

cover both the Greek contrast and the modern split, as follows. Both of the noetic emphases aim at knowing for the purpose of more complete being; but the theoretical emphasis finds the more complete being primarily and essentially in the very act of knowing itself, while the existential emphasis finds the more complete being in a full expression or synthesis of the positive tendencies of the self, to which knowledge is preparatory. In the former emphasis, knowledge itself, the vision of truth, is the culmination for man; in the latter, this may be true for some selves, but knowledge is looked upon in general as functional to, or at least only a part of, true selfhood. For the former, more knowledge means automatically more realization of essential selfhood; for the latter, this may or may not be so, depending on its use. One consequence of this contrast is that existential thinkers, including Socrates as well as Dewey, tend to regard as unimportant certain metaphysical questions which appear very important to the more theoretical pupil and grand-pupil of Socrates and to their philosophical followers.

The difference can be illustrated by a hypothetical glance at the one explicit discussion of piety in Greek philosophy, Plato's *Euthyphro.* The dialogue asks what piety essentially is; but no concluding answer is provided. Now I can well imagine Aristotle saying, first of all, that a good dialogue ought to have a beginning, a middle, *and* an end, and then supplying the end by arguing that true piety consists in the likeness to God which can be achieved through intellectual knowledge of divine truth, that is, the truth God knows. Piety toward God and self-realization for man are attained not through acts of will or states of feeling but through intellectual contemplation of the eternal truths found preeminently in the prime knower. In contrast, the dialogue may have been left unfinished by Plato to suggest Socrates' belief that piety involves a nondiscursive, mystical grasp of God, or being, or the order of things, or perhaps even just the good of man. It may also suggest that piety is an existential knowing of oneself in relation to the world order—a knowing which must be individual in character and about which formal statements are unfruitful.

It is doubtful whether we have ever had since, or will have again, as pure forms of noetic piety as are displayed in the valuations of these Greek philosophers. This is not merely because the circumstances of Greek living have not been duplicated to encourage a repetition. New historical patterns of piety have emerged to incorporate or at least modify the Socratic and the Aristotelian types of rationalism. Kierkegaard, in his passion for

existential truth, is perhaps the purest successor of Socrates; but
his noetic valuation is entirely subsumed within a wider context
of theocentric piety. Hegel is perhaps the purest rationalist
among the great philosophers since Aristotle; but his rationalism
is absorbed in a curious blend of cosmic and moral piety. History
is not so noncumulative that it can exactly repeat its earlier
phases.

Cosmic Piety

Cosmic piety is found in its purest and most comprehensive
form when there is an emphasis on the possibility of profound
experience of the unity of all things, the oneness of the cosmos,
plus an affirmation that such experience of cosmic oneness provides the illumination needed for human valuations. In this kind of
cosmic piety the appreciation of particular things is but a partial
awareness of, or a step toward, the goodness of the whole. The
zenith of this experience often is, on the subjective side, a sense
of mystical identification, and, on the objective side, a judgment
of metaphysical monism.

The clearest cultural expression of this form of cosmic piety
is in the Advaita Vedanta system of Hinduism. The identity of
Atman and Brahman, the absolute priority of Brahman over
Maya, the ideal of treating each thing as part of the All, the goal
of undifferentiated absorption into Brahman—these are some
characteristics of this purest of mystical monisms. The following
lines are illustrative:

> Manifest, [yet] hidden; called "Moving-in-secret";
> The great abode! Therein is place that
>   Which moves and breathes and winks.
>   What that is, know as Being and Non-being,
>   As the object of desire, higher than understanding,
>   As what is the best of creatures![5]

Of course, we are to identify this monism only with the Hindu
intellectual culture (and indeed not all of that), and not with
Indian culture as a whole. Indian popular religion, it seems clear,
is no mystical monism but rather a bewildering variety of truncated theistic allegiances—bewildering, we should add, to the out-
sider, since the Vedantist sees all this variety as acceptable and
unified because it is a progression toward, even an expression of,

the one Brahman that is beyond all difference and description. Despite the popular religion, however, no other intellectual tradition has emphasized so characteristically and so continuously the monistic form of cosmic piety. The West has its Plotinuses and Spinozas; but these are isolated figures, not cultural traditions.

Cosmic piety, even in its most comprehensive form, need not be pushed all the way to metaphysical monism in order to be felt. Such piety is in fact quite common without metaphysical sophistication. It is in one sense simply the extension of what we call natural piety. Once the retreat from monism occurs, however, cosmic piety tends to be immersed in one of the other principal modes of piety, theocentric or moral. One of the distinguishing features of Vedantic monism is that it is not theocentric: the cosmos, in the widest sense of the term, *is* Brahman, and personalistic theism is seen as but a lesser stage on the way to this final realization. But when the natural cosmos is not seen as one in essence with absolute being, not self-explanatory or self-sustaining through this essence, then the way in which it is conceived as entering our value system is altered. Where cultures are not monistic in tradition, this kind of cosmic piety does not have so dominant a position.

What is true of nonmonistic cosmic piety in general is also true of natural piety. Nothing is more common in human life than the simple, appreciative interest, and sometimes delight, that people take in the objects and living things in their surroundings. Yet it would be difficult to point to a culture in which natural piety has been as determinative and formative of values as has been theocentric piety in Judeo-Christian culture, noetic piety in Greek intellectual culture, cosmic piety in Indian culture, and moral piety in Chinese culture. There are times and places, however, in which natural piety has been relatively vivid or relatively vapid.

Perhaps we must count primitive culture as the most homogeneous instance of natural piety at the level of society as a whole, even though the attendant values are not the sort that civilized man always espouses. To the civilized mind, capable of a certain measure of detached contemplation and esthetic distance, this primitive piety smacks too much of the intensely practical, of the desire to coerce and cajole nature, of taboos and fetishes and magic, of the attitude "What will this object do for me if I behave, and what will it do against me if I don't?" to be of a high order of natural piety. But if, for the moment, we are not making critical assessments but are reviewing the actual modes of piety, we cannot fail to recognize the primitive man's involvement with nature, his intimacy with it, his addressing himself to it and its multifold phenomena as the key to whatever good or evil may come.

It has been claimed that the Chinese and Japanese people have maintained a distinctive natural piety, born from their more intuitive and less abstractive encounter with natural objects. In the West we do not think of classical culture or medieval culture, despite their peculiar greatness, as high points of natural piety. We *do* think of the Renaissance as a notable time in which there was a deliberate turning to the natural world as a source for shaping valuation. And may we not cite the founding centuries of American growth as a noteworthy reflector of natural piety, even though it is not fashionable to mention American civilization in connection with the world's more historic cultures? If we include under natural piety not only intuitive sensitivity to nature, not only a spectator's appreciation of it, but also a hearty, healthy, robust interaction with nature, a pragmatic grappling with it to rend from it its possibilities for good and its own nobility, a tangy zest for the out-of-doors world, then perhaps the Puritan settlers, the pioneer woodsmen, the frontier forerunners constitute a unique epoch in natural piety—lost for the most part to modern city dwellers who write about it. Lastly, there are the pastoral poets, the mountain climbers, the nature lovers, the natural historians, the farmers, the outdoor sportsmen, of any time and place, who suffuse more dominant values with their own seasoning of natural piety.

When does natural piety pass over into esthetic response? Somewhere, certainly, between the simple enjoyment of natural objects as the things they are and the more detached, yet more concentrated, more selective awareness of objects as instances of beauty or as stimuli to creative expression. I include esthetic emotion under cosmic piety because it seems to me that the esthetic response is necessarily related to the realm of real existence beyond the emotion itself. Even the imaginative constructions of the artist derive originally from contact with real existence and are symbolically related to it. But what if the artist's subject matter is man himself, or God, and not the natural world: is this not moral or theocentric piety instead? Not if the focus of attention is strictly on the esthetic, ignoring, for the occasion, the possible fusion with moral and theocentric interests. The artist *qua* artist sees man, or God, or nature as part of the objective cosmos he encounters, albeit imaginatively, and despite the fact that he may be more than artist.

All cultures, we are told by anthropologists, have some form of art and esthetic response. It is doubtful whether a claim could be sustained that any culture has made the esthetic its principal determiner of valuation, though it is certainly true that some cultures, such as the Greek, the Elizabethan, and the Japanese, have accentuated it far more than some other cultures, such as the Roman, or the Puritan.

The value in physical interaction with nature seems to be more of a biological prerequisite for culture than a possible center for it. Physical prowess alone, for example, would seem to be a tenuous basis of culture. Possibly the Spartans can be said to have emulated such a model, and doubtless various militaristic regimes in history have prized it. But there is a more profound ecological blending with nature that also can be called a valuational pattern of physical interaction. The American Indian culture and the Taoist culture are sometimes said to represent this pure, peaceful blending with nature, though here the religious and natural piety elements cannot be ignored either.

Moral Piety

It is in the historic Chinese society, under the influence of Confucianism, that moral piety has perhaps had its most exclusive position as the backbone of culture. I do not mean by this that the Chinese have been more moral than other peoples when judged by objective moral standards, nor even that the Chinese have been more concerned with morality than have other cultures. All I mean is that the ascendancy of the ethical interest as the determiner of valuation has been relatively less mixed here than elsewhere with the other principal modes of piety. It has not been theological. And as for the cosmos, Confucius' attitude set the tone: "His philosophy was the incarnation of common sense and practical wisdom. It contained no depth of metaphysical thought, no flights of speculation, no soul-stirring emotions of cosmic piety."[6] A certain qualification must be made in our general statement when we consider noetic piety, since the scholar has had a high place in Chinese valuation.

Chinese culture is also distinctive in taking that particular form of moral piety called filial piety as the basis of moral values. The chief duty is to establish correct relationships in external propriety and in depth of feeling toward those who immediately surround one, namely, family and friends. Unless this is done, one will not have peace with oneself and there will be no basis for reform in society; but if it is done there will exist the essential condition for personal happiness and social harmony. The *Analects* puts it this way:

> Few of those who are filial sons and respectful brothers will show disrespect to superiors, and there has never been a man who is not disrespectful to superiors and yet creates disorder. A superior man is devoted to the fundamentals (the root). When the root is firmly established, the moral law (Tao) will grow. Filial piety and brotherly respect are the root of humanity (*jen*).[7]

The other aspects of moral piety can be easily illustrated because of the importance to civilization of moral codes. Community loyalty is found everywhere, for it is the basis of village cooperation, regional organization, and national cohesion. Any nation that is highly unified politically or that shows unusual patriotism will exhibit this pattern of valuation to an eminent degree. Perhaps Roman culture and imperial Japan provide the most obvious illustrations, though we should like to think that community loyalty is no less present in democratic countries for its being integral with wider ethical concerns.

The most elementary form of moral piety, self-affirmation, which is also called self-love or prudence, occurs when there is genuine and active concern by a person for his own true good. This self-interest has been held by some philosophies, such as Epicureanism, Benthamism, and Freudianism, to be the sole determinant of valuation. Even some philosophers who have been primarily interested in political valuation and public duty, such as Machiavelli and Hobbes, have started from this premise. Some capitalistic economists have argued that this incentive of self-improvement is the real basis of capitalistic values in culture. In religion, when the motivation shifts away from loving God and loving one's neighbor to brooding on one's own salvation or furthering one's own ego, this self-interest has usurped dominance, and some have argued that it has dominated various portions of Christian history.

In the East, we find the egoistic emphasis in Chinese culture represented by the realist school of thought under such men as Han Fei, and in another form by the Taoist desire to withdraw from society, though the latter is blended with a mystical form of cosmic piety. In the Hindu hierarchy of valuation which proceeds from *kama* to *artha* to *dharma* to *moksha*, the first two stages are recognized as legitimate forms of self-interest before one reaches the stage of duty. It is well known also that Buddhism prescribes a program of self-salvation.

It is not hard to find both healthy and distorted forms of self-interest almost everywhere. Despite all these examples, however, the very demands of social survival, let alone the corporate good, mean that a higher level of moral piety, even beyond proper prudence, must prevail in a culture. There must at least be filial piety and community loyalty.

When community loyalty passes into a genuine concern for the good of all men, a sympathy with every individual, regardless of national or group attachments, there is universal moral piety or democratic feeling. This sentiment has doubtless been present in many isolated individuals throughout history, in various religious communities at their best, and in many movements of moral reform which attack social injustice and national prejudice. The most striking politically embodied expression of this feeling has come in the flowering of democracy in Western countries since the seventeenth century.

Mixed Modes

Every culture necessarily reflects, whether prominently or latently, all the modes of piety, for every culture confronts, though not always consciously, all the categories of the real. This situation does not prevent, as the above illustrations show, some cultures from displaying a predominance of one of the modes. It remains for us to note some instances in which the blending is itself dominant.

In the West, Stoic piety exhibits a striking synthesis of cosmic and moral piety, an outlook in which attitudes toward the cosmos are seen not only as inspiration for but as the actual solution of the moral problem. The aphorisms of the Roman Stoics are filled with this kind of simultaneity. Epictetus tells man that "he must bring his own will into harmony with events, in such manner that nothing which happens should happen against our will, and that we shall not wish for anything to happen that does not happen." In this way "each man spends his own life free from pain, from fear, and from distraction, and maintains the natural and acquired relations which unite him to his fellows."[8] Marcus Aurelius declares:

> This thou must always bear in mind, what is the nature of the whole, and what is my nature, and how this is related to that, and what kind of a part it is of what kind of a whole; and that there is no one who hinders thee from always doing and saying the things which are according to the nature of which thou art a part.[9]

An even more terse example of the theme is this: "Everything harmonizes with me, which is harmonious to thee, O Universe."[10]

In the East, Buddhism, I suggest, also displays this duality of cosmic and moral piety. Buddhism is often judged to be a purely moral teaching, and this judgment would be correct if we were to consider only original Buddhism and Gautama's injunctions against metaphysics. But in later Buddhism we find a concern with the analysis of *dharmas*, the chain of causation, and the indescribably *sunyata*, so that—and this is the key point—proper attunement to real existence, as immediately felt, is necessary for moral enlightenment. Some sects even personalize somewhat the cosmic dimensions of piety.

Gandhi's outlook, I suggest, represents a distinct fusion of moral and noetic piety. If truth is the one absolute value, as he declared, and if the road to freedom is through *satyagraha*, the nonviolent way of truth, then we see another unique blend of piety—an interesting contrast to Vedantic monism.

A more ultimate and comprehensive type of piety remains to be indicated. So far, we have not used the term "religious piety," which is doubtless the first meaning that will come to most people's minds upon hearing the word "piety." We have avoided the term so as not to suggest that the religious attitude can be referred to one specific sector of life. We may now use the term "religious piety" to indicate the pattern of synthesis of all the modes of piety that are developed within a culture. The religious piety of a culture is the ultimate form of emphasis and ordering given to the multiple valuations within the culture. It is the culture's way of reconciling itself at all levels to those realities it conceives as fundamental. In this sense we may say that religious piety is the heart or spirit of every culture.

Infinite Piety

The point we have just made suggests what might be a fitting conclusion to this survey, if we may strike a normative note at the end. Our contention has been that all the modes of piety result not from something extraneous to man but from his essential nature, as he discovers it in confrontation with the real objects of existence. Therefore all four modes need to be expressed and harmonized if a perfected scheme of valuation is to take place. In this scheme man himself achieves his total good because the modes of piety correspond to needs in his nature, and such good as is metaphysically beyond human experience is affirmed because the modes of piety acknowledge the objective perfections in being as such. And if by "religious piety" we mean the experience of total integration and proper direction of all our valuations, we may call the heightened sense of this experience, wherein it grasps us completely and joyfully, "infinite piety." In this sense infinite piety culminates the perfection of man. An experience never fully reached in empirical life, a point both approachable and receding, infinite piety is but a partial realization and therefore a lure, a goal. Yet even in a partial grasp it appears capable of indefinite intensification and expansion because it corresponds to the limitless possibilities in being itself.

A word should be added in conclusion about the relation between the notions of perfection and piety which we have discussed in these two chapters. Are we saying that valuation consists of conjoining the subjective act of piety with a perfection in these objects of reality? Not necessarily. It might seem so if we focused solely on theocentric piety, for God is considered supremely good, the *perfectissimum*, or, in Plantinga's phrase, "maximal excellence in every possible world."[11] But this is not necessarily so in the other modes. For example, the cosmos to which the Stoics sought attunement was not perfect or good but simply an eternal neutral fact. Even less is Schopenhauer's "world as will" a perfection. Moral piety does not presuppose the perfection of human beings but only their significance. So the relation is rather this: Man finds that he must relate himself appropriately to these various objects of reality in order to reach the perfection of his own being. "He must fit himself into the total scheme of creation and occupy the place destined for him by the kind of nature he has."[12] The piety and perfection are foci within the being of the valuer.

Whether these other objects of reality are themselves capable of perfection and good, and if so in what sense, we are to discuss in part 3. Meanwhile we may say that the varieties of human value are encompassed in some way by these several modes of valuation that we have surveyed. Thus the four categories of valuation will reappear in the next chapter, when we discuss the concept of needs, and in chapter 6 when we propose an extended classification of human values.

3: The Nature of Value

It is noteworthy that the solutions which philosophers give to philosophical problems are largely determined by the kinds of questions with which they begin. Thus, in attempting to solve the descriptive problem of the nature and status of human values and the normative problem of the standard for evaluation, ethics and the theory of value have been preoccupied with the question: What is the defining characteristic of value as disclosed in those experiences which are called value experiences, or in those objects, apprehended in the experiences, which are called value objects? This question is approached directly by examining or inspecting the value experiences, taken as end results or completed products, in order to discover some quality or characteristic of the experiences, or of the objects apprehended by the experiences, which alone gives the experiences or objects their value. The result is that some one characteristic, such as desire, interest, satisfaction, pleasure, conation, or the like, is alleged to be present in all such experiences; and accordingly value is defined in terms of this characteristic, which may, however, be only a concomitant, or at least not the entire essence, of the experiences. Having proposed such a solution to the descriptive problem in this manner, the philosopher goes on to the normative problem and tries to show that the norm consists in some balance or quantification of the one characteristic in terms of which he has previously defined value.

Our fundamental criticism of this approach is that it treats experiences and their content—interests, desires, and so on—in isolation from the experients or selves which have the experiences and, hence, tends to falsify the nature of the value involved in the experiences. We suggest, therefore, that adequate solutions to the two problems just mentioned cannot be given until we answer a further primary question, namely: Why do we as existential beings evaluate at all? Why do we regard things as good or bad, valuable or disvaluable? Our suggestion is that by failing to ask this primary question of *why* we value and evaluate, many approaches have also erred in saying *what* the nature of value is. Human values are so intimately connected with human selves that in order to know *what* value consists in, we shall have to know *why* we evaluate. Accordingly, we propose to begin not by inspecting value experiences as completed and atomic entities, to be dissected and picked apart in an effort to find some one feature which will define all value, but rather by returning, in a very literal sense, "to the sources of our concepts," to use Köhler's phrase.[1] We must find these "sources of our concepts" not in experiences taken as isolated, finished products but deep within the springs of human nature itself, in the selves who value, evaluate, and reevaluate. An answer to this prior question will allow us to come back to the central problems with more insight and confidence. We are, of course, in this chapter, confining ourselves to the range of human values, leaving till later the consideration of other kinds of good.

The Two Sources of Valuation

In speaking of the sources or springs of valuation we intend something analogous to what John Rawls asserts about the principle he calls the Aristotelian principle, which states:

> Other things equal, human beings enjoy the exercise of their realized capacities (their innate or trained abilities), and this enjoyment increases the more the capacity is realized, or the greater its complexity.[2]

Rawls describes this principle as a principle of motivation but also as a psychological law.[3] Analogously, the sources of valuation we shall speak of are at once the psychological conditions which (along with freedom) cause human beings to be valuers and the bases of motivation in their valuing activity. Thus these remarks about the Aristotelian principle, as well as the principle itself, are in accord with our approach, although our account in this and the next chapter is broader in scope and purpose.

If we probe into the value situation to discover the reasons why human beings are led to value things and to evaluate, the first suggestion that comes to our attention is the existence of needs. Man makes valuations and evaluations because he finds himself in existential situations in which he experiences lack, limitation, incompleteness; and he values those things which enable him to fulfill these needs and thus to persist in his being. It is interesting to note in this connection that the word "value," as originally employed in economics,[4] meant the exchange significance which objects have when measured in their capacity to serve human needs. From sociological evidence, too, it is a commonplace that the primary motivation of primitive man in his actions and evaluations is his basic needs of existence. And from our introspective experience it need hardly be added that one primary reason why we value things for ourselves, and why we judge things valuable for other persons, is that there is a recognition of some existential need or lack which must be fulfilled if our very being is to be maintained, either actually or more fully. Response to existential needs, then, is the first "spring" which leads man to make valuations and to evaluate.

But in addition to his existential incompleteness, which man finds to be his lot by nature, and to which he responds evaluatively, he is possessed of certain vital and creative impulses which lead him to evaluate, over and beyond the sole purpose of fulfilling needs or lacks. One of the marks that differentiates man from the animal nature which he shares in common with other animals is the fact that his valuations are initiated to a much greater extent by his sense of variety, of imagination, of personal taste, of esthetic appreciation, of curiosity, of ingenuity in activities, of multiform diversity in life patterns. Valuations arise not only in response to existential needs but also in response to these creative capacities. Let us adopt the term "variety," in a somewhat wide and technical sense, to cover all these latter kinds of valuation. "Variety," then, designates those springs of valuation by virtue of which man engages in valuation over and beyond his responses to need. "Variety" in this special sense is to be distinguished from the popular but analogous sense of mere diversity or absence of uniformity. "Variety" here applies to all those valuations which occur after or in addition to the fulfillments of needs.

These springs in human nature, then—the sense of need and the sense of variety—are the two general sources of man's valuations, the causes leading him to value and evaluate. In the one case, valuations are responses to his existential needs; in the other, valuations are responses to his "variety" capacities. Thus there is a twofold function of man's activities and judgments insofar as he is a valuing being: the "need" function and the "variety" function. To state the same thing in another way, we may say that from the standpoint of the valuing subject, the sources of valuation are his sense of need and his sense of variety; from the standpoint of the objects valued, these are required either as fulfillments of needs or as fulfillments of variety capacities; and when the subjective and objective components are taken together, we may say that human values consist in fulfillments either of needs or of variety capacities.

These two general sources of valuation must not be thought of as in a hierarchical order, so that the variety function takes over and becomes operative only after all needs have been fully satisfied. Such a supposition might have been formed after a cursory study of primitive societies, for there the pressing motivation to valuation is first of all the sense of need. Yet the variety function, though subordinate, is never absent. It could not be absent, for it is part of man as man. The evidence of artistry, for instance, in even the more primitive groups, as well as knowledge of diverse customs, amply testifies that creativity and variety are at work side by side with the responses to actual emergencies. But perhaps we get just as helpful a clue to the workings of valuation in primitive man if, as Bergson says, we temporarily divest ourselves of our cultural accretions and delve phenomenologically into our own conscious being—for if man is one thing rather than another, there must be continuities in his historical existence. When we do this, we see that man's very nature involves his being creative, in however limited a fashion. Very often he exercises his variety function in valuation in the same act in which he values things as fulfilling needs. No doubt primitive man had need for protection; but he did not necessarily have need for bows and arrows, still less for *this* particular arrangement and coloring of the arrow's feathers. He had need for clothing and social cohesion and religion, but no need for *this* particular attire or *these* customs or *these* superstitions. Similarly, we say that man has need of beauty, that is, of valuing beautiful things, for a being with no esthetic capacity is more like a computer than like a man; yet there is no *need* for valuing Shakespeare over Browning—we do this for another reason besides need. Thus, in the very valuation of things as need fulfilling, we also often call into play our variety capacities. We do not value beauty in the abstract; but the minute we value it in the concrete, the beautiful things fulfill both our sense of need and our sense of variety, in this case our esthetic impulse.

The two sources of valuation, then, are not to be regarded as wholly independent and compartmentalized, either historically or psychologically. There is a kind of valuational priority of the sense of need, since variety values have significance only beyond and in addition to the fulfillments of needs. But the two sorts of values are nevertheless intermingled. The totality of our valuations is interpenetrated with values arising from both sources.

Classifications of Needs

Various attempts have been made to classify and catalogue the natures and kinds of human needs. Probably the most common classification is that which regards all needs as biological and natural, including the economic. The basic needs are thus catalogued in terms of original drives, instincts, impulses, desires, and so on. Beyond these biological needs, the other achievements and values of mankind, often called spiritual, are then interpreted (depending on one's metaphysical outlook) either as explicable by reduction to the biological kind of need[5] or as acquired flowerings and frills, accumulated after all needs have been satisfied. But in the first case the interpretation leaves out what is distinctively human in our experience, namely, the awareness of lack and incompleteness in the spiritual as well as in the biological sphere. And in the second instance the interpretation involves a dual characterization of man which is equally untrue to experience; for man is a unity, and his experience of deficiency and longing extends throughout the whole of his being, not just a part of it. Thus need has reference to more than the biological instincts which must be satisfied in order to maintain the life process; it has reference to the whole of man's being. It might well be called ontological in character, involving incompleteness of being, existential deficiency, the presence of nonbeing with being. Thus the needs for knowledge, beauty, virtue, devotion, loyalty, and so on are just as properly needs as those economic and biological needs to which the word is usually confined. For only by these things can man fulfill the being which he experientially discovers himself to be in ideal, which he falls short of in fact, and which is the reason for his existential valuations.

In addition to this emphasis on biological and spiritual needs, needs can be characterized in several other ways. For instance, there is the difference between individual and group needs. The need for food or knowledge is peculiar to individuals; but the need for justice and law arises only for the social group. There is also the distinction between private and common needs—those which are peculiar to just this person and those which, though existing only for individuals, exist for all or many individuals. There are, finally, both persistent or permanent needs and temporary or changing needs—those which abide throughout man's historical existence or throughout a lifetime and those which are peculiar to a particular period of history or a particular period in one's life.

In a general way, then, needs may be described as ontological rather than simply as physiological or psychological. In more specific ways, they may be characterized as biological and spiritual, individual and social, private and common, persistent and temporary.

These are some familiar distinctions that serve to clarify the concept of need as it is relevant to value theory. A more systematic classification can be given by using the categories developed in chapter 2, in the delineation of contrasting orientations of piety. The assumption here is that there must be a direct relation between the value systems that men ideally affirm and the fundamental needs that are rooted in human nature. If this is so, then we may speak, in keeping with those categories, of theological needs, cosmic or natural needs, moral needs, and intellectual needs.

Theological needs indicate the importance to man of relating himself in thought and act to the ultimate ground of all being. This assertion represents the normative claim that though the physical and social needs of man may seem more immediate and accessible, nevertheless he remains, in the end, unfulfilled, apart from a nonillusory orientation toward being as it actually is: being as such. Metaphysically speaking, though not necessarily psychologically speaking, the soul is restless till it finds its primal source, as Plato and St. Augustine maintained.[6]

Secondly, relation to the natural cosmos supplies us with fulfillment of what are in many respects our most obvious and immediate needs. We shall call them natural needs. They include, first of all, the wide range of physical and biological needs whose satisfaction is essential for survival, health, emotional balance,

minimum comfort and well-being, recreation, and growth generally. We also include esthetic piety in this category on the grounds
that esthetic experience is an absorbing communion between man
and some medium in the materials of the natural cosmos. In view
of the depth of meaning which many sensitive spirits have found
in this experience, and in view of the universal occurrence of art
and esthetic feeling, we must be prepared to say that we are dealing here with a fundamental need of man through which, as we
say, he comes into his own. Finally, we must say that natural
piety itself corresponds to a need in man—a need in the sense that
for a person who has never appreciated nature as a whole or even
the common natural creatures about him, for a person to whom
nature is ever a stranger, for a person who has never said to himself, "These beings are something like friends, even kinsmen,"
there is somehow something lacking in his experience, something
that would be a genuine *perficiens* for him.

Moral needs indicate those normative relations among human
beings which are requisite for human perfection. They are usefully
divided into norms for social organization and norms for individual
response to other persons. The first group includes the needs for
economic production and distribution, political stability, fair and
just administration, equality, freedom, and peace. The needs of
individual response are summed up in the need for a person to
love his fellow men without discrimination. Lacking this response,
one must always fall short of the perfection of man, though this
self-perfection is not the motive of disinterested love toward
others. This one absolute requirement does not in the least dimin-
ish, but in fact is rendered concrete by, the more particular needs
of relatedness in our immediate sphere of living. Thus we may
speak of needs for proper self-love, for family affection, for
friendship, for social participation, and for supporting humane
causes.

Intellectual needs mean the necessity to use and cultivate reason in every relevant way, to love and seek truth, and to rely on
fact and not fancy. We hear much today about the limitations of
reason, and we are urged to subordinate our reason to feeling,
will, and other nonrational tendencies. This demand sometimes
has its point. But the radical views in this regard surely point the
way to folly, for fewer things have greater confirmation than the
fact that reason and intelligence are characteristically human, if
anything is.

One of the great advantages of beginning with the idea of need

as the basis of value theory is that it offers a point of convergence for many otherwise divergent approaches to human value—
approaches as diverse as classical philosophy, Judeo-Christian religion, and modern sociology, psychology, and psychoanalysis.
Partings of the way will generally result when the idea of need
becomes qualified and elaborated; but it can be a unifying category, a concept to which many approaches can make contributions. For this to happen systematically and progressively, however, it must be insisted that the concept of need is a universal
normative concept and not exclusively a variable and changeable
social product.[7]

We shall not go beyond this in classifying. Enough has been
said for the purposes for which this discussion is intended. Complete understanding and classification are not possible. "Conscious life is engaged quite as much in *trying to find out what* it
wants as trying to get it."[8] We are as ignorant of human nature
and of ourselves as of many other things. Hence needs must be
discovered progressively through experience, just as much as the
things which fulfill them.

More on Variety

The sense of "variety," that source of valuation by virtue of
which we value things over and above their capacity to serve
needs, is the spring of valuation which gives human life its richness and expansiveness, its self-transcendent possibilities, its
novelty and diversity, its infinite perfectibility. This spring of
valuation is what would give even a state of perfection the character of multiformity and variety in the literal sense. It affords
the answer to the charge that a heaven where all needs were
completely filled would be a dull and indolent abode; for where
the fulfillment of needs is complete, this source of valuation
would still allow endless outward expansion and creative valuation.

Although with this source too, as with the former, little advantage would be gained from an attempt to catalogue all the
creative impulses, the "variety" faculties, there are several points
concerning this source upon which we wish to lay stress.

First, the kinds of motivation to valuation which might be
classified under the sense of variety range in their *modus
operandi* from those whose resulting values are determined in

their nature exclusively or primarily by our physiological and psychological makeup and by the corresponding objects to those whose resulting values are the products largely of our free selectivity, inventiveness, and creativeness. An illustration of the first type is to be found in the fact that our likings of blue coats, fragrant breezes, and sweet apples are apparently completely determined by the nature of our psychological structure and by the nature of these objects. In such valuations there is no reason not to identify the value with the simple sensuous or esthetic pleasantness involved; and this is dependent on our conditioned makeup, over which we have little control.[9] At the other extreme, however, the valuations include quite as much inventiveness as conditionedness. If we consider artistic creation, scientific invention, or the diversity of recreational forms, which are valued quite apart from their capacity to serve needs, we see that these valuations receive their content in great measure from our own creativeness, our own molding of the materials given, our spontaneity in the presence of possibility. Although these springs to valuation are part of our determined human nature, the situations we finally value result from our own selectivity and inventiveness. To put the matter paradoxically but faithfully: we are indeed determined in such valuations, but we are determined to be free and inventive.

Secondly, the same distinctions between individual and group valuations and between private and common, which are noticeable in the case of needs, are also characteristic of the variety capacities. The valuations arising with respect to a new invention, such as the radio, are made by individuals, whereas the valuation of many forms of recreation has significance only for a group. Again, the motivation that leads to the valuation of a given time schedule for daily work may be a motivation that belongs to just this one person, whereas the motivation that leads to the valuation of a given art work is an esthetic sense which is common to many individuals, so that the resulting valuation is common or public. The distinction between biological and spiritual values is of less significance here, since variety values seem to be characteristically spiritual. The distinction between the permanent and the temporary, however, is equally applicable in the case of the variety capacities.

A further point to be mentioned is that the element of choice is much more dominant in the makeup of variety values than in need values. In the case of need valuations we have little

or nothing to say as to the nature of those things which will satisfy our needs. Only food will satisfy our hunger; in general,
only medicine will fulfill our need to recover health; only knowledge will fulfill our need for rationality. The objective conditions
of fulfillment, as well as the needs themselves, are set for us in
the nature of things, and we can only discover what the value
situations are, and then seek to actualize them. If we do not accept these valuations, we die, or at least fall short of the full
possibilities of our being. But in the case of variety capacities,
we have a range of choice as to what will fulfill them. We can
mold, sometimes even make, the objective counterparts which
please our esthetic sense or our inventiveness. Even in the case
of those variety valuations which, as we said, are determined in
content by our makeup, we can change them, ignore them, replace them; we have the power to choose among them, to bury
them or to actualize them, without danger to our existence, for
these values minister not to our needs but to our creative side.

Lastly, it should be pointed out that our fourfold classification of theological, natural, moral, and intellectual factors also
has relevance to the variety function in valuation. Each of these
patterns of piety has ample room for the exercise of creative
powers beyond pure need.

A Wider Polarity

If we look more closely at these two main springs of valuation, we see that they are aspects or manifestations of a more
inclusive polarity of structure which pervades man's entire being.
This polarity is that of necessity and freedom. In his existence
man is determined, necessitated, destined in certain definite
ways. But he is also a free being, capable of altering and modifying his life and actions through deliberation and choice. These
two features form a polarity which is characteristic of man's entire being, continuously present and operative, at least in potentiality. Man as man is necessitated, and man as man is free. From
a valuational standpoint, the sense of need is seen to be an aspect of the governance of necessity. Man is born with given pre-
dispositions and capacities, finds himself in a given environment
and given circumstances, and is destined by various lacks and in-
completenesses. Consequently, the valuations which arise from
response to these needs and which express their fulfillment are

necessitated by the structure of man and of the objective realities which are the conditions of fulfillment. It is interesting to note that one dictionary meaning of "need" is "necessity." What we need is what is necessitated. The sense of variety, on the other hand, is seen to be an aspect of the workings of freedom. Here the values are not altogether necessitated for us in the nature of things (except in the case of sensuous pleasantness, already mentioned). Rather we have a large measure of free choice and creation in the values which fulfill this side of our valuing nature.

Thus, since we can trace these springs of valuation back to a wider polarity encompassing man's whole being, we have still another reason for believing that these sources are grounded in the nature of man and constitute the original springs of valuation.

The preceding account of the sources of valuation is of interest in its own right. But for our present purposes the account will show its chief utility when we turn, as we shall immediately, to the problem of the nature and status of human values and the problem of the ground or basis for particular value judgments.

Value as Fulfillment

When we turn to the descriptive question of what constitutes human value, the first point to be learned from the foregoing discussion is that values must be inseparably related to the springs of valuation grounded in the human self. This means that theories which connect value with some factor which *might* or *might not* be present in the "value experience," whether it be desire, interest, pleasure, satisfaction, feeling, conation, emotion, approval, and the like, are analyses *ad hoc*. Two fallacies are frequently made at this point.

The first fallacy we have mentioned repeatedly, namely, the analysis and calculation of conscious states as independent entities, out of relation to the existential persons whose experiences those conscious states are. Strictly speaking, value does not characterize independent conscious states as such, but exists only in relation to the subjects behind them.

The second fallacy is the identification of value with some feature which may be only a concomitant, an ingredient, an accident, or a property of the value situation, but which does not constitute the essential character of it. Thus Perry maintains:

> This, then, we take to be the original source and constant
> feature of all value; that which is an object of interest is
> *eo ipso* invested with value. Any object, whatever it be,
> acquires value when any interest, whatever it be, is taken
> in it, just as anything whatsoever becomes a target when
> anyone whosoever aims at it.[10]

A truer account would have to maintain that, although interest
may be present in every value situation, we do not value things
because we first have an interest in them; rather we take an interest in them only because there are prior springs to valuation
which we are trying to fulfill and in which we implicitly believe
value to consist. The value judgment, therefore, must rest not on
interest but on this prior consideration, namely, on our view of
the existence of needs and the existence of variety capacities.

The same may be said of desire. It is our contention that we
would never desire anything at all unless there were prior existential needs and a sense of variety in multiple forms, in whose
fulfillment we had already presupposed value to consist, and
whose fulfillment we desired. We do not desire desires; rather
we desire the fulfillment of need and variety. Desires are thus
clues to the existence of needs, but are not the essence of value.
Furthermore, the fact that there are good desires and bad desires,
as everyone admits, indicates that there is a prior conception of
value in terms of which such discriminations are made.

Similar things may be said about other isolated features of the
value situation with which value is often exclusively identified.
We must be careful, therefore, not to identify the value of a situation with some factor which may be only the biological or
psychological means of initiating activity, or which may be only
a clue to the apprehension of value, or which may be only a
concomitant or property of the situation but not the essence of
it.

It seems necessary, accordingly, to define value not in terms
of any of the concomitants which have been suggested but in
terms of the fulfillment of the original springs to valuation which
we have discovered is the reason why we value things at all. The
nature of human value, then, may be defined as consisting in the
fulfillment of the sense of need and/or variety in any of their
diverse forms. This means that the multiplicity of valuation
which occurs in human life may be traced back to, and may be
said to consist essentially in, either the fulfillment of (a) some

need, biological or spiritual, individual or social, private or common, permanent or temporary, or (b) some aspect of the creative side of our nature—the esthetic impulse, curiosity, inventiveness, personal taste, and so on. From this viewpoint, desire and interest may be structural cues which implement the institution of these self-fulfilling situations; and pleasure and satisfaction might be clues to the apprehension of them. But, strictly speaking, the value consists not in these but in the fulfillment of some need or some variety capacity. Thus the decision as to which situations contain value, and which disvalue, belongs not to immediate experience or liking but to reflective judgment, for only judgment can say yes or no to various candidates.

Our present contention is that such a conception of value is what is presupposed in all of our value predications. To state the position summarily, we may say this: Granted that, as plain men, we have some kind of original, experiential knowledge of what the terms "good" and "bad," "valuable" and "disvaluable" signify—so that, for instance, if someone were to say that health is a good thing, we would understand enough of what was intended to be able intelligibly to agree or to disagree—granted this much, we maintain that when we delve into any value situation we will find that the reason why we finally ascribe good or value to some situations is because they are fulfillments of our sense of need or our sense of variety in some respect, either in ourselves or in others, and the reason why we finally ascribe badness or disvalue to some situations is because they hinder such fulfillments. Now in point of fact we *do* call some things valuable which do not fulfill our needs or capacities; but this is the very sign we ultimately use to measure mistaken valuations. That is, because we do not always know what our needs and variety capacities are, and what will fulfill them, we call things good which are not really good and we call things bad which are not really bad. We make false valuations in these cases. But this only shows further that the essential conception by which we determine such discriminations of value is to be found in the kinds of fulfillment we have suggested.

An Objection

We may as well answer immediately a criticism which might be raised against an account which defines value in terms of fulfillment. The criticism runs that some fulfillments are bad, that completions of some capacities and potentialities do not bring value but disvalue. The following formulation is typical:

> As for the "fulfillment of potentialities," I cannot see that this is good at all unless we first know that the potentialities are good potentialities. We cannot even say that right action or a good life fulfills more potentialities than does the reverse, since for each potentiality for good there must be at least one potentiality for evil (in fact many, since where you can do right in one way you can always deviate from it in many).[11]

For example, the fulfillment of one's potentiality to be a pyromaniac would be regarded by everyone as a disvalue rather than a value.

This criticism seems to presuppose a view of man as a bundle of potentialities, and the brunt of the objection is directed against the definition of value as the fulfillment of all these potentialities. But we, on the other hand, have regarded man as a being with definite existential needs and certain creative capacities, and have defined value in terms of their fulfillment. We are not forced, therefore, to maintain that the expression of every potentiality is a value, but only those potentialities which fulfill our needs and our sense of variety. Some fulfillments of potentiality thwart our basic needs and dull our creative sensitivity, and hence may be regarded as disvalues by us as well.

But does not arson fulfill the esthetic impulse and hence the sense of variety of the pyromaniac, and does it not satisfy his need for emotional adjustment? In the first case, arson may indeed satisfy one's esthetic impulse, but it must be remembered how we have defined the sense of variety: we have said that it is the spring of valuation by virtue of which we value things *over* and *above* their capacity to serve needs. This involves a kind of logical priority of the need function in valuation. Experience discloses that variety values are without significance when they block need values. No matter how esthetically satisfying arson may be for the pyromaniac, therefore, it can have little value if it runs counter to his essential needs, for in running counter it would destroy rather than fulfill his being. The burden of the present objection must accordingly rest on the second half of the question, namely, does the fulfillment of this potentiality for arson contribute to the fulfillment of his basic needs, for instance, the need for emotional adjustment? I do not know whether the people who raise the objection ask themselves this question seriously or not. Do they really believe that arson is evil and yet that it fulfills our human needs? The opinion of the human race in its long history has certainly been to the contrary; and clinical psychology does not advocate arson. What further evidence could be required? Although arson may afford temporary emotional relief, it does not fulfill basic emotional, psychological, intellectual, and moral needs, either of the pyromaniac or the other beings with whom he associates. There is no reason, therefore, to regard the fulfillment of all potentialities as values.

But then the question arises: How can we distinguish between what is needed and what is not needed? The answer to this question is that such knowledge must come through empirical discovery, both in our own lives and in the life of the human community generally. Knowing human nature and the individual self, on the one hand, and knowing the objective conditions of fulfillment, on the other, requires a process of discovery through experience, testing, self-analysis, reflection on the past, and accumulated wisdom. In this process some value claims are accepted and others rejected; some potentialities are deemed good and others bad.

The present objection, therefore, has no force against our view. It would hold only against a position which maintains that value consists in the fulfillment of every possible potentiality. But this is not our view. The central fallacy consists in supposing that, since the fulfillments of some potentialities are bad, therefore value cannot be defined in terms of any kind of fulfillments whatsoever. This inference is not sound.

The Status of Value

We are now ready for the third step in the argument of this chapter. The first step was the analysis of the springs of human valuation. The second step was the determination of the nature of values as consisting in the fulfillments of these springs of need and variety. In the third step we ask the question: What is the status of values as existents, either actually or potentially? The answer to the question must be, if the first two steps are correct, that human values exist, either actually or potentially, in the *relations* between valuing selves and the objective conditions and realities which fulfill the needs of the variety capacities of such selves. This is so because fulfillments cannot exist as objective qualities or properties of things, nor can they exist as purely mental states; rather, fulfillment can only exist as a relation between things. And if values consist in certain kinds of fulfillment, it follows that values must exist in situations which are relational in character.

To state the view briefly, we may say that values always arise in situations. These situations are relational in character, involving on the one hand a valuing self or group which is responding to its creative impulses and, on the other hand, the objective realities which complete or fulfill these springs of valuation. This is not to say that all such situations are already actual, as if all fulfillment were completed and all value achieved. Many situations are as yet only potential or possible, and are sometimes called ideals. We maintain only that the existent status of human values, whether actual or potential, is situational and that these situations involve relations of the kind we have described.

Such a relational theory of value, however, is often opposed by criticisms of the following sort.

> The value may appear to consist in relations which actually hold of certain objects. But it does so only because we identify value with the object valued. . . . The appeal to objective relations only shows that they are the ground for our attributing value to the object; not that they are themselves this value. Justice or fairness may consist in certain objective relations; but the value ascribed to justice is an added predicate over and above these relations. Harmony in the same way may consist in certain objective relations of color or tone; but the value of harmony does not consist in these relations; it is a further predicate which characterizes their presence.[12]

The fallacy here is the supposition that, since value does not consist in certain kinds of relations, namely, those which actually *define* justice or harmony, it cannot consist in any kind of relation whatsoever. Objects which exist in certain relations to each other, in terms of which something is defined, can, when so related, sustain other relations to valuing subjects so that value exists in these latter relations. For instance, the set of related colors or tones, in which harmony consists, becomes valuable by virtue of an additional relation to an esthetic person. Or again, a group of persons may be so internally related as to define what we would call justice or fairness; but it is also true that the group, so related, has additional relations to each member, so that the justice-related group has value for each and for all. In other words, any group of beings or entities, already internally related within itself, can have other relations either to itself, to each member, or to different beings, such that value consists in one or another of these latter relations.

Nicholas Rescher has shown how a relational theory can also lead reasonably to a belief in the objectivity of value judgments:

> Value—in this conception—is relational (in viewing the value of an object as something that arises from the nature of its interactions with people, or perhaps intelligent beings generally) but objective (since evaluation is, in general, based on objectively establishable and interpersonally operative standards).[13]

The reason for this objectivity ultimately is simply this:

> The existence of man and the nature of the conditions requisite to his well-being and welfare—and thus the characteristics of the humanly beneficial—are, after all, genuine *facts* about the world.[14]

Rescher himself seems desirous of bringing this objectivity in value under natural science, which I think is only partially possible. Nevertheless, we may accept the general point that, given the nature of man with his needs and his variety capacities, and given the nature of the world in which he lives, there are certain sorts of relations between man and world which are fitting, which conduce to well-being, and which therefore constitute, normatively considered, the basis of human values.

4: The Ground of Value Judgments

Our approach to value theory maintains that value judgments are objective both in the cognitive sense of being either true or false and in a distinctive valuational sense; that is, they are capable of truth or falsehood and yet, at the same time, are not reducible to the kinds of descriptive judgments found in the empirical sciences. On the basis of the previous chapter, we are able to say what this distinctive valuational import of value judgments is and to elaborate the ground of all judgments of human value.

The Nature of Value Judgments

Value judgments describe or define relational situations in which some objective condition, being, or reality fulfills some existential human need or is the completing object of some variety capacity. Thus value judgments do indeed present a descriptive aspect; but what they describe is not what the empirical sciences would describe, nor even what is necessarily actual at all—actual human prizings, for instance. Descriptions of actual human prizings are judgments of the ordinary factual sort to be found in psychology or sociology. The distinctive thing about value judgments is that they describe situations which may or may not be actual and to which actual human prizings and likings may or may not correspond. We may be unaware of these situations, may be ignorant of our values, or at least not realize them; yet the truth or falsity of the value judgments that describe these value situations does not depend on what human beings think or like.

To this extent we can agree with Hartmann when he writes:

> Not everything that "is" good or evil for everyone is felt by everyone to be good or evil. But that evidently is only a matter as to the acuteness or dullness of the sense of values. It does not touch the fact that one thing "is good for him" and that another "is bad for him."[1]

But we cannot accept the further inference that values must therefore be independently subsistent essences. The value situations have an objective status, but not as independent Platonic forms. Rather they are potential situations, in the Aristotelian sense, through whose actualization values would be realized in experience. Thus value judgments are descriptive. And they are also empirical in the wide sense, since our formulations of them are discovered through value experience. That is to say: What the value judgments describe, namely, the components of the value situation—the needs and variety capacities on the one hand and the objective complements on the other—can be discovered by us only in and through experience. Yet the potential value situations, and hence the truth or falsity of the judgments describing them, are not contingent upon actual human likings and opinions.

Value judgments have a normative as well as a descriptive aspect, and this is their principal function. We can now see how this is so. We have just mentioned the descriptive aspect; but in *describing,* the value judgments also exhibit and prescribe the norms by which we ought to weigh different value claims in order to evaluate them correctly. Our descriptive knowledge reveals that values consist in certain fulfillments (not necessarily actual), and they thereby become the particular norms by which particular valuations are to be measured. A particular liking or prizing is good or bad according to whether or not it is in fact an ingredient in a situation in which some need or creative faculty is fulfilled; and objects are valuable or disvaluable by a similar measure. The propositions in which these value claims are stated are warranted in the degree to which they conform to the judgments which prescribe certain value situations as normative.

Value judgments thus both describe and prescribe values. Of course, the range of normativeness which any single value judgment has, such as "This medicine is good for this man," is very limited, as is the range of normativeness of a particular factual judgment, such as "Lilies are white," since in both cases the judgments prescribe how we are to evaluate only one thing. The more universal norm would be one under which all evaluations could be subsumed. This would be the ground of all evaluation, and it is in that direction that we are moving.

Kinds of Evaluation

Before we move on, however, several necessary remarks must still be made about the nature of value judgments. The first point to be noticed is that, because of the immense diversity of value situations, a similar diversity in the meaning and import of value judgments must occur. All judgments are indeed true or false, but not all are so by virtue of the same thing. We have not attempted to produce a "general theory of value" in the empirical sense, in which one natural fact is alleged to be present in and to be the essence of all values. Rather we have traced valuation back to its springs and have discovered values to consist in their multiple fulfillments. It follows that there are needs to be fulfilled and creative impulses to be nurtured. The central question, therefore, is not simply whether the value propositions are true or false but what the value propositions *mean*. The criterion for determining the truth or falsity of the proposition will accordingly be directly related to what the proposition intends to assert. And the import of what is asserted varies with different judgments. There are many kinds of evaluation.

In the case of the first source of valuation, the needs involved may be relative to individuals, may be relative to a group, may be purely private, may be common, and so on. So too with the second source. The sense of variety—whether in the form of personal taste, the poetic impulse, the inventive urge, the curiosity impulse, the sense of noumenous awareness, and so on—may be individual, communal, private, common. Value judgments do not, therefore, designate some absolute value quality or some eternal form, which all can apprehend and to which all must conform in order to evaluate correctly. Rather, value judgments define situations which are infinitely diverse in kind. Values are highly relative in this sense. We may put the matter thus: Value judgments are cognitively absolute, claiming a truth or falsity to which everyone must consent in order to think and evaluate correctly; but the values to which the judgments refer are always relative to particular persons and particular groups and consist in particular fulfillments.

It follows that, in the absence of omniscience on our part, and in the absence of *a priori* intuitions of value qualities or eternal value forms, there must be a wide variety of practical tests and criteria for determining the truth or falsity of value judgments, that is, for discovering what the truly normative value situations are. When, for instance, a value judgment states that something is valuable, and the value in question is relative to just one person's need, or his esthetic taste, the subjective norm of whether in fact that person experiences the value may be the only applicable or even meaningful test of the judgment. In other similar cases, however, as in health or music, the doctor and the musician may provide a better test for what the individual's value is, and of what he would experience as valuable, than the individual himself. Similarly in the case of social values, the practical norms are those of social judgment and of qualified opinion of various kinds, depending on the nature of the value in the situation. In short, in learning what is good for us, in learning the truth about values (i.e., in learning about our needs and variety capacities and the objective realities which fulfill them), we must use the same practical criteria that we use for discovering the truth about anything— the criteria, namely, of consistency, coherence, correspondence, direct experience, workability, appeal to qualified authorities, and so on.

The present account also throws light on certain disputes which frequently occur concerning values arising from the sense of variety, especially concerning esthetic values. We often hear it said that a given art object—a poem, for instance—has a definite value which can be apprehended by qualified persons, so that one who does not apprehend the value must be mistaken and have a false sense of values. There is both truth and falsity in such an assertion. It is true that the dissenter must agree to the proposition that the poem has a definite value. But it is not true that if he does not apprehend the value, he must necessarily have a mistaken sense of values, for in many cases the only thing that is meant by a judgment stating that a poem has value is that the poem satisfies the esthetic impulse of a certain group of persons— artists, for instance. In such a case the qualified group of persons sets itself up as judge and determines the value of the poem accordingly. The dissenter can thus agree to what the value judgment asserts, even though he does not find the same value in the poem. After instruction, the dissenter may find the same value in the poem. But if in the end he does not, this does not mean that he has a false sense of values but only that he has a

different esthetic impulse; he may assign similar value to a poem
which the qualified company finds less valuable. Thus both parties can assent to the truth of both value judgments, but the judgments themselves assert different things: one that the former
poem satisfies the company of qualified persons and the other
that the poem does not have the same value for the dissenter.
There is no reason to suppose that the poem has an "absolute"
value, even if it has absolute beauty. It has one value for the
qualified artist and another value for the layman. The layman
may indeed wish to have an esthetic impulse like that of the
artist; but that is an idle wish if he does not have it. Such a view
accounts for the cognitive validity of all esthetic value judgments
and, at the same time, for the relativity of esthetic values themselves. The whole question is what do the esthetic value judgments
mean and for whom does the beauty have value? Thus the value
judgments are always cognitively valid; but the values themselves
are variant and relative.

Finally, a false charge of relativism must be dispelled. Against
our view it may be urged that anything is made good or bad according to taste. For instance, embezzlement, like the poem,
would be made valuable if it happened to please the taste of a
qualified group of criminals. But such a charge clearly mixes the
two springs of valuation. We have insisted over and over that the
sense of variety yields values only over and beyond the fulfillments of existential needs. Things are made good or bad in the
first place according to need, and only beyond this according to
taste. Embezzlement, then, must be measured first of all in its
relation to needs, both individual and social. And from this standpoint it simply has not been found to fulfill the enduring needs
either of the individual or society. The question of its value has
accordingly been settled at this level and the further considerations which the charge presumes are either irrelevant or trivial.
We can thus maintain the view that values are relative to situations and yet rigidly repudiate the kind of relativism which
makes anything good or bad according to taste.

The Ground of Individual Value

There arises now the question which has been latent throughout. If values consist in fulfillments of particular needs and particular creative capacities, what is the justification for saying

that some situations constitute such fulfillments and that others do not? What is the ultimate ground or reason for determining what is needed and what is creative, and what is not? To what do such fulfillments conduce as the ground and goal of particular value predications? What is the ultimate norm by which the particular normative judgments can be said to be warranted? These are various ways of formulating the same fundamental question.

Let us first confine ourselves to individual value. If the present account of the nature of human value is correct, the answer to the fundamental question can only be this: From the point of view of the individual, the ground or norm for particular evaluations is complete self-fulfillment or perfection of being. Only those lacks are genuine needs, and only those potentialities are genuine creative capacities, whose fulfillment contributes to or constitutes a partial institution of the complete self-fulfillment and perfection of the person involved. If the reason why man evaluates is because he is existentially deficient, then the ground or warrant by virtue of which things may be said to be good and valuable for man must be the degree to which they enhance the ultimate completion and perfection of his essential nature. The ground for particular value judgments, so far as they refer to individuals, then, is this self-fulfillment, and they are warranted in the measure to which the situations they describe contribute to such self-fulfillment. This is not to advocate a self-realizationist ethics of uncontrolled expression but to point out the ground which underlies our particular judgments of value for the individual self.

But such a view is not free from difficulties. It will be objected that everything man does is in some sense a fulfillment of his being, a realization of some aspect of his essential self. Thus many things that are commonly thought evil would turn out to be good, in our view. The argument is that the essence of the self includes all that it is, and since some realizations and expressions of the self are evil, the ground of evaluation cannot be self-fulfillment. A statement of this type of objection follows.

> Special value considerations aside, man may be described as "essentially" *anything* which he is or does, according to the dictates of *any* value conception. The bestiality, the triviality, the inhumanity of man is, if it be found in him, just as truly man as his rationality, his humanity, or his spirituality. Man is just as essentially, for instance, a thumb-twiddling

animal as a rational animal, and his value may be described
as validly in terms of his skill in thumb-twiddling as in terms
of degrees and varieties of rationality. To speak of *the* essence
of type or individual is a loose—though ordinarily a good
enough way—of meaning the "essence-in-view" or the *preferred*
essence. . . . The wise, the ignorant; the tolerant, the big-
oted; the moral, the immoral; the sensitive, the dull; the
plunderer, the benefactor; the "rich" in character and the
poor—all are equally and definitively types of "individuality
and value."[2]

Before answering this objection directly, let us recall what was
said in chapter 1 about the notion of the "essential self" and the
three meanings of "essence."[3] We distinguished there between
the ontological essence, consisting of those factual characteristics
that are needed to be a human person at all; the moral essence,
which is the self that one ought to be morally; and the valuational
essence, which is this very ideal self conceived of as the most native, most natural fruition of the ontological essence, the self
that *would be,* rather than another, apart from the obstacles that
prevent this fruition. In the previous quotation the author distinguishes only the first two of these meanings, does not consider
the third, and then charges the perfectivist theory with a fallacy,
based on a simple ambiguity. But suppose the valuational essence
is rooted in the very tendencies of the self ontologically conceived,
so that it has a certain ontological priority above any alternative
actualization? In that case the essential self would not be just the
"essence-in-view" or the "preferred essence," morally considered,
but a more basic ontological notion. It is from this hypothesis
that I shall formulate the response to the above objection.

We said earlier that the expression of all potentialities in man
does not constitute his value, but the fulfillments of his needs
and his creative capacities. In this section we added that the
ground for discriminating what is needed and what is creative, so
far as the individual self is concerned, is the ultimate self-fulfillment or perfection of the self's essential or ideal nature, as opposed to his presently existing, deficient, and therefore evaluating
self. The present objection against us maintains that everything
in the self is essential to it, that there is no such thing as an essential nature apart from one's presently existing nature; and it
maintains further that we are quite arbitrary in picking out some
of the features of the self and calling them the essential self. Thus

any definition of value that is based on self-fulfillment would presuppose some other criterion of selection of what is really valuable. But I do not believe either that we are unique in supposing a difference between the essential nature of the self, as distinguished from the existential self, or that we have arbitrarily defined the nature of the self. Let us consider each point in turn.

(a) Every theory of value must necessarily presuppose that the essential nature of individual persons is of the kind which will, when the highest good is attained, sustain and support that highest good in the particular way in which it has been defined according to the theory. If, for instance, perfect pleasure is set forth as the ground for all evaluations, it must be assumed that when perfect pleasure is attained, man's essential nature is such as would sustain the good life as so defined; for a being whose essential nature was different would find such a life intolerable or inadequate. This means that certain characteristics and potentialities of man—such as morbidity, pessimism, the potentiality for suicide, the potentiality of becoming bored with thumb-twiddling, and so on—are not really essential to the self but are accidental; for if these things were the most essential characteristics of man, the life of pleasure would simply be unattainable and would be irrelevant as a norm. Thus a difference between the essential nature of the self and certain existential, accidental characteristics is presupposed. If this were not so, nothing in the world could justify the choice of one thing as good over another—reasoning over thumb-twiddling, for example. If every characteristic of the present self were equally part of our essential nature, it would be wholly arbitrary to define the good life to include any one characteristic rather than another. Yet the fact that every theory chooses some characteristics rather than others in defining the good life (every theory, for instance, values reasoning, virtue, and happiness over thumb-twiddling in defining the ultimate good) is a clear indication that every theory presupposes that some features of the self are essential to it and can alone sustain the ultimate good in life, while other features are nonessential and can be completely rejected without loss of one's own being. It is only because we recognize the chasm between what we are in our presently existing, deficient selves—which we are trying to slough off and transcend as not most characteristic of our selves—and what we are in ideal essence—which we are trying to achieve more fully—that we evaluate at all and that we have a ground for calling some things good and other things bad; that is good for us which achieves this essential self more fully and that is bad for us which hinders such achievement. Even Sartre holds to the idea of responsibility for all mankind (rather than self-deception) as a norm, presumably on the assumption that man's nature (essence?) consists of nothing but free consciousness rather than something else.

To state the argument summarily, human values, including the ultimate good for man, must, when actualized, be necessarily experienced and maintained by the self, and, furthermore, by what is essential in the self's nature, for obviously they could not be maintained by that which does not constitute what the self really is. This means that many of the presently existing characteristics of the self and many expressions of potentialities, called evil, can and must be eliminated, yet leave the essential identity of the self to be active and to experience and to enjoy the values. The sole alternative would be to fall into the absurdity of holding that the ultimate good, the perfect life, however that be defined, will be maintained by a self whose very essence is nevertheless characteristically designed to maintain only the evil life, or at best the good life and evil life simultaneously. Every theory, therefore, which can possibly hope for both consistency and the improvement of valuations must recognize the difference between the essential, ideal self and the existential, deficient self, and must presuppose that some characteristics are essential to the self and that others are nonessential and eliminable.

This does not mean that man will not always be able to choose between good and evil, right and wrong, for certainly part of what makes a self a self is the power of freedom. In this sense man has the free potentiality both for good and for evil. But the *expression* of every potentiality which is possible to man must not be assumed to be part of his essential nature, even though the *potentiality* may be present. Rather it is the power of choosing between potentialities which is essential to him. Thus self-fulfillment must include the exercise and expression of freedom, but not necessarily the free expression of potentialities for evil. The paradox of freedom is that the self can choose the potentialities for good and thus fulfill its essential nature, or it can choose the potentialities for evil and thus destroy its essential nature, including its freedom. In the latter case, however, the destruction does not proceed from the self's essential nature but only from a part of it, namely, the capacity for freedom, at the expense of other aspects such as rationality, sociality, cooperation, and the like. The free expression of man's potentialities for good can alone sustain these other aspects of his nature, and hence must be assumed to be essential to him. The free expression of the potentialities for evil, however, destroys man's being and hence must be assumed to be nonessential to him; that is, such expressions can be completely eliminated without loss of essential nature, even though the power of freedom remains. Thus freedom, not the expression of potentialities for evil, is what is essential to man. Self-fulfillment demands only the expression of freedom, not the expression of every possibility open to man. And freedom can be expressed as much by sustaining and supporting the rest of man's essential nature as by destroying it. Therefore, while the power of freedom either to affirm or to destroy is part of man's essential nature, we cannot assume that those particular expressions of potentialities for destroying self-fulfillment are themselves part of man's essential nature. The destruction of a being's essential nature is not part of that being's essential nature, even though the freedom for doing so is present. On the other hand, the expression of the potentialities for good can alone sustain one's essential being and hence must be assumed to be part of one's essential nature.

(b) The other point to be insisted upon is that we have not arbitrarily defined the essential nature of the self. On the contrary, we have maintained that we do not know ourselves fully; that the knowledge of human needs, creative capacities, and the objective realities which fulfill them requires a process of discovery through experience; and that the content of ultimate self-fulfillment cannot be prescribed *a priori*. We *do* know what some of our needs and fulfillments consist in, such as sustenance, rationality, sociality, beauty, and so on, and that some things do not fulfill our essential being, that is, murder and thumb-twiddling. But our knowledge is partial.

Thus our view differs from those theories which select some one aspect of value experience, such as pleasure, and define it as the ground of value, for such theories always smuggle in a fixed definition of the essence of man, even though they do not always recognize it. The early utilitarians, for instance, in defining value as pleasure presuppose that the essential nature of man is that he is "pleasure-seeking man," for obviously the good life, consisting in pleasure, could not be lived and assented to by men whose essential nature is different from this. So, too, the theories which define value in terms of satisfactions, desires, or adaptation, to

mention only a few, often presuppose that the essential nature
of man is naturalistic and that it consists in his being exclusively
"satisfaction-seeking man" or "desire-seeking man" or "struggle-
for-existence man"; for a being whose essential nature is different from this would not find the ultimate good, as defined in
such terms, to be really ultimately good. Such arbitrary and fixed
definitions of the nature of the self, however, do not account for
all the aspects which man now finds in himself, or for the aspects
which may be discovered when he knows himself more fully, or
for the dynamic and reconstructive possibilities in his essential
being.

To summarize our reply to the objection: The view which finds
the ground of individual value to consist in ultimate self-fulfillment of perfection does not differ from other theories in presup-
posing an essential, ideal self, not yet attained, as distinguished
from the presently existing, deficient self. Rather it differs from
these other theories in (1) recognizing what is presupposed and
(2) not smuggling in an arbitrary, fixed conception of what the
essence of the self is.

Harmonious Perfecting

But the ultimate ground for evaluation cannot be stated, not
even for individual value, by reference to the individual self alone.
This is so both because the self is itself in part social and because,
in any case, there must be valuations resulting from the interactions of selves. What, then, is the ground for human value generally?

Following the line of thought of the previous discussion, we
shall have to say that if the ground of individual value is complete self-fulfillment, the ground of value in a community of
selves must be the harmony and integration of such perfected or
perfecting selves. But the term "harmony" often suggests mere
quiescence and even dullness, whereas the creative capacities
which man possesses would be able to make even a state in which
all needs were fulfilled into more than a state of quiescence.
There would be infinitely varied value possibilities. Therefore it
is necessary to add to the concept of harmony the notion of continuous perfecting, for even if all valuation for needs were ended,
perfecting could still occur—could occur horizontally, as it were,
even if the moral life were completed vertically. The condition of
harmonious perfecting, then, in which each self freely develops

and perfects its essential nature in the presence of those realities which complete its fulfillment, and in which each self is also in harmony with all other selves, stands as the ultimate norm or ground for human values. Particular valuations, as fulfillments of particular needs and variety capacities, gain their ultimate justification and warrant by the measure in which they contribute to such harmonious perfecting of the community of selves. Harmonious perfecting stands as the ultimate theoretical norm to which our practical norms for evaluation point and by which they must be justified; it is the norm which we presuppose when we evaluate correctly; and it would be the final *telos* if human values were the only values to be taken into account.

In summary: we have found one essential category in every value experience to be the "springs" of valuation. Without the original polarity of need and variety, which is present in every value experience, there could be no valuation. Furthermore, so far as human good is concerned, we have claimed that the final reason why we ascribe goodness or badness to certain situations, and why we judge ourselves mistaken when we are mistaken, is to be found in the degree to which those situations constitute fulfillments of the original springs of valuation. Thus another essential structure of every value experience is the relation of fulfillment between a subjective and an objective element. From this we proceeded to the inference that if the warrant for a particular valuation is a particular fulfillment, the ground for all evaluation must be, for the individual, total self-fulfillment of one's essential nature. For a community of selves, this ground of value would mean the self-fulfillment of each self in the relation of harmonious perfecting with all other selves and in the presence of those objective realities which complete their fulfillment. This judgment is *a priori,* not in the sense of being self-evident but in the sense of standing as the ground for particular evaluations, just as Kant's *a priori* judgments—that of causality, for instance—were said to stand as the ground for particular empirical judgments. The advantages of such an account as this, which is both *a posteriori* and *a priori,* over those empirical theories which claim the ground of value to consist in pleasure, interest, desire, and the like, and over those *a priori* theories which claim to make self-evident intuitive judgments of good and evil, are apparent; for the account we have given claims confirmability without falling into empirical contingency and it prescribes necessity without claiming dogmatic certainty.

Our next logical step, within the province of value theory

proper, is to outline the major types of value that are normative on this general ground of value. This we shall do in chapter 6. It seems wise, however, to deal with ethical theory first, and this we shall do in the next chapter. Preparatory to both of these discussions, this chapter includes a final section that relates the ground of value to morality, particularly the rationale for morality.

Morality and the Ground of Value

We may phrase the ultimate question concerning the rationale for morality as follows: What logical reason is there for anyone to seek to acquire and cultivate a deepened moral sense, that is, to participate in the moral institution of life?[4]

I will suggest that the final theoretical answer is this: One should be moral because this fits into a pattern of universal harmony of all things, both as a means to that end and as a part of the end itself, and, furthermore, anyone who possesses full understanding will see this relationship to be so and will see it as a sufficient reason for being moral. There are two main parts in this answer—two axioms, as they may be called. One I shall term the "axiom of universal harmony" and the other the "axiom of potential acceptance." The first is the strictly logical axiom in the sense of being a first principle. The other is more of a psychological axiom in that it claims what would be true of an individual under certain conditions of knowledge. Both are important because one gives us a metaphysical basis, the other an existential link, in the treatment of our question.

The universal harmony of all things can be regarded as the ultimate culmination of all existence, not indeed as a description at any particular moment of time but as an all-pervasive ideal. It is a normative concept. It is the underlying goal of life and conscious striving— a future goal when chronology is used, but more especially a qualitative goal. Thus it is a present, contemporaneous, dynamic, as well as future goal. Also, it may be regarded as rooted in the ultimate power of being that produces what is. It is the answer to the question of what God is about, namely, striving for the harmonious fulfillment of all beings. If we ask what this universal harmony consists in, or how we can distinguish objectively between a harmonious and a disharmonious state, the answer must be that we discover empirically what this means insofar as it is revealed in human experience. We must also add (or does it go without saying?)

that this conception involves the awareness and the value judgment that such universal harmony is in fact a good thing, an intrinsic value, the *summum bonum*.

Now it is into this pattern and process of universal harmony that human morality, that is, being moral, fits as an essential component. It fits in, first of all, as a means to the end, seen especially through the harmonization of human interests which morality promotes. We can infer from this human focus that being moral has a great deal to do with the harmony of the whole. But morality is also part of the end of universal harmony. That is, irrespective of its consequences there is something about being moral which, in Kant's words, shines like a jewel, and hence is one of the ingredients in the completeness of life and existence. This relationship to universal harmony is the sought-for justification, the *raison d'être*, for being moral.

But suppose a person does not accept this axiom, or does not receive it as a sufficient reason for his being moral? In this case we claim that he would do so under conditions of fuller understanding. This is the axiom of potential acceptance. Insofar as a person comes to have more knowledge of instances of harmony, more experiences of its worth, more awareness of what moral means, he will come to see that being moral is both mandatory and valuable. This axiom is an existential link because it immediately shifts attention from the purely theoretical contemplation of our question to the consideration of what practical steps can be taken to bring about the fuller understanding that is indicated. In other words, we do not claim that our final conclusion, our ultimate theoretical answer, even though logically adequate, will necessarily convince anyone who is in existential doubt. For this to happen, more vividness is generally needed, more immediacy, more concreteness concerning the experiential contents of morality and harmony. The first axiom gives only the logical principle that will resolve the doubt, if it is to be ended at all; it may not be a sufficient cause. How this concreteness of moral awareness, this fuller understanding, is to be attained will vary with individuals. But one thing would appear to be certain, namely, that some acts of decision and some decisions to act are necessary. Fuller understanding in these matters comes from decision, venturing, possibly from risk, and certainly from the willingness to go beyond the merely conventional to discover what being moral may really involve. Being moral may then be seen to be self-illuminating, self-authenticating, because of what it leads us to know and believe. The theoretical answer will then be reached by the road of decision.

5: A Theory of Ethics

The new analysis which A. C. Garnett has effected in ethical theory in his book *Ethics: A Critical Introduction*[1] strikes the present writer as so signal that it deserves wider attention and critical study from the philosophical community. I propose to give a brief account of the theory and to offer critical remarks upon it.

General Characteristics of the Theory

The reader may be assisted at the outset if some preliminary characterizations of Garnett's analysis are made. First, it is clear that Garnett believes an adequate ethical theory can be worked out by philosophical reasoning—a belief often called the autonomy of ethics. This does not mean that theology, religion, or science, for example, have no bearing on ethics but rather that there are distinctively philosophical questions which must and can be answered by the methods of philosophy. The subject matter of ethics, upon which these methods work, is taken to be "the moral judgments of mankind—of human beings at every stage of development" (p. 14). It is the business of philosophical ethics to reflect critically upon these judgments, to analyze the concepts involved, and to reach autonomous, rational conclusions of a normative character.

Second, Garnett says unambiguously that his theory is a teleological type of ethical theory (p. 374), inasmuch as the right is held to be what brings about good ends.

Third, the theory is naturalistic rather than nonnaturalistic in the ethical sense.[2] Garnett calls it "a revised conception of natural law" (p. 380). He believes that from a study of the actual nature of man, especially his volitional or moral conduct, we can learn what the good and the right *would be* if fully realized and therefore what they are as norms.

Fourth, the theory is what I shall call "perfectivist" in spirit. (I prefer the term "perfectivism" to "perfectionism" because the latter often has the connotation of "utopianism" in ethics, which is quite beside the point in the present case.) Garnett states the meaning of "perfection," as here intended, as follows:

> The concept of the perfection of any individual member is that of its efficiency as an organic whole of that particular kind, i.e., its possession and exercise of all the essential and variable characteristics of the species in such degree as makes for the fullest possible development and expression of every phase of its organic life [p. 220].

Perfection, in this sense, could be viewed as ethically neutral, even factual, in character; but there is inevitably associated with it a value connotation, and this happy conjunction makes the concept fruitful for the present theory, which seeks a connection between natural perfection and moral considerations. The evidence that perfection is good, that is, reasonably favored,[3] and is the key to the interpretation of ethical concepts, will appear concurrently with the process of presenting the theory that is constructed upon this contention. The presentation will be in two phases and eight steps.

First Phase: Analysis of Moral Concepts

Step 1. Analysis of "Ought"

Garnett begins his analysis with the concept of obligation or duty as expressed in the moral term "ought." The most general meaning of "ought," including its nonmoral uses, is found in the notion of requiredness. Following the psychologist H. L. Hollingworth, who prepared a list of ten uses of "ought" (p. 345), Garnett agrees that the common meaning is "what is required or prescribed within different situations." The "ought" is not simply a command, however, but an indication of what is required to effect or maintain certain conditions (p. 345). Judgments of "ought" are thus both prescriptive and informative in character (p. 346). The moral "ought" in particular, which is our concern here, refers to what is required in order to be a moral person, that is, a morally good man.

> To say "You *ought* (in the ethical sense) to do X" is equivalent to "It is *morally required* of you that you do X"; and this is equivalent to "It is *necessary* that you do X if you are to maintain a morally correct pattern or standard of voluntary conduct" [p. 349].

This interpretation is not yet the teleological principle that duty is contingent upon the production of certain good consequences, such as happiness. It is merely analytic, a tautology that spells out the common, accepted meaning of "ought" as that which is required to be a moral person, a person exemplifying the ideal conduct.

Step 2. Analysis of "Good"

A similar tautological definition is given for the term "good." After rejecting the identification of "good" with psychological states or with the elusive concept "ought to be" (p. 350), Garnett finds the common meaning in all uses of "good" in the notion of that which is reasonably favored. "Good" in general means "reasonably favored" (p. 351). " 'X is good' is equivalent to . . . 'X is an object toward which intelligent understanding tends to develop a favorable attitude!' " (p. 350). This definition replaces Sidgwick's "reasonably desired" on the ground that desire may not always be present. There is always present only a pro-attitude, suggested by the word "favored" and the connotation that such favor is extended reasonably and not irrationally. One other point is important: It is the object itself which generates the pro-attitude, and so this objective reference would seem to be indispensable. "We shall interpret 'good,' then, as meaning 'reasonably favored' or 'possessing characters which reasonably induce a favorable attitude' " (p. 352).

The moral sense of "good" in particular refers to those moral qualities, tendencies, and actions of a person which are reasonably favored. Moral goodness is that quality by virtue of which we say someone is a good man morally. It must be noted that the moral use of "good" in speaking of a good man is narrower than the use of "good" when the term "a good man" means "a perfectly developed or fulfilled man." Only a portion of this development is called moral development, namely, the perfection of the will, of the capacity for choice, of the voluntary conduct of man, and this portion is the moral good.

We must move, then, in the direction of finding out more about the specific content of this moral goodness, the good of voluntary conduct. As an aid in this process, Garnett distinguishes three further submeanings of "good," which of course, like the moral "good," include the general connotation of "reasonably favored." These three submeanings are "instrumental good," "intrinsic good," and "good of its kind" (p. 353). What are reasonably favored, in these three meanings, are, respectively, the external uses of something, the essential properties of something, and the perfection of potentiality in something. Moral qualities and acts are not judged good solely because of their extrinsic advantages (instrumental good), or even because of their intrinsic properties alone, for example, foresight (intrinsic good); for both of these sets of characteristics might be present in qualities and acts that we might judge to be bad from a moral point of view. The third submeaning, however, further analyzes the meaning of "moral good." Called by W. D Ross "attributive good" or "adjunctive good," this notion is defined by Garnett as follows:

> In this sense we consider the function of a thing that has a function, or the development of a thing that is capable of development, and such a thing is pronounced good in this sense according to the degree to which it is believed to fulfill the function or realize the potentialities of development of its kind.[4]

Moral goodness, Garnett finds, is judged good because of the measure of perfection in the qualities and acts involved in voluntary conduct. It is the intrinsic properties, however, thus perfected, which comprise the moral good; so the second and third submeanings are not entirely separate in this further clarification.

Step 3. The Convergence of "Ought" and "Good"

Both "ought" and "good" have led to a common point, the idea of perfection in volitional life. "Ought" does so because "what one ought to do is what one is required to do in order

to be the sort of person whose voluntary behavior can be reasonably favored or approved, considered simply as a specimen
of its kind."[5] And "good" does so inasmuch as the moral good
is precisely that "perfection of volitional life" in relation to
which the "ought" is defined. The perfection or ideal pattern
of personal conduct which defines the requirements of "ought"
is also the moral good. Garnett summarizes the convergence as

> what one (in the ethical sense) "ought to do" is what one
> is required to do to be a perfectly good man (morally), i.e.
> what is required for perfection of voluntary conduct or for
> perfect expression of man's capacity for control of imme-
> diate impulse by foresight and choice of goals beyond those
> of immediate impulse [pp. 357–58].

Step 4. Analysis of "Voluntary Conduct"

Garnett's definition of "voluntary conduct" is this:

> For the purposes of ethics "voluntary behavior" may be
> defined as "behavior so far as it is determined by foresight
> of and choice among the values seen as realizable by alter-
> native lines of conduct." And "a value," as used in this
> definition, may be defined, with R. B. Perry, as "any ob-
> ject of any interest."[6]

The elements to be emphasized in the above definition are
these:
First, voluntary conduct has alternative lines of action open
to it.
Second, the alternative lines of action involve values, so that
normally the different possible options would result in different
realizations of value. This provides the distinctively moral problem in voluntary conduct. Voluntary conduct becomes moral
conduct when values are involved. Value analysis does not, un-
fortunately, have much of a role in Garnett's theory, and he
finds it sufficient to accept Perry's well-known definition.

> Any interest fulfillment we may, for convenience, call a
> "value." Our primary values are, therefore, the fulfillment
> of our primary, or spontaneous, interests in *objects*, in-
> cluding the processes of our own bodies [p. 361].

Third, there must be foresight, deliberate decision, conscien-
tious choice for conduct to be voluntary.

Finally, voluntary conduct results in the control or direction of impulses by deliberately formed goals (or possibly the submission to immediate impulses, provided this is deliberate). In voluntary conduct, desire and impulse are subjected to reason and choice.

Now if these are the main characteristics of voluntary conduct, the perfection of voluntary conduct would be their perfection. Garnett makes the summary of this point as follows:

> An act in which the potentialities of voluntary control are fully or perfectly realized (a perfect specimen of its kind) will therefore be one in which (1) the process of consideration of alternative goals, with their means and consequences, is developed as fully as possible, (2) the interest in each of these goals is developed as fully as is possible when rational consideration of all the facts is uninhibited by partiality or prejudice, (3) the choice is an expression of the totality of interests thus developed selecting the goal most compatible with the whole [p. 357].

Second Phase: Determination of Moral Principles

Step 5. Levels of Voluntary Control

The positive norms and principles that will now be set forth do not result merely from logical and linguistic analysis, which has been the procedure thus far. The conclusions are synthetic and require substantiating evidence. The evidence is drawn from actual experience, as reflected upon by critical reason.

"Experience" here does not mean factual data alone, open to scientific observation, as if we were naïvely reading off the moral "ought" from the empirical "is" in a narrow sense. Human experience already contains normative and moral factors as well as describable facts, so that a careful study of it can in principle disclose moral criteria. The only assumption here is that there is such a thing as moral experience in some distinctive sense and that such experience has some acquaintance with what is ultimately the case in normative ethics.

Reflection from all angles leads, then, to the next step, namely to the conclusion that the perfection of voluntary conduct, regardless of completion, is approached through a process of development. Garnett distinguishes three principal levels of voluntary control, although it may be assumed there are degrees within each level (p. 359).

Below the level of volition altogether there is involuntary expression of interests and impulses. When these come to be controlled, selected, and organized by deliberate choice for achievement of individual purposes, there is the first stage of voluntary conduct. Its goal is the direction of our own behavior for maximum benefit to ourselves. The attainment of this personal control is the virtue of prudence (p. 360).

Beyond the concern with self is the interest in the welfare of others, and this is as much a fact of moral experience as the former concern. This interest is expressed, first of all, in obligations toward specific individuals or toward groups or communities to which one may belong. Moral attainment at this level Garnett calls loyalty; it is the second stage of moral development. Such loyalties may require sacrifice of personal interests.

Finally, there is the level of disinterested good will, shown toward all men equally, regardless of any distinguishing marks. The perfection of this level is the virtue of *agape*, or love (p. 363). It is the supreme attainment in moral experience.

These levels of volition represent progressively inclusive and sympathetic advances in the capacity for dealing with human interests and values. It may seem as if the levels were described as automatic stages in individual growth. In fact, however, there is nothing automatic about it, and in any case the criterion for ranking conduct by levels is not chronological but moral.

Step 6. Principles of Moral Obligation

The ideal of conduct just sketched is what Garnett calls the natural perfection, that is, the good of its kind, in the realm of voluntary conduct. But it is simultaneously the moral norm for our action. The norm is affirmed in our moral experience and embodied in our more developed moral codes. It is supported by empirical disciplines that are concerned with needs of personal growth, maturity, and well-being. Here, then, we find that union of natural perfection and moral norm which was forecast earlier. This being so, it is possible to state, on the basis of the levels of voluntary control, the principles of moral obligation which they exemplify. The principles are three and are named the principle of prudence, the principle of loyalty, and the principle of *agape*. Garnett formulates them as follows:

(1) Act in accord with the requirements of prudence except when this would conflict with those of loyalty and *agape*. (2) Act in accord with the requirements of loyalty except when these would conflict with those of *agape*. (3) Act always in accord with the requirements of *agape* [p. 364].

These are all synthetic and necessary propositions.

Step 7. The Right and the Good

Some further remarks may now be added about the relation of the right to the good. Morally right actions are, analytically, those which ought to be done. The principles just given provide the criteria for judging actions right or wrong. Actions which are in accord with these principles, that is, with perfect voluntary conduct as defined, are right actions. This is a synthetic proposition. But must every aspect of the action—motive, intention, attitude, consequences, and all—be in perfect accord with the principles in order for the action to be right? No, says Garnett: In common usage it is sufficient that an action's "intended consequences" be in accord with the principles for it to be considered morally right. That is, actions may be right if they are consistent with the principles, even if the motives involved are not as perfect as they might be (p. 358). To be morally good, however, in the fullest sense, one's motives and other aspects of actions must be perfect as well.

This last point suggests another contrast. Since morality displays a development, there may be degrees of moral goodness, that is, relative approximations of perfect voluntary conduct. The right, however, cannot exist in degrees. Actions which are right simply ought to be done (p. 355). One thing that this entails, according to Garnett, is that only *perfectly* good actions are *necessarily* right. Relatively good actions, those with admixtures of evil, may be the right ones in given situations; but they are contingently right, for they may be wrong in other situations. On the other hand, it would be self-contradictory to say that a perfectly good action is wrong; it is necessarily right.

Step 8. Good Reasons in Ethics

In concluding the exposition we shall refer to a topic very prominent in recent ethical analysis. It has been pointed out that one important function of ethical discourse is to supply the in-

formal logic of moral conduct, to give good reasons for moral action. In the present theory, good reasons in ethics consist of the
principles enumerated above.

> If we want to give good reasons for any statement as to
> what is ethically right or wrong we must show that, in
> the circumstances to which it applies, it follows from one
> of these three principles and does not conflict with any
> one of them.[7]

Critical Modifications

An ethical theory, Garnett maintains, must have the support
of actual moral intuition in practice, of general or prephilosophi-
cal criticism, and of philosophical analysis and synthesis (p. 368).
The support from philosophical analysis must be the adequacy of
the analysis itself and the clarity it may introduce into our ethical thought. In addition, Garnett says that, from the vantage
point of overall synthesis, we must expect an adequate ethical
theory (1) to explain both the agreements and disagreements in
moral judgments, (2) to bring consistency into the body of our
actual moral judgments, and (3) to provide criteria for forming
further moral judgments without distorting the insights of previous moral intuition. Discussion is not extensive either on the
claim that these are the criteria to be employed or on the claim
that the present theory fulfills them most adequately. Obviously,
the whole presentation is intended to affirm both assertions *en
route.* Candor must admit, however, as Garnett would agree, that
there is in philosophy no linkage between theory and criteria
which could amount to formal proof and so the affidavits must
simply be delivered to other philosophically minded readers for
their scrutiny.

For my part, I think the theory goes a great distance in the
direction of adequacy but is still subject to certain key modifications. Most of the modifications that I shall suggest are intended
to make the theory more thoroughly perfectivist and less eclectic
in character. I do not believe they change its entire structure.

The weakest point in Garnett's presentation, I think, is its
theory of value, because of omission and commission. Value
theory is obviously important in the whole theory, for on it rests
the claim of a teleological, utilitarian orientation. The nature of
moral endeavor, according to Garnett, is that it promotes ends in
the form of fulfilled human interests. And yet value analysis is

given almost no place in the theory. This is the omission. The failure of commission is that of too easily taking Perry's conception of value.

The omission leaves us wondering whether the term "value," in Garnett's borrowing from Perry, is intended as a descriptive or a normative term, or both at once. In the cases of "ought" and "good," Garnett distinguishes between a general descriptive meaning, covering all uses, and the specific normative meaning that is relevant in ethics. This is not done in the case of "value." The ambiguity about "value" is serious, for it is the nub of our criticism of Perry's definition. To define "value" as "any object of any interest" may be very useful as a descriptive definition for certain sociological and psychological investigations, but it can hardly stand the strain of the fully normative sense of the term that is implicit in moral discourse. It is true that people consider any object of any interest as a value to them, but such values are apparent values from a normative point of view; they are value candidates, and may or may not be "reasonably favored" when critically examined. Many of these objects of interest, when so examined, turn out to be harmful, enervating, or no values at all. If we say this, as we commonly do in ordinary appraisals, the term "value" must contain, in the normative use, an essential element that is not conveyed by the descriptive report: "any object of any interest."

Again, what is moral endeavor in the form of prudence, loyalty, and *agape* attempting to do? Does it promote any interest indiscriminately? Certainly not. It seeks to promote what will genuinely benefit or perfect the persons concerned. It does not concentrate on interests as such but on those that are values in the normative sense. We need, then, a conception of value that is consistent with this fact.

The analysis of "value" can be readily given, and I believe with greatest accuracy to moral experience, by the same concept that Garnett employs to analyze "ought" and "good." Just as the moral "good" means "perfection of voluntary conduct" and the moral "ought" means "that which is required by such a standard," so "value" may be interpreted in relation to the notion of perfection. "Value" may be defined as "that which is a part of, or in some way contributes to, the perfection of man's nature, considered both essentially and individually." If we do not press the analogy too far, we might say that "value" in general is related to "the good of man" in general, as the moral "ought" is related to the moral "good." That is, "value," like "ought," is definable by relation to a standard of perfection, a "good of its kind." In the case of "ought," this is the perfection of voluntary conduct alone; in the case of "value," it is the perfection of man's whole being. I do not mean that "value" by itself is a moral term, without the additional premise that values ought to be realized; there the analogy stops.

We may designate the characteristics of anything whereby it is constitutive of or contributory to man's perfection as "perfective characteristics" and may then define "value" more simply as denoting such characteristics; that is, "value" means "perfective in character." "Intrinsic value" would designate the experience or experiences in which self-fulfillment is directly felt, and "instrumental value" would indicate anything which in any way contributes positively to such experiences. It should be added that "value," as here defined, includes as part of its very meaning the general notion of "good" defined by Garnett as "reasonably favored," and this is why we often speak interchangeably of human value and human good. But my further contention is that the "perfective" character, not the "interest" factor, gives the distinctively normative element to "value" and is the real source of the "reasonable favor" attached to what we take as normative values. We come back, then, to Garnett's view that "when a man's attitudes are intelligently determined, or reasonable, they tend to favor the more perfect rather than the less perfect development of the activities conceived as essentially involved in the concept of man" (pp. 221-22). I believe this account gives a sounder explanation of what moral endeavor is attempting to do: It is concerned not solely with the balancing of interests but more with the perfecting of man, although it must be admitted that the balancing of interests, or (as I prefer to put it) selecting from among perfective possibilities, is a great part of the immediate moral problem in most moral situations.

The second sequence of modifications that I would like to introduce has to do with the moral principles enumerated by Garnett. To begin, I believe that his use of *agape* is more sprawling than is the usual, and certainly the original, sense of the term. For him, it includes any attitude or behavior that involves general "good will." But general "good will" may not reach the level of *agape,* which I believe includes, among other things, the element of unreserved self-sacrifice wherever needed.

Take, for instance, a wealthy man who freely gives away a large part of his holdings for charitable purposes and becomes known as a philanthropist. This action might be done, to be sure, for more than prudential reasons, and from more of a general philanthropic motive than is present in a particular loyalty, but still with no intensity of concern for other people and certainly with no self-sacrifice. The motivation might simply be the feeling that where economic goods are plentiful they ought to be shared, and this would represent "good will" but not exactly what is meant by *agape*. The action would be, I should say, an example of what is conveyed by the term "benevolence."[8]

Furthermore, it is difficult to derive the principle of justice as an obligation from the previous principles alone. Loyalty focuses on specific individuals and communities; benevolence is concerned with general welfare; *agape* is unqualified affirmation of another person. On the other hand, "justice is the first virtue of social institutions," says Rawls at the opening of his *A Theory of Justice*.[9] Justice requires fair and equitable treatment of all members of society. "Each person possesses an inviolability founded on justice that even the welfare of society cannot override."[10]

I suggest that these virtues of benevolence and justice are distinct from the three Garnett acknowledges and that therefore there is need of an expanded list of principles. To summarize: Prudence requires us to act for our own highest perfection; benevolence requires that we share the goods of this world with everyone in a spirit of disinterested good will; loyalty requires the fulfillment of our obligations to particular persons and groups; justice demands moral equality and fairness in the entire social realm; and *agape* requires a passionate concern for any individual person, even to the point of unreserved self-sacrifice.

I also suggest that, in the hierarchy of obligations, general benevolence may sometimes need to be superseded by duties of loyalty and justice. That is, I agree with Prichard and Ross that sometimes particular duties of loyalty, such as keeping a promise, may take precedence over our duty to promote general welfare, and with Rawls and Frankena that sometimes the demands of justice outweigh considerations of benevolence. Thus the ascending order of obligations would be more like this: prudence, loyalty, benevolence, justice, *agape*, with the first four being considered *prima facie* duties and *agape* an ideal virtue, accompanying all of our other obligations.

I believe, finally, that a sixth and more general principle is needed to complete our analysis of obligations. This principle designates not so much a sixth level of voluntary control as a dimension of conduct which permeates all the other levels and clarifies their basic intent. The principle expresses the obligation always to act so as to promote—consistent with the other obligations—the maximum realization of perfections in the world. The virtue or perfection of voluntary conduct from which this principle derives is universal respect for being as such. It may be called the principle of universal piety. Each of the other ideals, at a different quantitative and qualitative level of demand, fulfills this principle.

In addition, the principle of universal piety has some application beyond the realm properly designated by the other virtues. Garnett himself has spoken of the duty to tend to the interests of animals (p. 376). It is also fitting that we take up an attitude of natural piety, rather than wanton destructiveness, toward nature as a whole. Such attitudes and obligations seem not to be describable as prudence, loyalty, benevolence, justice, or *agape*. They are readily covered, however, by our all-encompassing sixth principle.

Clarification of the moral principles enables us to state more specifically, if more cumbersomely, whether perfectivism in ethics is teleological or deontological. It is both. For Garnett, the theory is thoroughly teleological; but this seems too simple an answer. The principle of universal piety is a teleological principle since it directs all obligations to the end of actualizing perfections in the world. Thus the theory can be said to be ultimately teleological, although the term "teleological" here is somewhat wider than in its usual application to systems of ethics concerned with satisfying desires and harmonizing interest. The principle of *agape* is, I believe, mainly deontological since its central emphasis is not upon the calculation of consequences but upon the spirit of uncompromising self-giving for human needs. The principle of benevolence is a teleological principle in the usual sense, and the principles of loyalty and justice are deontological principles. The principle of prudence is a teleological principle of limited scope. Moral requirements may thus be seen in a hierarchy involving both sorts of factors, so that a simple designation does not fully reflect the complexities of the moral situation.

I now want to comment on an ambiguity in some of Garnett's language. The problem is that moral principles and the whole moral enterprise may seem in the end to be justified merely because they are instrumental in fulfilling one's own self, in realizing oneself. This makes the final appeal self-interest—enlightened self-interest, to be sure, based on prudence—but nevertheless something far less than the highest moral level. Garnett clearly does not intend this result, but some of his language suggests it. He says, for example: "Moral laws, in this view, are rules of essentially similar kind to the rules of health, of athletic training, or of the acquirement of knowledge" (p. 380). Now these sorts of rules are essentially rules of self-improvement, and one who follows them does so to benefit himself. When one seeks health, athletic skill, or knowledge, he is cultivating himself and not other people, although he may be benevolent with his attainments afterward. But I should have thought that the reason for being moral would involve acting intrinsically and essentially for the good of others, at least at the levels of loyalty, benevolence, justice, and *agape*. One will, to be sure, perfect oneself as a by-product in the process, but this is not the rationale for it. If analogies must be used, we might say that moral principles are like rules of medical practice by which physicians promote the health not primarily of themselves but of the community.

The source of the ambiguity is Garnett's careless shifting between two conceptions: (1) that moral principles may be derived from the notion of perfection in voluntary conduct, which is one part, the moral part, of man's total good, and (2) that moral principles may be derived from what is required for an individual's self-realization. The theory is essentially based on the former conception; but in the end it seems to come down to the latter. The latter is, however, largely a prudential consideration, and this despite the fact that working for the good of others is required as a means to one's own self-realization, I believe that this catering to the older self-realizationism[11] is quite unnecessary, and in fact misleading, for the new analysis, which I have called perfectivism, is able to stand without it. I acknowledge that self-realization or perfection is what we mean by the total good of the individual, if that is all we are considering, but this is quite different from saying that it is the warrant for morality. It is also true that the requirements of perfect voluntary conduct are the requirements for a partial self-realization, namely, the fulfillment of the moral self. But the whole point in this realization is the common good of all, so far as that can be achieved, and it may or may not bring the complete realization of oneself.

One further point should be clarified, and I think it expresses Garnett's intention, although he does not state it as such. It might be argued that the entire structure of the theory rests on the general definition of "good" as "reasonably favored." This definition is included in the meaning of some of the basic concepts: perfection, moral good, value. Without this inclusion, the principles that are set forth could not have the approved status they have. And yet this general meaning is described by Garnett as naturalistic and nonnormative. Now this situation might lead someone to conclude that the ethical theory, and indeed morality itself, has no warrant other than the fact that it happens to correspond to a pro-attitude, a social approval, as indicated by the common, conventional, ethically neutral word "good." And I must confess that this seems to me a very precarious basis for an ethics which obviously is intended to have cognitive validity.

The inference can be avoided, however, by two considerations. The first is that reasonable favor in ethical judgments includes the cognitive factor. Reasonableness requires the acceptance of what is objectively true in ethics. Reasonable favor is assigned because ethical principles are thought to be true, and ethical principles do not become true merely because favor is assigned.

The other consideration is that the term "good," as defined by Garnett, is not really a nonnormative term. To be *reasonable* in favoring things is to follow a norm. Of course, this usage of "good" is applied in other contexts besides the moral one; but it is nonetheless normative. The definition differs from other uses of "good" which are really nonnormative. For example, when a child says of candy "It is good," he means simply "It is tasty," and no thought of *reasonable* favor is involved. We thus have a very general, normative meaning of "good," which Garnett properly isolates, and this general meaning covers a variety of submeanings, but it excludes a number of other equivocal uses of the same English word which are not normative. When, in ethics, we employ the general meaning of "good" which Garnett has isolated, there is already a critical selection, a normative element, and not merely conventional approval.

Summation

I would like to incorporate these modifications into a final summation of this ethical theory of perfectivism. I shall not elaborate on the numbered points.

1. The term "perfection" refers to the full development or

actualization of the nature of anything, considered generically first of all, but also individually where that is possible.

2. If we omit equivocal nonnormative uses, the most general normative meaning of "good" may be taken to be "that which elicits reasonable favor," the favor being extended because of the inherent characteristics of anything and not because of any extraneous consideration.

3. The term "value" refers specifically to the "perfective" characteristics of anything—those characteristics of things or experiences by virtue of which these things and experiences enter into man's perfection. It is these values that moral endeavor seeks to further.

4. Man's total good or supreme intrinsic value would be his complete self-fulfillment, the perfection of his generic and individual nature. In actuality, such good exists in degrees.

5. The moral good is that part of man's total good which comprises the perfection of voluntary conduct. It too may be spoken of as actualized in degrees.

6. The term "ought," used in the moral sense to signify our duties or obligations, refers to those acts that are required to effect or maintain the perfection of voluntary conduct.

7. Duties or obligations are acts that are "right" for us to do; but such acts are objectively and necessarily right only when they embody all the qualities of moral goodness, that is, of a perfect voluntary act.

8. Since in given situations perfection in voluntary conduct may be either impossible or unknowable, it is proper that many actions be judged right provisionally and contingently, even if they do not possess all these qualities, provided only that their consequences are in intent consistent with the moral standard.

9. Actual moral experience reveals that there are levels of attainment in the voluntary control of conduct, ranging quantitatively from concern for oneself to concern for mankind and qualitatively from prudence to *agape*.

10. Six moral principles may be formulated which state the ideals involved in these levels of perfection: prudence (acting for one's own highest good), loyalty (fulfilling specific obligations to other individuals or groups), benevolence (promoting the general welfare), justice (ordering society fairly and equitably), *agape* (acting with unselfish devotion to the needs of anyone), and universal piety (furthering the perfections of being at any level).

11. The moral standard may be expressed as follows: Act always

in accordance with the requirements of prudence, loyalty, benevolence, and justice—normally in this hierarchy but allowing exceptions in priorities—and always act from *agape* and universal piety
throughout, so that the end of maximizing perfections to the
highest degree possible in the moral situation may be accomplished.

12. The principle of universal piety has a quantitative extension
beyond the other principles, in that it sometimes requires action
for the nonhuman good as well as for the human.

13. The moral standard is ultimately teleological in a perfectivist sense; but actual moral demands exhibit a complex network
of varying teleological and deontological priorities.

14. Moral judgments, being cognitive as well as prescriptive, are
appropriately regarded as true or false as well as obligatory or non-
obligatory.

15. Good reasons in support of the truth of moral judgments
consist in appeals to the ethical principles that comprise the
moral standard, which in turn is considered cognitive and warranted both by moral intuition and by philosophical analysis and
synthesis.

6: The Classification and Choosing of Values

We have before us in this chapter a task that represents the culmination both of the psychological-epistemological groundwork of our value theory and of the ethical theory intrinsic to it. It is a culmination of the former because, having traced the psychological sources of value to human needs and variety capacities and having propounded the epistemological ground of value judgments to be harmonious perfecting, we must fill out this general framework by knowledge of specific values that fulfill human needs and capacities and that are justified by the ground of value judgments. It is a culmination of the ethical theory because, though we may explain right and obligation by reference to the principles of prudence, loyalty, benevolence, *agape,* and universal piety, questions naturally arise as to what, after all, are the prudent things to do, the loyal things to do, the *agape*-istic things to do, etc. These principles, whether deontologically or teleologically oriented, are concerned with choices among values, and therefore we must decide what the principal values are and whether there are secondary principles that will serve as guidelines for choosing among values. To this important task we now turn.

Three Questions Distinguished

To ask about the meaning of "intrinsic value," "intrinsic good," "highest good," *summum bonum,* and similar terms is often to imply that there is a single question involved which requires a single answer, namely, the indication of that characteristic which is believed to meet the meaning requested. Actually there are three questions that could be involved, so that the attempt to give a single answer is confusing, because it is not clear which question is being answered or how the other questions would be answered if they were answered.

The three questions are these: (1) What is the factor (or factors) in anything, regarded as intrinsically good, that makes it intrinsically good? (2) What are the chief types of experience or situation in which this factor is exemplified? (3) Of all the exemplifications, is there one in which the factor that makes for intrinsic good is found supremely, or at least more dominantly than in the others? We shall call these three questions the question of intrinsic good, the question of man's principal values, and the question of the highest value. Some references to other ethical theories will help to delineate these questions and to introduce our alternative account.

For Aristotle, the factor of intrinsic good is *eudaimonia* or happiness, which he interprets as activity of the soul in accordance with virtue. This factor must be present for anything to be considered good, or, alternatively, only that which is constitutive of *eudaimonia* is good intrinsically. The experiences in which this factor is found, that is, the principal values, are all, for Aristotle, instances of man's natural functioning, realizations of some aspect of his essential being. Some of them would be physical vigor, sensory functioning, artistry, political activity, friendship, moral virtue, and intellectual pursuits. Among all these values, the one that Aristotle regards as the supremely highest is rational contemplation.[1]

According to Spinoza, the factor that makes for intrinsic goodness is desire, more particularly rational desire. We do not desire things because they are good, he maintains, but they become good through our desiring them. The objects of rational desire, that is, the principal values, would include the survival of our being, love and other positive emotions, political freedom, true or adequate ideas, happiness, and self-knowledge. The highest of all the values he calls blessedness, or the intellectual love of God.

Kant's view is more difficult to state in this tripartite fashion, but I think we may say that the quality of intrinsic goodness, for Kant, is the coordinate experience of virtue plus happiness, or, more accurately, happiness proportioned to virtue. This is what he calls the *summum bonum*. To be intrinsically good, something must be constitutive of such an experience. Among such constituents, that is principal values, we could mention doing one's duty, prudence, theoretical knowledge, esthetic delight, perpetual peace, friendship, and love of humanity. Of all these values, the preeminent one, and the only one without qualification, is moral worth or the good will.[2]

For W. D. Ross, the factor of intrinsic goodness is the presence of a nonnatural quality of good intuited by the discerning experiencer of values. The kinds of experience he lists as possessing this quality are pleasure, knowledge, virtue, and the apportionment of pleasure to virtue.[3] He does not suggest that any of these is the highest single value; rather some synthesis of them is the chief intrinsic good in any particular circumstance.

For John Dewey, the good is related to the problems of men in specific life situations, so that the factor of intrinsic goodness would be whatever brings a satisfying resolution into a problem situation. Peculiar to this view is the contention that there can be no list of permanent intrinsic values because there is no clear-cut distinction between intrinsic and instrumental values. Emphasis is certainly given, however, to those values such as democracy, art, and learning, which have a proven generality of worth in resolving human problems. Dewey suggests that among all human values, growth itself, which involves continual change, is the only enduring end,[4] and this may be said to be his highest value.

These illustrations show how the three questions mentioned above can be used for analysis, even though they are not distinguished as such by the writers. Now as far as our own interpretation is concerned, only the answer to the first question has been elaborated up to this point in this book. We have been expounding the theory that the factor of intrinsic human good is that which is experienced by man to be perfective in character, that which perfects his nature, that which fulfills his generic and individual potentialities essentially.[5] It will be clear that this is basically the Aristotelian concept, though to use the term "happiness" for it only obscures the central meaning nowadays. Our difference from Aristotle comes at two fundamental theoretical points. First, a considerably changed conception of human nature as a result of Christian theism, philosophical reflection, and scientific study implies a correlative shift in outlook as to what values in fact perfect man's nature essentially. Second, a recognition of individualized potentialities means a more radical emphasis on the individual as a unique value center than was possible within Aristotle's subordination of the individual to type or generic essence.

We are now ready to deal with the second question by indicating the principal values according to perfectivism. Our answer to the third question has already been intimated in another connection, when we spoke in chapter 4 of harmonious perfecting as the ground of value judgments. A further word on this will be added after the upcoming classification of values.

Metavalues

The classification of values, to be proposed below, proceeds according to the fourfold scheme used in chapter 2 to delineate the modes of piety and in chapter 3 to suggest a classification of human needs. Logically prior to these principal values, however, are certain prerequisite values, such as being alive, which are preconditions for all the others. I shall call these prior values "metavalues" and define them as preconditions for other values in a way that the latter are not preconditions for *them*. For example, life is a precondition for esthetic experience, but esthetic experience is not a precondition for life. It is not that these metavalues cannot be fitted into the four categories and therefore form an extra, fifth category on the same plane. Rather they belong to all the categories and not just to one, in much the same way that good English style is essential to all the liberal arts without being something different from the liberal arts. We could make a classification of liberal arts and then say that good English style is not simply one liberal art, to be listed alongside others, and yet is not something outside the liberal arts altogether but rather a liberal art that pervades and is essential to all other liberal arts. So it is with values and metavalues.

I wish to indicate these metavalues in this section before going on to the main classification.

We may divide the metavalues into three classes, which I shall call "protovalues," "supravalues," and "epivalues." Their meanings, let alone their experienced value, cannot be rigidly demarcated, for they are all foundational preconditions in order for other values to have their full significance. Nevertheless, we shall stipulate that "protovalue" suggests a temporal priority and a valuational substructure out of which other values emerge. "Supravalue" connotes a contemporaneous and supervening presence of conditions for other values to flourish, once they have been made possible by the protovalues. "Epivalue" suggests an ultimate valuational end or goal toward which other values point and in the light of which they are illumined. We might also say that the three classes of metavalues refer, in a very rough way, to past, present, and future, provided we understand that all of them come together and are actively involved in the present.

The first of the protovalues is life itself. In a wider context, we could say existence itself; but for the human realm we must at least say life and, better, self-conscious life. Such terms as *pour-soi* or *Dasein* often do more to indicate the concrete, vivid, unique conscious awareness that is human life. For elementary purposes, to speak of life itself is sufficient.

It might be said that the value of life is really contingent on other values, rather than the reverse, in the spirit of Socrates, who said in *Crito* that it is not life but a good life that is worth seeking. This way of putting the matter, however, refers to a special moral problem which comes up in crises when we have to ask whether life is worth preserving at all costs, including the sacrifice of cherished values. This special problem is not involved in the self-evident valuational truism we are making here. The difference is brought out easily by pointing out that while it was morally right for Socrates to drink the hemlock and not surrender his ideals to mere survival, it remains true that in doing so, he also ended the inquiry into truth he was carrying on among the Athenians and with his friends. Life is needed for human value.

Life as a precondition of value cannot be thought of today, if it ever could be, as referring solely to the life of the individual. So bound up is the possibility of individual life with the total environmental balance in the biosphere that we must think of life as a whole as the precondition. The protovalue of life must necessarily encompass this larger ecological harmony, within which, only, individual life can flourish.

To life itself we must add the development of those physiological processes that sustain and further life. We may speak of these organic protovalues collectively as maturation and growth. It is difficult to know how much of the normal human maturation and growth is necessary for a meaningful life of value. Individuals vary considerably on this factor. Certainly an abundant life of value is possible with rather serious retardations in physiological development. On the other hand, we also know that, without minimum normal development, barely staying alive may be the result, and this will afford only the simplest physical feelings and pleasures.

We must think of physiological development as including physical and mental factors. Failure to develop physically may prevent

an expanding life of value, and severe mental retardation will do
likewise. Moreover, in either eventuality the one seems to influence the other, even if the other might have been rather normal
apart from that influence. Again, it is not possible to say how
much maturation of each kind is necessary. All we seem to be
able to say is that a modicum of psychosomatic maturation is
necessary for higher human values, and that more is often necessary for more comprehensive achievements.

In the category of protovalues I would also like to place the
value of mental health. It is possible to grow and mature psycho-
somatically in a normal way, from a physiological point of view,
but still to suffer mental illness and neurotic crippling psychologically. Value experience is not impossible in neurosis, of course,
though it may be all but impossible in psychosis. It is sometimes
suggested that neurotic tendencies are an aid to some pursuits of
value. But that is not said by psychologists and psychoanalysts
who study the cramping and thwarting effects of these compul-
sions. It is absurd to suggest that mental illness is to be preferred
to mental health. So important does the latter now seem that we
must count it as a central intrinsic value, and this despite the
fact that, in given instances, lines of demarcation between illness and health are not always sharp.

There is a further condition of value which today has become
so vital that I believe it must be listed in this primary category.
It is world peace. With the threat of nuclear destruction, men
are asking, as well they might, what life of value would be left,
or even possible, if a nuclear war befalls mankind. In former
eras this condition could conceivably have been thought of as a
purely instrumental state, or perhaps not even paramount in
value considerations. Not so today. And peace has also acquired
a more positive connotation, signifying not only the absence of
war but active cooperation and the replacement of enmity by
mutual concern. Thus we tend to view world peace today not
only as an instrumental aid or necessity but as something praise-
worthy, even joyful, in itself—as part of human fellowship.

We cannot think of any of these protovalues as solely instrumental in their value, in the way we would think, for example,
of a washing machine or a fifty-cent piece. The experiences of
being alive, of maturing and growing as normally as one's given
potentialities permit, of acting from mental stability, and of
being at peace seem to be good in themselves, in addition to being the instrumental substructure for many other values.

As first among the supravalues—those which have a special pervasive requiredness and power for the actualization of other values, such as the seasoning in foods which might otherwise be somewhat insipid or a catalyst in a reaction which would not otherwise take place—as first in this group I shall list freedom. I intend "freedom" here in all of its practically important senses: ordinary freedom, to choose for oneself and to act from choice without compulsion or duress; political freedom, to help mold society without totalitarian control; civil freedom, to speak and to exercise other human rights; psychic freedom, to be productive and humane without enervating emotional blocks. Only in such a climate of full freedom can the life of value genuinely flower. "Freedom is . . . that faculty which gives unlimited usefulness to all other faculties. It is the highest order of life, which serves as the foundation of all perfections and is their necessary condition."[6]

The term "creative self-expression" or simply "creativity" usually adds a positive, active content to the idea of freedom alone, unless one deliberately qualifies his use of "freedom," as Erich Fromm does, for example, by a term like "positive freedom" and spells out the intended meaning. Without this verbal qualification we may think of freedom as giving one condition of human value but as requiring creativity to make its possibilities realized. We mean by creativity the quality of, as we say, being alive, being aware of constructive possibilities, being imaginatively and resiliently productive. In this sense, it can be listed as an additional supravalue. It might be argued that this is not needed to experience all intrinsic values—simple pleasures or knowledge, for example. Granted. But we are not suggesting the absence of all value apart from the metavalues. We are claiming that the metavalues have a peculiar pervasiveness without having specific objects—God, nature, man, truth—and that they have a highly catalytic and seasoning effect in relation to other values.

It must be kept in mind that in this chapter we are concerned with the value that various conscious states have for the human individuals who experience them. This does not exhaust the meaning or significance of those states but only indicates that they have, as it were, a reflexive character as value for the experiencing person. Thus, for example, the main import of benevolence is not that it brings value to the benevolent person but rather, by very definition, that it brings many other kinds of value to other people. Yet we may also talk about the reflexive value that benevo-

lence has, as a by-product, for the benevolent person insofar as
it perfects his moral will and thereby his total self.

It is in this way that we must distinguish between religion and
the value of religion. Religion, the third of our supravalues, may
be thought of *per se* as basic commitments and endeavors directed toward reconciliations among men, nature, and God. But
religion also has a reflexive value for the individuals who practice
it, for he who loses his life shall find it. This value is that of a
unifying and integrating directiveness in life. Thoughts, feelings,
and actions are unified around purposes that are conceived as
supremely worthy, and one's life is directed toward these objects
with conviction and often with zeal. This is no mean value when
we consider the terrifying possibilities for disintegration and loss
of self to which human beings are prey. Since we do not like to
think of religion as a purely private phenomenon, involving just
one's own solitude or just a soliloquy with God, with no implications for fellow men and perhaps the whole of being, it is well
to think of religion as a metavalue rather than as a specific type
of value.

The epivalue, alluded to before, will appear best after our survey is completed, and so we shall turn directly to the main classification of values.

An Outline of Principal Values

At this point the reader is referred again to the classification
of the modes of piety suggested in chapter 2 on page 26. This
will provide the basis of our classification of principal values.
However, since we are concerned here not with the objective re-
ferents as such but with their reflexive values for the individual,
it will be more appropriate to adapt the terms and emphases for
the purpose at hand. My procedure will be to make some inter-
pretive comments with regard to the chief categories of value
and then to show the proposed scheme in another synoptic outline.

The outline of values is not a recommendation for new values
never known before. It is not a transvaluation of values, though
one may hope that concentration on an adequate list of values
will help to transvaluate the disvalues that are prevalent. I take
it that what the philosopher is attempting to do in a proposed

outline of values is to say—on the basis of his own experience and on the basis of a considered judgment of mankind's moral consciousness, his value awareness, his social experience, his ordinary language, his psychology and religion—what types of value tend to fulfill man's nature, both in its generic needs and its individual variety capacities.

To begin with, in speaking of the four broad objects of value—God, the natural cosmos, man, and truth—as entering into culturally embodied systems of life, we suggested the terms "theocentric," "cosmic," "moral," and "noetic" piety. But in focusing now on the felt value states of the individual self, it will be better to use terms that bring out more immediately the value feelings involved. I suggest that this can be done most instructively if we speak of the values of reverence, the values of appreciation, the values of human relatedness, and the values of knowledge.

Under theocentric piety, the distinction was made between the piety of adoration and the piety of acts. Looking on the human value of these experiences, as contrasted with their theological intention of worship, we suggest that the first is best described in Rudolf Otto's phrase "numinous awareness," or the experience of the holy. That is, man in such an experience finds himself overwhelmingly transfixed by an awareness of the sacred or holy and he finds this to be of inestimable value to him. It is noteworthy that Otto specifically refers to the holy as a category of value,[7] though he should not be interpreted as one who describes religion as a purely subjective phenomenon.

The value of the other aspect, acts, comes in the realization that one's endeavors are, in intention, though not with certainty in fact, in accord with the best one knows, more particularly with the supreme creative will that makes for value in the universe. If such realization is rare, it is nevertheless cherished when felt. I distinguish this theocentric emphasis in acts from religion in general, for the term "religion" is usually defined more broadly today, so that, for example, a naturalistic religion like Buddhism will afford the integrating directiveness of religion without being theocentric. The term "service" is not quite apt here either, for it too is often used with exclusively humanistic intent. The term "vocation" is sometimes used for this emphasis in a theological setting. Whatever descriptive terms are employed, they will refer, in this value context, both to a man's God-inspired occupation and to

His little, nameless, unremembered, acts
Of kindness and of love.[8]

The values of appreciation, which we are defining as those
which emerge from man's relation to the natural cosmos, may
also be called natural values. First among these we must mention the values associated with our relation to our own psycho-
physical organism, insofar as this can be viewed as a natural phenomenon. Without going into detail about this obvious source of
value experience, we may perhaps divide these values into two
classes: pleasures and skills. Bodily pleasures would include the
satisfactions derived from our senses and our natural desires. Mental pleasure may be thought of as pervading all other value experience in varying degrees, but it may also be listed as a separate
category to cover such more obviously hedonistic experiences as
entertainment, amusement, humor, light reading, revery, and the
like. Physical skills would include the value found in all those
pursuits which involve some artful, skilled use of the body, as in
craftsmanship, athletic feats, games, hobbies, and manual work.
Mental skills would include the achievement value inherent in
any special development of our mental powers, as in well-trained
noticing, accurate memory, valid reasoning, solving problems,
mental discipline, and the like. This kind of value comes under
physical interaction in the modes of valuation listed in chapter 2.
    The other three divisions we listed under cosmic piety—natural
piety, esthetic emotion, and mystical awe—also suggest to us,
without much need for comment, further sources of natural
value. People find joy in natural piety, in beholding, appreciating,
and moving among the natural objects that surround them, provided, of course, these things are of such a sort, and are so arranged in the environment, as to call up this appreciation instead
of stifling it. They take delight in the various esthetic qualities in
art works, natural scenes, and the human form. And beyond these
is the value feeling of cosmic awe, often described as mystical,
which has the whole natural universe as its object. This feeling
might be entertained, for example, in contemplating the enormity
of the physical universe, with its countless galaxies and its vast
distances, or in meditating on the sort of unity that an individual
may be said to have with all things. All of these types of experience are found to be value laden, to be somehow perfective of
man.
    In surveying the values of human relatedness we must also
consider a relation to ourselves, viewed this time as a personality

or personal self. Value is experienced, first of all, in simply being a distinct, self-directed, individual person. Many terms have been employed to indicate this value: self-love, self-respect, a sense of dignity, authentic existence, proper pride, individualism, self-reliance, and so on. It will be sufficient if we refer to this value as "individuality."

Expanding outward to our relation to others, we find the closest is the value of living and developing in a family situation. Here we must also include sexual love, but not limit this to bodily pleasure alone.

Next is the value of friendship, which has always been highly prized by the value consciousness, and still is, even though it is becoming somewhat of a lost treasure in modern society. More common today perhaps than friendship are the hosts of other associations with people whose congenial and often convivial character is intrinsically valued by those who experience them.

The wider relationships that we have to more public groupings—community, state, nation, and world—are all aptly summed up in the term "citizenship." To be an active participant within the social units to which we belong—local, national, and international, and perhaps in the future interspatial—is considered to be of high value, not only for the good it might bring in society but for the individual who participates.

Finally, in this category we must emphasize that culminating quality whereby we become related most effectively to other people, namely, concern for the general and particular welfare of others. This is that very perfection of voluntary conduct which we discussed in the last chapter as the basis of duty and right, but which we can also see as a reflexive value for the individual through contributing to the perfection of his own nature. Again, many terms are current for this value: moral goodness, virtue, a sense of duty, reflective conscience, moral sensitivity, and so forth. Perhaps the value connotation involved is suggested best by speaking of "having a moral character," for this phrase connotes not only moral goodness in the strict sense but also what has traditionally been called "the virtues," that is, such further traits as humility, courage, resoluteness, friendliness, generosity, etc., which are not strictly equivalent with the sense of obligation. Though the virtues in this sense are not equivalent with duty, yet they are generally classified along with moral virtue or worth, because, in Socrates' way of putting it, the virtues are in a sense one. The term "moral character" connotes this wider complex of traits.

Little gloss need be added for the intellectual values. It seems self-evident that men find great value in the use of their minds in seeking truth, and this value is felt both in the actual attainment of truth, which we call knowledge, and in the very pursuit of it. Thus we may speak summarily of knowing and inquiring as the intellectual values.

With these remarks we shall propose our outline of chief types of human value. It must be remembered that such an outline can hardly be exhaustive, nor is it intended to be, for human values could be named, categorized, divided and subdivided almost indefinitely in detail. Nicholas Rescher has classified classifications of values under six headings (and even these are said not to be exhaustive) according to whether they refer, respectively, to (a) subscribership to the values, (b) the objects valued, (c) the sort of benefit at issue, (d) the sort of purposes at issue, (e) the relation between subscriber and beneficiary, or (f) the relation of the values to other values.[9] Our own classification (below) is probably of the "c" type, whereas our outline of the modes of valuation in chapter 2 might come under the "b" type, but possibly under a new category, that is, the relations between self and reality in which values arise.

The function of a short outline, such as the one below, is to focus on the kinds of things which, in general, we ought to seek in life, both from moral duty and for the perfection of life.[10]

Outline of Human Values

I. Metavalues
  A. Protovalues
    1. Life itself
    2. Maturation and growth
    3. Mental health
    4. World peace
  B. Supravalues
    1. Freedom
    2. Creativity
    3. Religion
  C. Epivalue: harmonious perfecting
II. Principal Values
  A. Values of reverence, or theocentric values
    1. Experience of the holy
    2. Experience of accord
  B. Values of appreciation, or natural values

      1. Psychophysical states
        a) Pleasure—bodily and mental
        b) Skill—bodily and mental
      2. Natural piety
      3. Esthetic experience
      4. Cosmic awe
    C. Values of human relatedness, or moral values
      1. Individuality
      2. Family life, including sexual love
      3. Friendship and association
      4. Active citizenship
      5. Moral character
    D. Values of knowledge, or intellectual values
      1. Knowing
      2. Inquiring

Are these not the values we seek?

The Highest Value

We can now take up the third question, which we distinguished at the beginning of the chapter. By the term "highest value" we mean the value which is to be preferred to all others, insofar as it is the end or goal to which the others contribute. Our proposed answer to the question of the highest value is found in what we call the epivalue, harmonious perfecting. In addition to what was said in chapter 4 about this concept, we shall make several further comments in the light of the foregoing survey.

Harmonious perfecting is an ideal that is simultaneously individual and social. The locus of value is the individual, and therefore the perfecting of individuals and their value experience is fundamental. Yet the ideal is not limited to some individuals only but is for all alike; hence the valuational aim is the enhancement of all. And since this aim demands harmonious interaction of individuals with one another, the end is also social or communal. Thus do we arrive at the highest value, namely, *the perfecting of each in harmony with all.*

The concept of harmonious perfecting is, however, a rather empty abstraction when taken by itself. This is why we needed the survey of principal values before attending to it further. We can now say that what we mean by harmonious perfecting is the coop-

erative attainment by individuals of this whole range of values
that perfect man's being, with due consideration of particular
needs, abilities, and circumstances, with discriminating emphases
according to the principles of ethics, and with the recognition
that finiteness demands of men that the life of value—like poli-
tics—must be the art of the possible. Harmonious perfecting will
involve a "symphony of values,"[11] or if not as replete as that, at
least chamber music.

I use the participial form of the noun, "perfecting," to indicate that, from our human vantage point, the highest value of
perfection remains for us ever an ideal to be striven after, and
that the most we can hope for as relevant to our daily endeavors
is progression toward it.[12] "Perfecting" also suggests a more ultimate characteristic, namely, that the highest value is no static
stoppage but implies continuous creativity and variety even if
qualitative ultimacy be reached.

To speak of harmonious perfecting is obviously to intimate
through a philosophical abstraction what in a religious context
would be referred to by more convictional terms. Christianity
speaks of the kingdom of God, Judaism of the Messianic age.
Buddhism speaks of *nirvana*, Hinduism of *moksha*. All these
terms are not equivalent by any means, but they indicate that
religions refer in convictional language to some highest state or
ideal. What is the relation between the two sorts of terms, philosophical and religious?

The philosopher—or at least this philosophical treatise—is attempting to say what can be said about values, including the
highest value, on the basis of rational inquiry. He therefore uses
more general, neutral words rather than specifically convictional
religious phrases. Furthermore, philosophy is limited—as religious
interpretation, based on faith, is not—to the ideals of human life
as we know it, and is not—as religion often is—concerned with an
eschatological state involving a radical transformation of present
life conditions. Now with these different perspectives some philosophers have, of course, arrived at conceptions incompatible
with a theological outlook. But this is not necessarily the case,
as in Josiah Royce's discussion of the "beloved community,"[13]
which he thought coalesced with the Christian ideal. One advantage of the term "harmonious perfecting" would seem to be
that, like Royce's term, it not only points very directly to an
ideal that is highly relevant to our known human life but is
not entirely inappropriate in meaning to an eschatological state.

Principles of Choice

We now come to the last task in this chapter. We are to consider whether, in view of the foregoing review of values, there are any subsidiary principles of choice concerning these values that are based on the ethical principles that were developed in the previous chapter, namely, prudence, loyalty, benevolence, *agape,* and universal piety.

To advocate any principles of choice is to imply that some kind of ranking or priority among values can be established. But there is at least one kind of ranking that is not possible, and that is the kind in which there would be, in the abstract, a definite and permanent scaling of all values by their respective priorities, just as one might list all the colors by their respective wavelengths and see them all in a fixed spectrum. In such a scheme one would simply choose from top to bottom at all times, insofar as one were able. This sort of ranking is impossible for three reasons: first, what is found meaningful and perfective depends very much on individual needs and abilities; second, because of the importance of individuality, variations of choice are justified due to preference; and third, since most choices involve social consequences, priorities must vary due to different or changing social circumstances. We must therefore seek our invariant guiding principles amid a context of variable rankings and priorities.

For convenience of perusal I shall state, under each numbered paragraph below, a subsidiary principle of choice which seems warranted and indicate its derivation or its relation to the general perfectivist framework.

1. First, and most generally, it is clear that if this survey does indeed cite the types of value which are perfective of human nature, we ought in all our choices to be scrupulous to enhance in some way these values, rather than the disvalues which are their opposites. This is a direct consequence of the principle of universal piety, that we ought to promote perfections generally. It is also a concretization of the first principle of classical ethical thought, that we ought to seek the good and avoid evil.

2. In our choices to actualize the values of life we should see to it that we are furthering the perfection of individual persons, unique selves, in their value experience. This is implied by the metaphysical thesis that the very locus of value is the individual and also by the great significance we attach to individuality in its own right in the list of values. It is likewise implicit in all the ethical principles, especially *agape.*

3. If we are correct in relating value basically to human need, as set forth in chapter 3, rather than to interest, preference, or the like, then in our choices among these values we ought to seek first of all to meet these needs wherever possible. Then subsequently—in a logical, not necessarily a temporal, sense—will we seek to enhance variety values beyond needs.

4. If the above values are indeed our intrinsic values, those that are constitutive of human perfecting, then we will keep them, rather than purely instrumental values, uppermost as we deliberate about intermediate ends and goals in our attempts to apply the principles of prudence, benevolence, etc. Having money, for example, will always be subordinate to meeting human needs for physical well-being, freedom, or beauty. This is not to say that instrumental values may not be vital as short-range goals or as abiding means. In fact, this subject needs more attention in philosophy; it is curious that philosophers have neglected instrumental values in favor of intrinsic values. The deficiency ought to be repaired, though it is not within the scope of this work to do so.

5. If the metavalues have the foundational character we suggest, it is clear that they will have a certain valuational priority over other values and that, at times, acting accordingly will be paramount. What would happen to other intrinsic values, for example, if a vast, worldwide fresh-water shortage prevented normal life, maturation, and growth? A painter, confronted with a choice between continuing to work at his easel while totalitarianism crept in or striking some decisive blow for freedom at the expense of his painting, ought, we may presume, to do the latter, for freedom is essential for the very possibility of art, as well as for many other values. Happily, the values of life can often be pursued together without conflict; but this does not negate an inherent priority which bursts clear at certain times.

6. We must always consider how context demands particular emphases. Some would call this the pragmatic principle or the contextual principle. It will be enough to refer to the idea involved as the "priority of the fitting." It has an important place in value theory, if it is not the dominating principle. It means that, over and above the concern for basic human needs and capacities, value priorities are often suggested or demanded by varying life problems, contexts, or situations, personal or interpersonal. We are then obliged to choose among values so as to do the fitting, to resolve the problem, to bring some release, to open some avenue of further values, to reconcile some breach, and so forth, and

to choose thus even if some tentative rule is not followed that might otherwise be relevant.

7. We must give priority—provided the context shows that other needs have been adequately satisfied—to those value capacities which most distinctively and uniquely perfect man as man. We have already suggested that life, growth, material necessities, and physical pleasure can have an intrinsic as well as an instrumental value, and that at times they must take priority in decisions. But if they are reasonably accommodated and are causing no special contextual problem, we must surely rank the values of the mind and spirit as higher, for they perfect man and his unique, his distinctively human, being. This would be an Aristotelian way of rescuing—if it is worth rescuing—the phrase "moral and spiritual values" from total vagueness, namely, by accepting their supremacy, provided moral values are understood to mean the values of human relatedness on our list and spiritual values are understood to signify all the others which are not predominantly physical, biological, or egoistic.

8. It is good to remind ourselves that while choice among values often requires the choice of one value over another, the exclusion of some values in favor of others, it is nevertheless frequently true that many values can be furthered abundantly together. It is well to stress this latter ideal as important on principle. A scientist with a blind spot for all art, an artist with no concern for citizenship, a philosopher with no love of people, or people with no tincture of philosophy are examples of disappointing narrowness that need not be.

9. Since moral goodness is a human value and in turn requires, through loyalty, benevolence, justice, and love, that values be sought for other persons and not just for oneself, we have the principle of value extension for everyone. Intrinsic values are open to all, and universality takes priority over exclusivity. Human values are to be promoted for all persons.

If we give names to these principles, we can list them summarily in the form of brief injunctions:

1. The principle of value furtherance: Further these values rather than their opposites.
2. The principle of individual perfecting: Enhance the perfection of individual persons.
3. The principle of basic needs: Meet need values before variety values.
4. The principle of intrinsic priority: Further these intrinsic values ahead of instrumental values.

5. The principle of metavalue priority: Promote metavalues as requisites to other values.
6. The principle of contextual priority: Consider how context makes particular value emphases fitting.
7. The principle of spiritual priority: With basic needs met, give priority to those value capacities which most fulfill man as man.
8. The principle of wholistic development: Promote as many intrinsic values together as possible.
9. The principle of human extension: Promote these values as far as possible for everyone.

Conclusion

Our chain of thought in this and the preceding chapter arrives at the following summary.

The discussion of ethics presupposes some rudimentary sense of obligation, some concern about what is right with respect to values. This is a precondition for the entire subject. Obligation can also be considered a value, as in our reference to the value of moral character; but in a more primordial sense it is really a prevalue, without which any discussion of principles and values is impossible. Inquiring into obligation and right, we concluded that they are most adequately conceived in relation to a hierarchical standard of moral principles, namely, prudence, loyalty, benevolence, justice, *agape,* and universal piety. These are principles of moral choice concerning values, and to complete the discussion we turned to the topic of major values. (Our survey of major values is shown in the table of values in this chapter.) We could then determine various value priorities and subsidiary principles of choice, even though an absolute ranking of values is not feasible. There are invariant priorities of the definite values over their opposing disvalues and of individual development over miscellaneous or indiscriminate value production. And there are, in general and depending on circumstances, the priorities of need values over variety values, intrinsic values over instrumental values, metavalues over other values, the fitting over inflexible rules, spiritual fulfillment over material pleasures, all-round development of values over narrow tastes, and values for all persons over self-interest.

7: Esthetic and Religious Value

There is a perennial fascination in relating the two kinds of experience we call, even if not very clearly, esthetic and religious. In this chapter we shall explore, for its own inherent interest, this relation between two of our primary (some would say our most ultimate) values.

What kind of program do we need to carry out in order to make this exploration profitable and slake our fascination? Certainly we would need, first of all, some characterization, independently, of the esthetic dimension and the religious dimension of life. Then we should want some comparison of features to show wherein the two converge toward and diverge from each other. We may then wish to consider situations in which one of the principals is the invited guest in the other's house. For example, is there a religious art, and is there an esthetic religiousness? Also, is there anything about these situations that would come under the headings of desirable or undesirable? This last question suggests a moral dimension, and we may well conclude by relating results to this focal point of all values, the sphere of obligation and action. Here is a program which, if we cannot do justice to it in full, at least points out directions for us and harnesses the interest of a brief chapter.

The Esthetic Dimension

To simplify, I shall begin by putting forward a thesis from which all else regarding the esthetic in this chapter will unfold, like the design of a rug emerging as the rug is unrolled on the floor. The thesis is that what we intend by the esthetic dimension of experience is a unique interplay of three factors: the esthetic attitude we bring to certain experiences, the objects focused on in those experiences, and the psychoemotional responses engendered by those objects; and furthermore that the main factor, the anchor, what we might call the *primary esthetic fact,* is the esthetic object. By "primary esthetic fact" I mean that by reference to which other esthetic terms are definable, such that the reverse is not the case.

Experiences that have this interplay of esthetic attitude, object, and responses are properly what is meant by esthetic experience. The term "esthetic experience," however, is sometimes used in a narrower sense to mean merely the subjective reactions involved in the complex of factors. To avoid confusion about this term I shall refer to these subjective reactions as "psychoemotional responses" and to the entire complex of factors as the "esthetic dimension" of life or of experience.

In support of the claim that the object is the primary esthetic fact, there is first the need to recognize the centrality, phenomenologically, of what is focused upon in the esthetic dimension, which is always the object; and there is, second, the demand to acknowledge the presuppositions of normative esthetic judgments which claim at least some kind of objectivity, such as would be provided by the primacy of the object. I also offer the following phenomenological speculation about the emergence of the esthetic dimension into the cultural foreground. We may imagine that primitive man brought to his world no prefigured and already conditioned esthetic attitude; rather he was first struck, fascinated, transfixed by certain features of his environment, certain esthetic objects, probably first in nature and then of his own making. This initial fascination merely arose, subjectively, from what we called in chapter 1 the transcendental (in Kant's sense) valuational capacity in man, his primordial piety. Once having savored such qualities in objects, man's attention eventually turned to what needed to be cultivated by way of attitude in order to reap more fully the delights afforded by such objects. So along with the making of art objects came the refinement, heightening, and fostering of the esthetic attitude so necessary for appreciating, what?—the *object*—and so necessary for wringing valuable psychoemotional responses from objects.

But our purpose here is not to investigate the object as such, since we are not engaged primarily in general esthetic theory. Our concern here is with the human-value aspect of the esthetic dimension, and for this we must turn to esthetic experience in the narrower sense, the psychoemotional responses. It is in these responses that what is humanly valuable is found, even though we may wish to say that beauty and the esthetic qualities of objects comprise an independent good in their own right.

Many have been the attempts to isolate some one reaction, or some group of reactions, that will uniquely define the esthetic response or experience. Without elaborating on this problem, I will merely suggest what seems to me the best line of solution to it. That would be to hold, first, that in general terms the esthetic response is simply any response which notices and appreciates the distinctive esthetic qualities of objects (which would have to be specified), and, second, that there is a variety of factors in such responses, some one of which, or some group of which, is always present. These factors could be thought of as displaying a "family resemblance,"[1] such that the entire group of traits is never wholly absent collectively from any individual esthetic response, yet they might not all be present together in it. These factors or traits could be identified as including perceptual content, images, physiological reactions, pleasure or delight, emotions of various kinds, ideas, empathic tendencies, and perhaps a higher noesis.

Now for our immediate purposes we are interested in noting, from among these factors or from among their relations to esthetic objects, any characteristics that will be especially significant for comparing esthetic and religious experience.

A first characteristic is what we might call immanent concentration. The esthetic response concentrates on an individual object, artistic or natural, just for the sake of the immanent qualities of the object. Though a person may be carried far beyond the object, especially through the ideational content, still the primary and culminating attention is focused on the object, just as a camera is focused on a scene to take a picture or a rifle is focused on a specific target to hit it.

The immanent concentration which takes place outwardly in relation to the object is correlated with a like unity within the psychoemotional responses themselves. The esthetic experience enfolds its elements, gathers them into a unity, and is enjoyed in its own immanent being. It is *sui generis* in value, a delight unto itself.

Back to the relation to objects again. The very function of the esthetic response is to apprehend with autonomous delight cer-

tain objective features of things and of works of art—features like
form, arrangement, rhythm, skillful composition or performance,
line, color, symbolization, beauty. All of the psychoemotional responses are in some way the means of picking up and dwelling
upon such features.

As a consequence of the above characteristics, it may be
pointed out that esthetic response is essentially contemplative
and not an incitement to action. This claim might be disputed
by "activist" poets, novelists, dramatists, and other artists. There
need be no quarrel, of course, if we are willing to make the distinction between what art is esthetically and what it might do
socially as a by-product. One may hope, socially speaking, that
art will lead to social betterment. But that is quite a different
thing from saying that art is, by its very nature, esthetically, a
call to action. A resounding "no" to that thesis is certainly the
consensus.

However, esthetic response has also been spoken of as cathartic
for the individual, if not society. Without vying for any particular theory about catharsis, Greek or otherwise, we can agree that
art often has a transforming influence on the individual beholder.
Esthetic response, though sometimes but a minor and passing delight, may at other times bring an immense elevation in spirit,
and even be a sustaining staple in life.

Both contemplation and catharsis suggest a certain vicarious-
ness, that is, involvement yet detachment, which the individual
experiences in esthetic response. The emotions one feels at a play
or at a gallery are real emotions, but the context is not the same
as one's ongoing daily life. To feel the jealousy of the Othello
situation or the pathos of the Lear story would not be the same
as feeling these emotions in relation to one's own family or
friends. One becomes involved in the esthetic object, yet a certain detachment or distance remains in esthetic response and is
essential to it.

Perhaps a word should be ventured on how esthetic response
relates us to existence as such by its particular objects. The
answer for many is that through esthetic response the world of
entities, usually so common, routine, and prosaic, becomes alive,
fresh, vibrant, vivid, shattering. "By dealing with things, by
making use of them, by becoming accustomed to them, as we
say, we lose sight of them." But esthetic response "gives the
world back . . . in all its original strangeness, the shock of its
first surprise."[2]

We have said enough to lay the first stone in our edifice. Let us place the second.

The Religious Dimension

The same problem concerning the dominance of the object or the subject is present in religious interpretation, as it is in esthetics. And it also seems most reasonable, and for similar reasons, to hold that the *primary religious fact* is the religious object. Religious feelings do not loom up in isolation but in response to the way in which the object is conceived or how it impinges on experience.

But again our interest centers not on the object as such but on the human-value factor of religious experience, and this is found in the felt significance of religion. And if we treat here of religious experience in general terms, this makes no presumption about the importance of the general over the particular. In fact, it can hardly be said that the general traits occur apart from particular forms; so it is the particulars that must be examined for the choosing of a religion. Our aim here is more limited.

G. Van der Leeuw, in his exhaustive phenomenological study of religion, finds that the most essential characteristic in all religion is the response to some awe-inspiring power. His conclusion is: "Religion exists always and universally. . . . And in each case its essence is powerfulness, always in the religious sense of this term."[3] The religious sense of power is not that of sheer brute might, not even always that of supernatural force, but rather that of power felt as mysterious, dynamic, efficacious, awesome, practical, sacred, holy, capable of engendering fear and terror on the one hand or love and obedience on the other.

Van der Leeuw also finds that, phenomenologically considered, religion takes surprisingly fewer forms than might be expected from first beholding the great diversity of religious phenomena in the world.

> History offers in religion, as elsewhere, only a restricted number of possibilities: the religion of Form, or of formlessness: that of Will, or of nothingness: the religion of asceticism, or of strain: of compassion or of obedience—with these the entire wealth of history appears to be practically exhausted. Just as, in the course of history, mankind turns again and again to some few symbols, so there are also

but few traits wherewith the essence of Power can be depicted, and only a few attitudes that can be adopted towards it.[4]

Now what is common in these human responses to sacred power, these "few attitudes that can be adopted towards it"? The answer is given in terms of a double movement, withdrawal and attraction, occurring simultaneously in religious experience. More vividly stated:

> In the human soul, then, Power awakens a profound feeling of awe which manifests itself both as fear and as being attracted. There is no religion whatever without terror, but equally none without love, or that *nuance* of being attracted which corresponds to the prevailing ethical level.[5]

Here, then, is a first element in religious experience: the response to holy power whose nature causes both withdrawal in fear and marvel, and attraction in love and obedience. In theistic religion the latter is emphasized because the holy power is believed to be itself love.

I believe this base can and must be supplemented by other characteristics that are seen as equally essential from other angles, and that in fact they are implicit in Van der Leeuw's account.

One of these characteristics that is immediately evident is the fact that the power is apprehended as a value object, and often, it may not be too much to say, as the supreme good. To go this far might seem to exclude a religion of the demonic. But "demonic" reflects a judgment, from our point of view, and though we may rightly regard certain views as perversions, this does not mean that the power is not (pervertedly) felt as supremely good by those who are attracted by it. Again, our statement might seem to exclude religions which have no supreme being but are drawn by myriads of finite objects filled with *mana*. But here the supreme value is simply the general power of *mana*—certainly not the particular sticks and stones, for these are sacred only because they possess *mana,* and they might lose it.

A further characteristic is seen when we focus not just on the practicality *of the power* but on the practical import *for the action of the religious experiencer.* Here the central aim must surely be thought of as some kind of reconciliation, of the individual or the group, with the value power in question. From this angle, reconciliation appears to be of the essence. This characteristic might not seem to accord with the movement of withdrawal cited by Van der Leeuw. But the withdrawal can be interpreted simply as an alternative strategy that seeks proper adjustment or reconciliation. If the flames are too hot in proximity, one withdraws for a more favorable adaptation to the fire. Beneath both attraction and withdrawal is a yearning to effect that mode of reconciliation which will be efficacious—not necessarily in a selfish sense—for the individual or the community.

This leads us to another distinctive characteristic, namely, that religious experience is suffused with what concerns man ultimately in life. If "ultimate concern" is not enough to define religion, it must at least be recognized as an important ingredient. Religious experience points to what men address themselves to above all else, what their ultimate commitments and endeavors are. And if every religious experience, as distinguished from the entire fabric of religion, cannot be said to lead equally to the heights or the depths, still none is totally detached from or devoid of some involvement with what is taken as ultimate concern.

Another set of characteristics might flood in if we attempted to draw a clear distinction between what has variously been called dynamic, open, higher, or ethical religion, on the one hand, and static, closed, lower, or amoral religion on the other hand. Let us settle for two points because of their central role in religious experience as it would commonly be thought of today. One is the ethical dimension, certainly a culminating facet of any form of religious experience that has come of age. The other is the element whereby the symbols and objects of the world are employed to help free the individual from bondage to that very finite world and to loft him to transcendent meaning and being. In theistic religion this would all be summarized in the term "worship" or "adoration." Others speak of elevation, liberation, mysticism.

Essential Convergences and Divergences

I use the terms "convergence" and "divergence" instead of "similarity" and "difference" or "identity" and "contrast" in order to keep clear that the esthetic and religious dimensions are different phenomenologically and that no useful purpose is served by suggesting that they are "just the same" in some respects and "just different" in others. We can, however, speak of ways in which they tend to converge toward or diverge from each other. First, convergences.

If we may take the esthetic experience of the artist, admittedly a special case of the esthetic dimension, as normative in some respects for esthetic experience generally, we may suggest that both the esthetic and the religious dimensions converge in displaying a charismatic spontaneity, a living in the spirit, as distinguished from binding rules and routine rigidities. Both elevate—today perhaps we should say "launch"—the individual into a state of creativity, of freedom, of grace, wherein he surpasses, for long or short periods, his ordinary humdrum self. He can feel in both a sense of the heightened being which is potential in human life. They both approach, if not a transvaluation, at least a supersession at times of ordinary ways of feeling and valuing.

As for what is sensed in these experiences, we notice immediately that both kinds embody a selectiveness in approaching the world. The things to which attention is paid or which are used as symbols are perceived not merely as ordinary sense objects, that is, complexes of sense data that are useful for practical purposes, but as objects that illustrate the particular characteristics of the given perspective, esthetic or religious. Both, in other words, are selective interpretations of existence, or, more primitively, selective responses to it. Paul Weiss refers to this convergence in the following example.

> The character of being "sacred" has a role similar to that characteristic of the features of aesthetic objects. . . . If we look at a cave with an architectural vision, we see something not in neutral nature (since this is irrelevant to us) . . . but the contoured space of an external aesthetic object. If we look at that very cave in a religious spirit, we see it instead as sacred, with a unitary nature at once divinely qualified and grounded in God.[6]

Not only are both types of experience selective in their emphasis concerning objects, they also show some convergence in what is selected and emphasized. That is, both select for emphasis various forms and symbols that are drawn to a large extent from particular cultures and societies, yet both seek to extricate the individual from mere conditioning, from local narrownesses, and to reach something more universal, more essential, or more eternal. If it is true of the esthetic dimension that it reflects some "unique perspective, historical period, and culture, but it may simultaneously be universal and abiding in human significance,"[7] this may certainly be said to be the emphasis and aim of the religious dimension too. They accomplish this aim in different ways and for different purposes, but the general convergence of interest is noteworthy.

All of these convergences point to what might be considered a culminating convergence, namely, that both esthetic and religious attitudes bring the respondent into fresh and insightful awareness of real existence. Both bring a rediscovery of the world, a new vision of what it is and how it can be viewed. They differ of course in what is noticed and under what perspective it is seen; but that real existence can take on new and vivid meaning through both art and religion is abundantly evident. Also, we need not argue at this point whether the respective experiences are cognitive in character, such that we can be said to know something we did not know before. Suffice it to say as a minimum that there is new significance, rediscovery, renewal of awareness, altered consciousness in relation to the world of real existence which we otherwise contact, for the most part, merely through the means of practical adjustment.

Now, divergences. And first—though it may seem too obvious to stress—the distinction between the beautiful and the holy, or, we may say, between esthetic quality and sacred power, is foundational for defining the very difference between the two responses and also as the basis of other divergences. Despite the convergences, the patent fact remains that the esthetic dimension of life pays attention to immanent qualities of form, harmony, rhythm, and sensory content, while the religious dimension is absorbed in qualities of sacredness, supreme good, adorability, and worshipfulness. In the words of two apt titles of poems by Hopkins, we may say that the esthetic consciousness sees the world as "Pied Beauty" and the religious consciousness sees it as "The Grandeur of God." All of the convergences are, to be sure, present in these two different modes of awareness, yet the two address themselves to divergent aspects of existence and, accordingly, give rise to contrasting emphases in interpretation and interest.

With this obvious difference in mind, let us consider some more subtle divergences which are implied by it.

Van der Leeuw indicates one of them when he speaks of the esthetic as being dependent on form and of the religious

as seeking freedom above form. A statement of the divergence is
as follows:

> Art always seeks the "foothold in the finite," the closed
> form. It must do so by its very nature. Formless art, art
> which has no style, is a creature of the imagination. Reli-
> gion, too, is subject to form. It also has its shells, and there
> are all too many of them. But it knows that the "foothold
> in the finite" stands in inmost contradiction to its essence.
> . . . But a novel, a drama, a symphony, a painted picture
> are the more perfect the more they approach the ideal of
> perfect form, beauty which rests in itself.[8]

One is thus tempted to speak of the simple difference between
form and formlessness. But religion seeks not so much the absence of form as the superseding of form in the life of the spirit.
Art, on the other hand, demands and seeks form for the very
fulfillment of its spirit, and this is true not merely in reference
to a strictly formalist theory. of esthetics but in reference to the
very nature of art.

A similar assertion about art, but with more emphasis on the
finite as temporal limitation rather than as form, is made by
Whitehead:

> The merit of art in its service to civilization lies in its arti-
> ficiality and its finiteness. It exhibits for consciousness a
> finite fragment of human effort achieving its own perfection
> within its own limits. Thus the mere toil for the slavish
> purpose of prolonging life for more toil or for mere bodily
> gratification, is transformed into the conscious realization
> of a self-contained end, timeless within time.[9]

Thus the esthetic experience slices out, as it were, some finite
portion of time or some finite extent of space and discovers
within that limit some immanent perfection, some inherent harmony, some objective perceptual delight. And if we can say this
is a fair way of describing the esthetic approach to existence, we
can also say that the religious experience directs us beyond the
finite to the infinite. In the religious dimension is the awareness
of eternal goodness and being undergirding the finite, of sacred
power as the ground of our existence. The very function of religious forms is not to rest with finite things but to see them as
divine instrumentalities and traces.

In the light of these phenomenological divergences it is easy to see yet another contrast—the most significant one from a practical point of view: Esthetic experience involves a certain detached, distanced contemplativeness, whereas religious experience of necessity escalates itself into practical life commitments and the direction of life's course. Man appreciates and enjoys esthetic forms, but he lives and dies for religious ideals. The esthetic is more discrete, self-contained, autonomous; the religious is more continuous with the convictions and ideals of an individual or a sacred community. The esthetic is a penultimate interest; the religious is an ultimate conviction.

Interfusion

Now we consider the possibility of merger. The question is whether, in view of the striking convergences, the esthetic and the religious dimensions can coalesce, unify, interfuse. If they did so in a predominantly esthetic context, we would have religious art or, more widely, religious estheticism; if they did so in a predominantly religious setting, we would have esthetic religion or, more widely, a religion of the esthetic.

The answer to the main question must surely be a qualified "yes": the two dimensions tend at times to merge or interfuse, at least in inward experience if not in outward manifestation. If there are the convergences at the phenomenological plane that we have suggested, then we can certainly recognize cases of interfusion, without risking ontological confusion. The heightened awareness of the world, or the insight concerning man, which is achieved in the esthetic dimension may reach a point where the beholder finds it religiously revelatory and decisive for his convictional commitments. Likewise, the context and symbols of the religious dimension may be so enshrined in esthetic quality as to magnify the feeling of the sacred and make it seem less possible without the beauty of that context or symbolic setting.

Can we then, to take the first case, speak of religious art or religious estheticism? Yes, provided we understand this in phenomenological terms and not in terms of subject matter employed or themes introduced. We are accustomed to speak of religious paintings or religious novels merely on account of the

content they deal with. No harm is done if it is clearly understood that this is but a convention for speed of communication.
There is no *essentially* religious art, however, unless some awareness of ultimate meaning or purpose, some illumination of the
ground of all existence, is mediated through the artistic vehicle,
and in that case no particular subject matter is necessary since,
as theism puts it, the divine is omnipresent and can be found
everywhere.

> The possession of God in beauty can be latent; it can also
> come to light at any moment. As soon as something "of
> the total meaning of life" shines forth, the aesthetic ex-
> perience has become a religious experience.[10]

What of the other case? Can we also speak of esthetic religion
or a religion of the esthetic? If the intention is merely to assert
that there are patterns of religion which are ornately clothed in
esthetic garb, then the claim is obviously true. One frequently
speaks in this sense of a highly esthetic service or church or
scene, as compared with plain, unadorned settings. But an *essentially* esthetic religion is a more difficult concept. For this to
occur, one would have to say, in effect, that esthetic experience
is one's ultimate concern, or, to paraphrase, that God is beauty
and beauty God and this is all one knows or needs to know
about religious experience.

In this sense, a religion of the esthetic is a possibility, though
it seems rare in occurrence. It appears to be held at times by
individual artists. I believe the only substantial organized form
of it is to be found in Zen, though some may differ from me
in the interpretation that Zen is properly to be characterized as
a religion of estheticism. But I take it that the aim of Zen is
simply that of having a heightened awareness of things—no revelation, no mystical union, no worship—just purity of awareness,
satori; and this can occur in relation to anything: a painting, a
flower, a mountain, a cup of tea. In ordinary language, this practice may be called religious because it takes the place, say, of
union with Brahman in Hinduism or fellowship with God in
Christianity. But in more exact usage it might better be called
an esthetic response, or a religion of estheticism.

Now we face the question of whether total interfusion is
desirable. We can agree at the outset, no doubt, that if ultimate
meaning can shine through the forms of art, then religious art is

eminently desirable, and if esthetic quality can enhance the religious experience, then esthetic religion is equally desirable. But is total interfusion, complete union, desirable, either in the context of religious art or in the context of a religion of the esthetic?

Aside from a specific religious commitment on this matter, there are two good philosophical reasons for not supporting or recommending total interfusion.

The first reason is a moral one. To hold consistently and absolutely to the esthetic as one's ultimate concern, one would have to place nothing above it in importance, not even the political defense of freedom merely to live one's life and to determine one's own goals in a peaceful world. From such a perspective, esthetic ultimacy seems narrow and self-centered. There are many values besides the esthetic, and one's moral concern in the world would seem to require more than a consistent, uniform penchant for having esthetic experience.

The other reason is phenomenological. If we were correct in depicting the divergences as well as the convergences, it would follow that much of the religious dimension of experience would be lost if it were simply identified with the esthetic. Phenomenologically, one would then be centered on the finite, the formal, the immanent, the self-contained, the sensorily delightful; and, valuable though these are, one would have but an attenuated grasp of the infinite, the eternal, the transcendent, the holy, the needed commitments for life and death. One would be grafted to the particulars of existence but would not be suffused with the ground of all existence. The religious experience which claims that this intimation of the transcendent is a possibility even without esthetic emphasis would be greatly impoverished if it had to be restricted to specific esthetic objects and qualities. One may add that the esthetic also would lose by total interfusion. There is certainly esthetic delight—probably most of it—which is valuable for itself but which does not rise to the level of revealing ultimate meaning and purpose. It seems an unreasonable restriction on art and esthetic experience to say that they must always be religious in character.

I do not say that the two would not be interfused in the kingdom of God. But we are in no position to effect such an eventuality without grave distortion setting in.

The Moral Dimension

The preceding discussion brings us straight to the realization
that the practical relationship between the esthetic and the religious, as distinguished from phenomenological description of
their relationship, cannot be settled apart from the moral dimension of life. As long as we are dealing with human values, it is
our ethical principles that determine priorities among them. The
esthetic cannot supersede the ethical, and the religious does not
negate moral insight. It is true that at times in history it is proper and necessary to abrogate what has been a prevailing moral
outlook in the name of a more ultimate religious concern. Then
a new wave of moral insight may take place. But the aim of
religion is not, as such, to dispense with the ethical but rather
to give it sanction and guidance.

What the moral dimension demands first of all, it would seem,
is that our ultimate concern among values *be* our ultimate concern, that is, that religious conviction take precedence over penultimate interests. To say this is nothing other than to advocate
personal integrity, self-consistency, honesty. To say otherwise
would be to countenance duplicity, hypocrisy.

This demand would mean for most people that the esthetic
is a subordinate value and must serve its role within more ultimate convictions. But, curiously enough, warrant is also given
here to those who claim that for themselves the esthetic is the
religious. Here too there may be integrity. Is there a contradiction in our position?

Not at all. For the demand that one's ultimate concern *be*
one's ultimate concern is not the only demand made by the
moral dimension in this area. Integrity is necessary, but it is not
enough. The moral dimension also demands, of both esthetic
and religious interests, that the cause of human perfection be
served. This is a direct consequence of the principle of universal piety. The case insisted upon by morality is that neither the
estheticism of an individual or a group, nor the religiousness of
an individual or a community, can be isolated from the ideal
of universal perfection of all individuals. If one's religiousness
gives divine sanction to this ideal, as it does in theism, and if
one's estheticism gives aid to and spurs this ideal, as it does in
great art, there is no conflict but, on the contrary, added im-
petus and harmony. But if such is not the case, if special priv-
ilege or moral negligence is fostered at the expense of human

good, then the moral dimension demands reassessment and readjustment. No doubt more could be said on this theme from the perspective of a particular religious conviction, but these remarks would seem to hold on the basis of general philosophical ethics.

Esthetic, religious, and moral, along with intellectual, values form a natural crown of the human value system. In its own way and in its own context, each of these has some valuational priority: the esthetic in its awakening of the soul to fresh harmonies in all existence, the religious in its impelling the soul to sacred worship and meaning, the moral in its direction of the soul toward the perfection of each in harmony with all, and the intellectual in its uniting of the soul with truth. Blessed indeed is he whose soul is integrated in regard to these values—in time, in space, in proper proportion, in contextual priority. His is a single-minded response, active and passive, to being itself, seen now as the beautiful, now as the holy, now as the good, now as the true, and each suffusing though not becoming the others. His is an infinite piety.

Summary

Much of what has been emphasized in this chapter can be summarized in the following outline of propositions.

1. The esthetic response is characterized by
     Immanent concentration outwardly
     Immanent unity inwardly
     Focus upon specific features of particular objects
     Contemplative rather than activist mood
     Catharsis of some sort
     Detachment and vicarious involvement
     Rediscovery of the world of things
2. The religious response is characterized by
     Awareness of awesome power
     A sense of the sacred or holy
     Acceptance of the holy as value
     Ultimate commitment
     Endeavors to reconcile
     Ethical demands as divine sanctions
     Worship, or liberation, or mystical identification
3. The esthetic and the religious converge with respect to
     Charismatic spirit

Seeking the permanent or universal through particular
conditioned forms
Selectivity in grasping existence
Heightened awareness of existence
4. The esthetic and the religious diverge with respect to
The beautiful versus the holy
Form versus transcendence of form
Immanent finite perfections versus transcendent infinite
meanings
Distanced contemplativeness versus active commitment
5. The esthetic and the religious fuse at the point of religious
art and esthetic religion, but total interfusion is undesirable for moral and phenomenological reasons.
6. The moral dimension of life demands that one's ultimate
commitments be followed consistently and with integrity,
and that both the esthetic and the religious serve the
cause of human perfection.

PART THREE

Nonhuman Good

8: Voices of Natural Piety

The idea of nonhuman good has long been a matter of controversy in analytical and speculative philosophy. The question is whether the term "good" or its derivatives are properly applied to anything other than human states of consciousness or, by extension, animal consciousness. The classical doctrine is that goodness and being are convertible terms, whereas the modern preference appears to be substantially in favor of restricting "goodness" to consciousness. In this part we shall inquire into this question and shall see that the two doctrines are not in all respects opposed, allowing us to reconcile their respective claims.

In this chapter I want to begin with data. I want to display a wide variety of quotations, which I have been collecting for some time, to show how extensive has been the belief in or the feeling of the reality of nonhuman good. I shall call this intimation of nonhuman good, whether in belief or in feeling, "natural piety," using the term in a somewhat generous sense. The quotations will not give proofs of nonhuman good; rather they will illustrate what may be called the data of natural piety, that is, the primitive awarenesses in human experience on which constructive theories draw.

I like to think of this chapter as affording, with respect to natural piety, a miniature parallel to what William James accomplished with respect to religious experiences in his *Varieties of Religious Experience*. The undertaking will remind us of the range of experiences that must be taken into account in devising our formal theories about the good.

I shall select the quotations first of all from poetry, then from religion, then from miscellaneous quarters, and finally from philosophy itself. These are my sources, these are the voices of natural piety.

Poets Sing the Good in Nature

Along with common sense, natural piety poetry is our most
fertile source for the awareness of good in the natural world,
for poetry embodies an immediacy of thought and feeling that
are unprejudiced by elaborate assumptions, philosophical speculations, or theological deductions. I shall not claim, by any
means, that poets are unanimous in their value responses to nature. There are those who find it "red in tooth and claw," and
little more; those who are dismayed by it or dread it; those who
find it wayward and indifferent; those who ignore it. But I believe these attitudes are not typical and that poets for the most
part through the centuries have celebrated in their many linguistic ways a valuational kinship between themselves and nature, a kinship which is mutual and not merely an empathic
projection of the ego on the natural world.

I shall suggest by illustration that there are at least ten ways
in which poets celebrate (I am tempted to say demonstrate) the
good they find in the nonhuman realm. To give advance notice
of these ways, I shall summarize by saying that a poet may, in
relation to nature,

1. Sing its beauty;
2. Acclaim its purity, innocence, or perfection;
3. Express love of it;
4. Lament its transience;
5. Compare it favorably with man;
6. Appeal to it as teacher;
7. Adumbrate its mystery;
8. Regret alienation from it;
9. Withdraw to it in mystical retreat;
10. Declare its goodness didactically.

(1) So common is it for poets to sing of nature's beauty that
even a cursory study will bring floods of examples. Let us illustrate—and begin our cantata—with these lines from Gerard Manley Hopkins:

> Glory be to God for dappled things—
>   For skies of couple-colour as a brinded cow;
>   For rose-moles all in stipple upon trout that swim;
> Fresh-firecoal chestnut-falls; finches' wings;
>   Landscape plotted and pieced—fold, fallow, and
>   plough; . . .

> He fathers-forth whose beauty is past change:
>   Praise him.[1]

From another poet, here is a more simple feeling of beauty:

> Lord, when I look at lovely things which pass,
>   Under old trees the shadow of young leaves
> Dancing to please the wind along the grass,
>   Or the gold stillness of the August sun on the
>   August sheaves;
> Can I believe there is a heavenlier world than this?[2]

(2) Until recently, perhaps, when confidence has been shaken, nature has stood among poets for what is pure, innocent, or perfect. Despite evil and human contrivance, nature at least remained undefiled, untainted, a haven for pure enjoyment. Thus Shelley, who abounds in this feeling:

> Away, away, from men and towns,
> To the wild wood and the downs—
> To the silent wilderness
> Where the soul need not repress
> Its music lest it should not find
> An echo in another's mind,
> While the touch of Nature's art
> Harmonizes heart to heart.[3]

Solidly unequivocal is Coleridge's climactic line in the following:

> "Most musical, most melancholy" bird!
> A melancholy bird? Oh! idle thought!
> In Nature there is nothing melancholy.[4]

And here is an older witness to something objectively perfect in nature:

> What pleasure were to walk and see,
> Endlong a river clear,
> The perfect form of every tree
> Within the deep appear.[5]

(3) A poet may, with minimum ulterior intention or intellection, simply express his love and joy in being among the things of nature. A nice illustration is from Lord Byron:

> I love not man the less, but Nature more,
> From these our interviews, in which I steal

> From all I may be, or have been before,
> To mingle with the Universe, and feel
> What I can ne'er express, yet cannot all conceal.[6]

A quatrain from Walter Savage Landor tells us his value priority in the second line:

> I strove with none, for none was worth my strife,
> Nature I loved and, next to Nature, Art:
> I warm'd both hands before the fire of life;
> It sinks, and I am ready to depart.[7]

Also, it is not amiss to quote in this connection these famous lines of Coleridge:

> He prayeth well who loveth well
> Both man and bird and beast.
> He prayeth best who loveth best
> All things both great and small.[8]

And can we forget the primitive affections of our American *enfant terrible,* Walt Whitman?

> All truths wait in all things, . . .
> The insignificant is as big to me as any,
> I believe a leaf of grass is no less than the journey-work of
>   the stars,
> And the pismire is equally perfect, and a grain of sand, and
>   the egg of the wren,
> And the tree-toad is a chef-d'oeuvre for the highest,
> And the running blackberry would adorn the parlors of
>   heaven,
> And the narrowest hinge in my hand puts to scorn all
>   machinery,
> And the cow crunching with depress'd head surpasses any
>   statue,
> And a mouse is a miracle enough to stagger sextillions of
>   infidels.[9]

(4) Poetry is filled with regrets over temporal passage in the natural realm, particularly the ending of that which is beautiful or enthralling. If time is viewed in one respect as an arena for decision, a vale of soul making, it is seen in another respect as a thief. But why would this be so if what is regretted were not a cherished good? Robert Herrick is but typical when, in addressing the lovely blossoms, he says:

> What! were ye born to be
> An hour or half's delight,
> And so to bid good night?
> 'Twas pity Nature brought you forth
> Merely to show your worth
> And lose you quite.[10]

(5) A poet may see nature in a very favorable light, compared to man, thereby showing not only the disappointment felt toward man but the good or worth experienced in nature. Shelley's exaltation of nature has this byplay—as well as other sentiments, as indicated in our previous quotation from him—and even more in these lines:

> I love snow, and all the forms
> Of the radiant frost.
> Everything almost
> Which is Nature's, and may be
> Untainted by man's misery.[11]

The pungency of the comparison is asserted economically if we juxtapose three short lines from a poem by Edward Thurlow:

> May! queen of blossoms,
> And fulfilling flowers, . . .
>
> Thou hast no need of us.[12]

An engaging twist of emphasis is achieved when the harshness of nature is frankly recognized and still is compared favorably with man, the implication being that even the worst in nature has something better to commend it than human dealings:

> Blow, blow, thou winter wind,
> Thou art not so unkind
> As man's ingratitude; . . .
>
> Freeze, freeze, thou bitter sky,
> That dost not bite so nigh
> As benefits forgot;
> Though thou the waters warp,
> Thy sting is not so sharp
> As friend remember'd not.[13]

(6) A poet may submit to nature as the all-knowing or at least all-

inspiring teacher of man. Here we encounter the relation of pupil
to master, whose motto might well be:

> Come forth into the light of things,
> Let Nature be your teacher.[14]

And thus we come to Wordsworth, the master builder, if not the
master craftsman, of the whole sentiment of natural piety. Wordsworth seems to unite all the approaches and attitudes of this sentiment:

> For nature then . . .
> To me was all in all.[15]

But he is insistent at times on the pedagogical status of nature:

> One impulse from a vernal wood
> May teach you more of man,
> Of moral evil and of good,
> Than all the sages can.[16]

We truly learn, he thinks,

> Not with the mean and vulgar works of Man;
> But with high objects, with enduring things,
> With life and nature; purifying thus
> The elements of feeling and of thought.[17]

We can be confident in her teachings,

> Knowing that Nature never did betray
> The heart that loved her. . . .[18]

Let us now look at a longer passage in which Wordsworth summarizes his natural piety and relates it to a kind of pantheism of
nature:

> . . . And I have felt
> A presence that disturbs me with the joy
> Of elevated thoughts; a sense sublime
> Of something far more deeply interfused,
> Whose dwelling is the light of setting suns,
> And the round ocean and the living air,
> And the blue sky, and in the mind of man;
> A notion and a spirit, that impels
> All thinking things, all objects of all thought,
> And rolls through all things. Therefore am I still
> A lover of the meadows and the woods,

And mountains; and of all that we behold
From this green earth; of all the mighty world
Of eye, and ear,—both what they half create,
And what perceive; well-pleased to recognise
In nature and the language of the sense,
The anchor of my purest thoughts, the nurse,
The guide, the guardian of my heart, and soul
Of all my moral being.[19]

(7) Nature may fascinate, intrigue, or mystify a poet by its inscrutable workings or depths. And while adumbration of mystery may portend a hidden evil as well as a captivating good, poets often connect mystery in a circuitous tie with some difficult but not illusory good in nature. This must be at least part of what the tiger represents to Blake:

Tyger! Tyger! burning bright
In the forests of the night,
What immortal hand or eye
Could frame thy fearful symmetry? . . .

When the stars threw down their spears
And water'd heaven with their tears,
Did he smile his work to see?
Did he who made the Lamb make thee?[20]

A cosmic exchange in mystery is hinted at in the following lines:

O be prepared, my soul!
To read the inconceivable, to scan
The million forms of God those stars unroll
When, in our turn, we show to them a Man.[21]

Mystery can lure even those who are not inclined toward reading back any objective natural good from the world. Thus Hardy, not noted for rosy optimism, can say to the thrush:

So little cause for carolings
Of such ecstatic sound
Was written on terrestrial things
Afar or nigh around,
That I could think there trembled through
His happy good-night air
Some blessed hope whereof he knew
And I was unaware.[22]

(8) A poet may express a feeling of alienation or estrangement

from nature. But why would he do so unless he feels that that from which he is separated is a loss to him, an objective good, to which reconciliation would be of great value to him? Thus the thesis of natural piety is present here also.

This estrangement is the theme of an interesting poem, "World-Strangeness," by a minor English poet, William Watson:

> Strange the world about me lies,
>   Never yet familiar grown—
> Still disturbs me with surprise,
>   Haunts me like a face half-known.
>
> In this house with starry dome,
>   Floored with gemlike plains and seas,
> Shall I never feel at home,
>   Never wholly be at ease?
>
> On from room to room I stray,
>   Yet my Host can ne'er espy,
> And I know not to this day
>   Whether guest or stranger I?
>
> So, between the starry dome
>   And the floor of plains and seas,
> I have never felt at home,
>   Never wholly been at ease.[23]

The poetry of estrangement is of course profuse, expressing the anxiety and disillusionment of an age. But not all of it refers to natural objects as paradigmatic for man, as do the lines below from Hopkins. He is contrasting sea and skylark as representative of nature with man's state.

> How these two shame this shallow and frail town!
> How ring right out our sordid turbid time,
> Being pure! We, life's pride and cared-for crown,
> Have lost that cheer and charm of earth's past prime.[24]

(9) A poet may turn to nature in a mood of mystical identification, somehow finding human good and natural good merged. William Blake, in one of his prose etchings, states the mystical sense:

> He who sees the infinite in all things, sees God. He who sees the Ratio only, sees himself only. Therefore God becomes as we are, that we may be as he is.[25]

This is the unity theme of mysticism. But a poet may also simply
have empathy with nature in a mutual longing for a final good:

> Ah, Sun-flower! weary of time,
> Who countest the steps of the sun,
> Seeking after that sweet golden clime
> Where the traveler's journey is done: . . .
> Where my Sun-flower wishes to go.[26]

Blake is a religious poet; but mystical feeling can also be naturalistic. For example, Robinson Jeffers, in "The Rock and the Hawk,"
speaks of "the mysticism of stone."

(10) A poet may, picturesquely or even prosily, simply proclaim
the goodness of nature in a didactic fashion. Pope is our eminent
instance in point:

> All nature is but art unknown to thee,
> All chance, direction which thou canst not see;
> All discord, harmony not understood;
> All partial evil, universal good.[27]

Emerson's poem on the world soul is another instance. In the
portion quoted below we hear first a kind of invocation, then didactic interpretation, and lastly a note of optimism:

> Thanks to the morning light,
> Thanks to the foaming sea,
> To the uplands of New Hampshire,
> To the green-haired forest free; . . .
>
> The inevitable morning
> Finds them who in cellars be;
> And be sure the all-loving Nature
> Will smile in a factory.
> Yon ridge of purple landscape,
> Yon sky between the walls,
> Hold all the hidden wonders
> In scanty intervals. . . .
>
> Over the winter glaciers
> I see the summer glow,
> And through the wild-piled snow-drift
> The warm rosebuds below.[28]

A further example, from a poet laureate:

> Love, from whom the world begun,
> Hath the secret of the sun.
>
> Love can tell, and love alone,
> When the million stars were strewn,
> Why each atom knows its own,
> How, in spite of woe and death,
> Gay is life, and sweet is breath.[29]

We began our poetry selections with Hopkins and we may well conclude with his unmatchable two-line summation of a poet's natural piety. After noting the ills that man has done to nature, he says nevertheless:

> And for all this, nature is never spent;
> There lives the dearest freshness deep down things.[30]

The Religious Revere the Good in Nature

Next we turn to our second major source, the expressions concerning natural good that appear in religious literature. Here we frequently find the qualification that assertions are made not of a good in nature *in se* but of the conviction that nature is a good or value to God and thereby indirectly good, objectively, from a human point of view. Sometimes even this qualification is not present and we have a direct statement.

The classical source for Western religious natural piety is, of course, the creation story in the book of Genesis. After the recounting of each act of creation comes the refrain: "And God saw that it was good." Then, at the end, there is the climactic utterance: "And God saw every thing that he had made, and behold, it was very good" (Gen. 1:31). In commenting on the attitude toward physical nature to which this biblical view gave rise in Jewish life, Huston Smith writes:

> One specific element in the Biblical account . . . deserves special notice; namely, its estimate of nature, the physical component of things.
>   Much of Greek thought, notably that dominated by Plato and Plotinus, takes a dim view of matter. In Hinduism and Theravada Buddhism the basic outlook is optimistic in spite of the material world rather than because of it. In India matter tends to be regarded as a barbarian,

spoiling everything she touches. Liberation lies ultimately in
extricating spirit from its material involvement.

How different the first chapter of Genesis. . . . Pressing
for meaning in every direction, the Jews refused to abandon
the physical aspects of existence as illusory, defective, or
unimportant. Fresh as the morning of creation, they were
to be relished with zest.[31]

Later biblical references can be found to echo or amplify this
attitude. The Psalms are not didactic in style, but perhaps something of their approach to nature can be captured from these
verses:

The heavens are telling the glory of God;
and the firmament proclaims his handiwork. [Ps. 19:1]

Thou crownest the year with thy bounty; . . .
The pastures of the wilderness drip,
  the hills gird themselves with joy,
the meadows clothe themselves with flocks,
  the valleys deck themselves with grain,
    they shout and sing together for joy. [Ps. 65:11–13]

Let the heavens be glad, and let the earth rejoice;
  let the sea roar, and all that fills it;
  let the field exult, and everything in it!
Then shall all the trees of the wood sing for joy
  before the Lord. [Ps. 96:11–13]

We find the Genesis theme continued in an Apocryphal book:

For thou lovest all things that exist, and hast loathing for
none of the things which thou has made, for thou wouldst
not have made anything if thou hadst hated it.[32]

St. Paul gives a theological interpretation of nature when he
suggests that the natural creation has shared in the downfall which
has befallen man:

For the creation waits with eager longing for the revealing of
the sons of God; for the creation was subjected to futility,
not of its own will but by the will of him who subjected it
in hope; because the creation itself will be set free from its
bondage to decay and obtain the glorious liberty of the
children of God. We know that the whole creation has been
groaning in travail together until now. [Rom. 8:19–22]

The inference from this passage might seem to be that nature is not good but evil; but the deeper, presupposed truth is that nature is basically and originally good—only it has been temporarily spoiled.

Now let us shift abruptly to some examples from Eastern religion, before returning to some later allusions in Western religious thought.

We must agree in general with Huston Smith's estimate, in a quotation above, of the Hindu view of matter. We could mention, however, as a qualification, matter which is informed by life, which is given great reverence in India. We could also point out that nature in Hindu thought gains a certain stature, a certain elevation, by being seen, from the vantage point of the sage's mystical monism, as one in essence with all being. For is not everything Brahman to him? Thus in the *Bhagavad-Gita* it is said of the yogin:

> He rests in the inner calm of the Atman, regarding happiness and suffering as one. Gold, mud, and stone are of equal value to him. The pleasant and the unpleasant are alike. He has true discernment.[33]

The teaching concerning life, mentioned above, seems to have been carried to its extreme in India in the Jain religion. This *ahimsa* doctrine shows how the nonhuman realm is revered for one reason, the presence of life. Matter is valued for its association with life. The following quotation from a pamphlet on Jainism expounds this association as well as the general teaching:

> The Jain religion teaches that even the smallest of the small living beings (Jeevas) should be given protection and should not be hurt. It is the teaching of Jainism that all living beings in the world desire to live. . . . Therefore, every living being should protect every other living being whether it is endowed with one sense or five senses, whether it is an animal or a man. There is life (jiva) even in earth, water, fire, air and vegetables. The soul in all living beings is like the soul in us.[34]

From Japan, I choose some scattered sentences from *The Book of Tea* which hint at a beauty in things despite their impermanence and disharmony, as seen by Japanese Zen:

> Teaism is a cult founded on the adoration of the beautiful among the sordid facts of everyday existence. . . . Let us dream of evanescence, and linger in the beautiful foolishness of things. . . . We have even attempted to speak in the language of flowers. How could we live without them? . . . Their serene tenderness restores to us our waning confidence in the universe.[35]

Some think the Chinese have the most direct appreciation of nature for its own sake, perhaps because the Chinese approach is more naïve and uncomplicated by metaphysical presuppositions. I quote two short passages from Smith, drawing a comparison:

> How should man relate himself to nature? On the whole the modern Western attitude has been to regard nature as an antagonist, something to be squared off against, dominated, controlled, conquered.

> There is a naturalism in Chinese thought, but it is the naturalism of the artist and the romanticist instead of the scientist, the naturalism of Thoreau and Wordsworth rather than Galileo or Bacon. Nature is something to be appreciated, intuited, communed with, reverenced; there is no sustained thought of using it or suggestion that it might be mastered.[36]

Following the emergence of Jewish natural piety, we can probably take this description of a leading Jewish figure, Israel Ben Eliezer or Baal Shem Tob, as both luminous and typical:

> Informally and aphoristically he taught that God dwells in all things in nature and man. Since God is thus in all things, the good is in all things and all men. . . . The pervasive attitude was a humble, unaffected, and generous love for all God's world.[37]

And now let us hear from the greatest of the medieval Jewish thinkers, Maimonides. In the words below he stresses the intrinsic significance that each thing has just in being what it is.

> I consider therefore the following opinion as most correct . . .; namely, that the universe does not exist for man's sake, but that each being exists for its own sake, and not because of some other thing.[38]

For a modern example we turn, as we so often do, to Martin Buber. The world of nature, according to Buber, can enter to a certain extent into the I–Thou relation, thereby revealing its own inherent worth. Here is his description of our possible relations to a common tree:

> I consider a tree.
> I can look on it as a picture. . . .
> I can perceive it as a movement. . . .
> I can classify it in a species and study it as a type. . . .
> I can subdue its actual presence and form so sternly
> that I recognize it only as an expression of law. . . .

> I can dissipate it and perpetuate it in number, in
> pure numerical relation.
> In all this the tree remains my object, occupies space
> and time, and has its nature and constitution.
> It can, however, also come about, if I have both will
> and grace, that in considering the tree I become bound up
> in relation to it. The tree is now no longer It. . . .
> The tree is no impression, no play of my imagination,
> no value depending on my mood; but it is bodied over against
> me and has to do with me, as I with it—only in a different
> way.[39]

Next we follow through on some further Christian expressions
of natural piety, or, to repeat, intimations of some good that is inherent in natural things. St. Augustine is a prime example. In the
first quotation below he contrasts appreciative and practical attitudes toward nature, and in the second he gives voice to the doctrine
that goodness is a transcendental coincident with being.

> Thus the reason of one contemplating nature prompts very
> different judgments from those dictated by the necessity of
> the needy, or the desire of the voluptuous; for the former con-
> siders what value a thing in itself has in the scale of creation,
> while necessity considers how it meets its need.[40]

> All natures, then, inasmuch as they are, and have therefore a
> rank and species of their own, and a kind of internal harmony,
> are certainly good.[41]

Since Augustine is commonly regarded, not without reason, as
unduly scornful of the world of the senses and the flesh, the following quotation may be a partial antidote to this interpretation and
serve to give a truer picture of his meaning:

> There is no need, therefore, that in our sins and vices we accuse
> the nature of the flesh to the injury of the Creator, for in its
> own kind and degree the flesh is good; but to desert the Crea-
> tor good and live according to the created good, is not good.[42]

Boethius also, in one of his theological tracts, declares the goodness of being:

> Things which are, are good. For all the learned are agreed that
> every existing thing tends to good and everything tends to its
> like. Therefore things which tend to good are good. . . . But

those things whose substance is good are substantially good. But they owe their actual Being to absolute Being. Their absolute Being therefore is good; therefore the absolute Being of all things is good.[43]

It is one thing to state an abstract belief about the good in nature; it is another to live daily in a spontaneous love of natural things. As an example of one who practiced the latter, it is generally thought that few can parallel St. Francis of Assisi. His biographer says of him:

> Whence we who were with him used to see him rejoice, within and without, as it were, in all things created; so that touching or seeing them his spirit seemed to be not on earth but in heaven. And by reason of the many consolations which he used to have in things created, a little before his death he composed certain Praises of the Lord for His creatures.[44]

These "Praises," contained in "The Song of Brother Sun,"[45] celebrate sun, moon, stars, wind, water, fire, earth, and all natural things.

From the mystical tradition I choose Meister Eckhart:

> The least one knows of God as, for example, to see a flower get its Being from him, is more perfect knowledge than any other. To know the least of creatures as one of God's Beings, is better than knowing an angel. . . . I once said that wood is better than gold, which is a fantastic thing to say, and yet a stone, to the extent it has Being, would be better than even God and the Godhead without Being.[46]

And from the devotional tradition Francis de Sales:

> Behold, Philothea, how one may extract good thoughts and holy aspirations from everything that presents itself amidst the variety of this short life! Unhappy they who withdraw the creatures from their Creator, to make them the instrument of sin; and thrice happy they that turn the creatures to the glory of their Creator, and employ them to the honor of his sovereign Majesty.[47]

Pascal, both devout and scientific, sees nature, in his characteristic way, as a mixture of perfection and blemish:

> Nature has some perfections to show that she is the image of God, and some defects to show that she is only His image.[48]

In either case, "We must not judge of nature by ourselves, but by it."[49]

Coming to more contemporary writers, I offer Henry Drummond's vivid portrayal of Robert Burns:

> Carlyle said of Robert Burns that there was no truer gentleman in Europe than the ploughman-poet. It was because he loved everything—the mouse, and the daisy, and all the things, great and small, that God had made. So with this simple passport he could mingle with any society, and enter courts and palaces from his little cottage on the banks of the Ayr.[50]

In speaking of love in the context of work, R. L. Calhoun can say:

> What we mean here is, first, a lusty, sensuous delight in things men see and handle, and in the seeing and handling of them: well-planed wood or a sweet-running engine, good soil or well-bred livestock. Such love of the things with which one works —materials, tools, books, plants, and animals—is the best solvent of the paradoxes that complicate the worker's living. It gives reality to the assurance that in the devotion of his life, a man will find it.[51]

C. S. Lewis, amid some thoughts on prayer, mentions "the behavior of stars and trees and water, . . . sunrise and wind," then adds: "May there be *here* (in my heart) the beginning of a like beauty."[52] Later, in reference to the creation of the world, he says:

> This creative act . . . is for the sake of each human soul. Each is an end. Perhaps for each beast. Perhaps even each particle of matter—the night sky suggests that the inanimate also has for God some value we cannot imagine.[53]

Lastly in this section I shall present an extended excerpt from contemporary philosophy of religion. It is from William Temple, who sets down what he considers to be a condition for the appearance of good in nature, and also speculates on the sort of good that nature has for God.

> Till Mind appeared as an episode in the world process, all other episodes had value in potentiality only, not in actuality —so far at least as the process itself supplied the condition of its actualization. In the sight of God, and it may be also of spirits other than those born in the world process, that

process and its episodes had value. But with the coming of minds there came also for the first time episodes within the process supplying to other episodes the condition for the actualization of their value. . . .

In the inorganic world we may imagine that the divine mind takes delight, as that world in vast expanse and tiny detail expresses the perfection of quantitative relationships. It is a delight both scientific and aesthetic, and if here perhaps the scientific preponderates, we may assume that there is preponderance of aesthetic satisfaction in the loveliness exhibited by every form of organic life from the "Tiger! Tiger! burning bright" to the delicacy of a butterfly's wing, so that in every changing phase of nature "God renews his ancient rapture." He looks upon His own creation and finds it "very good", and therein also finds the fulfillment of the purpose with which He made it. It is His work, and in it He finds the counterpart of His own mind, so that the human student of creation is, in Kepler's words, "thinking God's thoughts after Him."[54]

A Mixed Chorus Augments the Theme

For this third section I have brought together a potpourri of illustrations which, from their varying origins and interests, give expression to other nuances of natural piety and show how pervasive this valuational sentiment is.

Earlier we quoted extensively from poetry; but the novel is also a fruitful source for us, and I shall quote from several. In *The Brothers Karamazov* we find this conversation between Father Zossima and a peasant lad, who begins:

> "I know nothing better than to be in the forest," said he, "though all things are good."
>
> "Truly," I answered him, "all things are good and fair, because all is truth. . . . It's touching to know that . . . all, all except man, is sinless, and Christ has been with them before us."
>
> "Why," asked the boy, "is Christ with them too?"
>
> "It cannot but be so," said I, "since the Word is for all. All creation and all creatures, every leaf is striving to the Word, singing glory to God, weeping to Christ, unconsciously accomplishing this by the mystery of their sinless life."[55]

In Hardy's *Tess of the d'Urbervilles* appears this description of
Angel Clare:

> Unexpectedly he began to like the outdoor life for its own
> sake, and for what it brought, apart from its bearing on his
> own proposed career. . . .
> He grew away from old associations, and saw something
> new in life and humanity. Secondarily, he made close ac-
> quaintance with phenomena which he had before known
> but darkly—the seasons in their moods, morning and evening,
> night and noon, winds in their different tempers, trees, waters,
> and mists, shades and silence, and the voices of inanimate
> things.[56]

At the end of his little novel, *Benito Cereno*, Melville includes
this conversation between Don Benito and Captain Delano, who
begins:

> "But the past is passed; why moralize upon it? Forget it.
> See, yon bright sun has forgotten it all, and the blue sea, and
> the blue sky; these have turned over new leaves."
> "Because they have no memory," he dejectedly replied;
> "because they are not human."
> "But these mild trades that now fan your cheek, Don
> Benito, do they not come with a human-like healing to you?
> Warm friends, steadfast friends are the trades."[57]

Santayana offers an apt illustration in his novel *The Last Puritan*:

> Why is human conscience so exacting, so impertinent? In na-
> ture, if things were let alone they would be perfect. No doubt
> they can't help interfering with one another and making a
> dreadful mess of it. But how lovely each natural thing would
> be, if it could only be true to itself.[58]

From the novel we turn to the essay. Earlier we heard Emerson
the poet; here is Emerson the essayist:

> To the poet, to the philosopher, to the saint, all things are
> friendly and sacred, all events profitable, all days holy, all
> men divine.[59]

And again: "In nature there are no false valuations."[60]
Now we hear from a literary critic of some note, Nathan Scott:

> The artist whose art is essentially mimetic would, indeed, be
> in a bad way were he convinced that Plato's account of his

situation in the *Republic* is a true account and that the world
which is at his disposal is unreliable, unsubstantial, and illusory. But if, on the other hand, he has a deep confidence
in the trustworthiness of the created orders of existence, then
he will be able really to face the world, and, given his com-
petence as a craftsman, he will make us face it also, in all of
its cosmic wonder and tragic glory. . . . What one feels to be
formative in much of the representative literature of our time
is a deep need for a deep restoration of confidence in the
stoutness and reliability and essential healthiness of the things
of earth— . . . such a confidence as it is precisely the genius
of an Incarnational faith to provide.[61]

Unamuno is quotable for passionate statements on many themes.
Here he speaks of the expanding character of love toward the
world:

For this love or pity for yourself, this intense despair, . . . will
lead you to pity—that is, to love—all your fellows and brothers
in this world of appearance. . . . And this compassionate feeling for other men, for your fellows, beginning with those
most akin to you, those with whom you live, will expand into
a universal pity for all living things, and perhaps even for
things that have not life but merely existence.[62]

I believe an instructive avenue to pursue for our purpose—though
lack of knowledge and space prevent my doing so here—would be
science, or rather scientists speaking in their nonscientific moods.
This would be especially relevant since scientists have gotten the
reputation of looking at nature in exclusively quantitative, value-
empty categories. But such is far from the case in many instances.
Loren Eiseley, for example, can say of his aim in *The Firmament
of Time:*

I shall want to look at this natural world both from the empirical point of view and from one which also takes into account that sense of awe and marvel which is part of man's
primitive heritage, and without which man would not be man.
For many of us the Biblical bush still burns, and there is
a deep mystery in the heart of a simple seed. If I seem for a
time to be telling the story of how man came under the domain of law . . . , it is only that we may assess more clearly
that strange world into which we have been born—we com-
pounded of dust, and the light of a star.[63]

Another scientist, C. A. Coulson, quotes with approval these
words of Thomas Traherne:

> He that knows the secrets of nature with Albertus Magnus,
> or the motions of the heavens with Galileo, or the cosmog-
> raphy of the moon with Hevelius, or the body of man with
> Galen, or the nature of diseases with Hippocrates, or the har-
> monies in melody with Orpheus, or of poetry with Homer,
> or of grammar with Lily, or of whatever else with the greatest
> artist; he is nothing if he knows them merely for talking or
> idle speculation, or transient and external use. But he that
> knows them for value, and knows them his own, shall profit
> infinitely.[64]

Reviewing the history of science, Sir James Jeans, writing on
the effect of atomism in Greek thought about nature, gives this
pertinent account of changed outlooks:

> These doctrines . . . stressed the existence of an objective
> world external to man, independent of man, indifferent to
> man. . . . The world which hitherto had been man's play-
> ground and pleasure ground became his prison. Hitherto it
> had been permeated by beauty, sweetness and warmth—the
> gifts of the gods to men—but these were no longer part of
> nature; they were imaginings of man himself.[65]

Naturalists—in the botanical sense—are in a closer position than
most people to develop the appreciation of nature that is characteristic of natural piety. The following is taken from an interview
with one of them.

> I feel conservation is as close to an act of faith as I can
> readily bring to mind. . . . When we say conserve, we mean
> for the future. We cannot say what is in it for me. We
> are doing it for future generations, and the importance
> of it is so overwhelming that we must, in effect, start
> a crusade for preservation of certain things that we find
> around us today. . . .
> If a person lives in one place long enough, I think that his
> personality perhaps changes along with the landscape, and he
> becomes more of a wiser person, shall we say. . . .
> Like any knowledge, I think that a person who appreciates
> something opens vistas that would not be there without this
> knowledge. I think it's fairly evident that a knowledge of
> anything, particularly of beautiful things, is an advantage in
> its own right. . . .

> ... It should be obvious to anyone who does think about it that because of the interrelationship of organic nature, we start a whole chain of results when we tamper to any great degree with this beautifully integrated system.[66]

From the naturalist to the ecologist is a short step these days. There are those concerned with ecology who think we shall never solve our environmental crises without a fundamentally new attitude toward the goodness of nature. Thus a physicist, Harold K. Schilling, even speaks of the desecration of the natural order as blasphemy.

> We are indeed talking about blasphemy . . . arrogant violating of what is sacred and infinitely precious to the God of the universe. This is what pollution is, as is the littering of the earth and outer space, the wasting of natural resources, the wanton destruction of plant and animal life, the irresponsible upsetting of ecological equilibria, the crushing of human and nonhuman spirit. All of this is blasphemy at its worst!
>
> To speak of blasphemy in this situation is to be religiously sensitive in two ways: first, to the sanctity of natural relationships, and second, to the evil and sacrilegious side of man.
>
> The Biblical ethic has had an essentially twofold focus, calling for love of God and love of neighbor. It should now become threefold, demanding also love of nature.[67]

Ian Barbour, in less impassioned language, suggests that the needed new attitude can actually be recovered from the biblical perspective: "We can recover its convictions that nature has intrinsic value and that man's dominion must be exercised responsibly."[68]

A single sentence from Jane Addams reminds us how elemental is the love of natural things among children:

> It is hard to reproduce the companionship which children establish with nature, but certainly it is much too unconscious and intimate to come under the head of aesthetic appreciation or anything of the sort.[69]

The next five quotes I shall use are from student papers. They are particularly valuable because in all cases they were written in the context of other topics and not on the theme of this chapter. Thus they afford access to a more spontaneous, not a manufactured, natural piety. I shall present them without comment.

> To me everything in the world, inorganic and organic, is important; so this philosophy is meaningful to me.

In my ideal religion, you do not have to go to church, only
if you really want to, but you must be able to see and love
nature; plant, animal, and human nature.

As I look at the hazy, gray shadows on the smooth snow—so
pure and bright, as I raise my eyes to the soft clouds and
sunny blue sky under which bare branches sway in the winter
wind, I think how exciting and yet peaceful are these natural
things.

Man and the stars are brothers because they both have mass.
Man and the stars both have existence. And one wonders
whether they both have a purpose, too. One wonders
whether the brilliancy of the stars is not matched by the
brilliancy of the human consciousness and will. . . . This
is what man was created for, what each individual must
live and die for, to be a part of the perfect continuum,
existence.

At the present moment I feel that he [man] needs somehow
to blend himself with the timeless perfection of the universe,
and to do this he must know the spirit that governs the universe itself.[70]

Before going on to philosophical expositions of natural piety, I
want to acknowledge that writers can certainly be found who hold
vigorously for the opposition, who deny any good in nonhuman
nature. Their counsel should be heard even in these courts of praise.
Thomas Hardy, for example titles a poem "Neutral Tones" and concludes it:

> Since then, keen lessons that love deceives
> And wrings with wrong, have shaped to me
> Your face, and the God-cursed sun, and a tree,
> And a pond edged with grayish leaves.

In the passage below, John Dewey records his opposition.

As long as the notion persists that values are authentic and
valid only on condition that they are properties of Being independent of human action, as long as it is supposed that their
right to regulate action is dependent upon their being independent of action, so long there will be needed schemes to

prove that values are, in spite of the findings of science, genuine and known qualifications of reality in itself.

Such statements as we have been making are, therefore, far from implying that there are values apart from things actually enjoyed as good. . . . There is no value except where there is satisfaction.[71]

Strictly speaking, my use of the word "value" is also restricted to the human scene; but since Dewey clearly intends, as I do not, the word "value" to cover the whole range of "good," the passage must be taken as counter to the meaning of natural piety as I have defined it.

Bertrand Russell once penned a brief for the opposition that is even more outspoken, even defiant:

But the world of fact, after all, is not good; and in submitting our judgment to it, there is an element of slavishness from which our thoughts must be purged. For in all things it is well to exalt the dignity of man, by freeing him as far as possible from the tyranny of nonhuman power. When we have realized that power is largely bad, that man, with his knowledge of good and evil, is but a helpless atom in a world which has no such knowledge, the choice is again presented to us: Shall we worship force, or shall we worship goodness?

Blind to good and evil, reckless of destruction, omnipotent matter rolls on its relentless way.[72]

I cannot refrain from juxtaposing to the above quotation from Russell a remark of Archibald MacLeish on the same topic, the power in matter. What a different conclusion a poet comes to!

Furthermore, there has been nothing in human history that has brought mankind closer to the immanence of an infinite creativity than the revelation that the minutest particles of inert matter contain an almost immeasurable power.[73]

But we can find contrary quotations from the writers just quoted (though not of course from all opponents). Two quotations from Hardy appeared earlier in the chapter on our side of the bench. The later Russell can be found to say, in words just as impassioned as those above:

> The love of knowledge to which the growth of science is due
> is itself the product of a twofold impulse. We may seek knowl-
> edge of an object because we love the object or because we
> wish to have power over it. . . . Science in its beginnings was
> due to men who were in love with the world. They perceived
> the beauty of the stars and the sea, of the winds and the
> mountains. Because they loved them their thoughts dwelt
> upon them, and they wished to understand them more in-
> timately than a mere outward contemplation made possible.[74]

Dewey also makes statements elsewhere which, if not inconsistent with the above quotation from him, at least give a counter-
emphasis. For example:

> Natural piety is not of necessity either a fatalistic acquies-
> cence in natural happenings or a romantic idealization of the
> world. It may rest upon a just sense of nature as the whole of
> which we are parts, while it also recognizes that we are parts
> that are marked by intelligence and purpose. . . . Such piety
> is an inherent constituent of a just perspective in life.[75]

And he quotes sympathetically these words from W. H. Hudson:

> I feel when I am out of sight of living, growing grass, and out
> of the sound of birds' voices and all rural sounds, that I am
> not properly alive. . . .
>   . . . When I hear people say that they have not found the
> world and life so agreeable and interesting as to be in love
> with it, or that they look with equanimity to its end, I am
> apt to think that they have never been properly alive, nor
> seen with clear vision the world they think so meanly of or
> anything in it—not even a blade of grass.[76]

Of all modern thinkers, the one who best captures the spirit of
natural piety in its most comprehensive significance is, I believe,
Teilhard de Chardin. His "Hymn to Matter"[77] is a superb expression of it. He celebrates matter and nature not only for themselves
but for the great potentiality they bear. He will also appear in a
later chapter (11), but I shall insert one specimen from his poetic
prose to end this section.

> Never say, then, as some say: "The kingdom of matter is worn
> out, matter is dead." Till the very end of time matter will al-
> ways remain young, exuberant, sparkling, new-born for those
> who are willing.
>   Never say, "Matter is accursed, matter is evil."[78]

Philosophers Expound the Theme

We come now to a sampling of the ways in which philosophers have stated the conception of good in nature. We shall see that philosophers from all major schools of thought—realism, idealism, naturalism, pragmatism, process philosophy, neo-Thomism, analytic philosophy, existentialism—have followers who support the doctrine in question. I am not saying that all of these schools necessarily entail the doctrine, nor am I saying that philosophers cannot be found within most of their ranks who would explicitly reject the doctrine. Neither of those propositions would be true. Nevertheless, there is apparently nothing within these schools to exclude the doctrine, and, furthermore, supporters can be found in each of them. These two facts I consider to be of great significance as convergent evidence or data.

Let us begin with Aristotle. Typically cautious, he seems to hold, due to his teleological concept of nature, that whatever attains a certain objective perfection in its being has attained something better than a failure of attainment would be, and has thereby achieved a good. There is a universal scale of such good, depending on the potentialities of things and their gradation throughout nature.

> The productions of nature have an innate tendency in the direction of the best condition of which they are capable, and so have the creations of the craftsman and artist and whatever has an efficient cause of any kind, especially if that cause ranks highest in the scale of excellence.[79]

The position of St. Thomas Aquinas is similar to that of Aristotle, except that for Thomas the good in nature, while independent of human value, is related to a supreme valuing and value-endowing consciousness. Copleston states the position succinctly:

> Thus Aquinas did not deny or belittle a "dynamic" concept of the universe. On the contrary, he saw in all things a natural tendency to realize or develop their several potentialities, and he regarded this tendency as something good.[80]

Gilson gives us an amplified view of Aquinas's view, as follows.

> Pure matter can, therefore, not exist by itself, since it is only a being in potency; it is, however, not merely potentially good, but really and absolutely good, because it is ordered in view of a form and constitutes for that reason a good. There is, therefore, an aspect under which the Good is wider Being. . . .

... For if matter were bad in itself, it would be nothing;
and if it is something, then, in the very measure in which
it is, it is not bad. Like everything else within the range of
creation, matter is therefore good and created by God.

Further: not only is matter good in itself, but it is also a
good and a source of good for all forms capable of combining
with it. ... The doctrine of St. Thomas is pervaded by a radical optimism, because it interprets the universe as created out
of pure goodness, all parts of which, in the measure of their
subsistence, are as many reflections of the infinite perfections
of God.[81]

For an idealist like Berkeley, it might be thought that no such
doctrine as natural piety is possible since the material substrate
has disappeared. But the denial of matter does not mean the elim-
ination of nature, and the idealist is likely to hold that if nature is
really psychic, that is the only condition under which it would be
meaningful to characterize it as independently good. In any case,
Berkeley has included a beautiful passage on the value qualities in
nature in his *Dialogues between Hylas and Philonous*. Philonous
is speaking:

Look! are not the fields covered with a delightful verdure?
Is there not something in the woods and groves, in the rivers
and clear springs, that soothes, that delights, that transports
the soul? At the prospect of the wide and deep ocean, or
some huge mountain whose top is lost in the clouds, or of
an old gloomy forest, are not our minds filled with a pleasing
horror? Even in rocks and deserts is there not an agreeable
wildness? How sincere a pleasure is it to behold the natural
beauties of the earth! To preserve and renew our relish for
them, is not the veil of night alternately drawn over her face,
and doth she not change her dress with the seasons? How
aptly are the elements disposed! What variety and use [in the
meanest productions of nature!] What delicacy, what beauty,
what contrivance, in animal and vegetable bodies! How ex-
quisitely are all things suited as well to their particular ends,
as to constitute opposite parts of the whole! And, while they
mutually aid and support, do they not also set off and illustrate each other? ... Is not the whole system immense, beautiful, glorious beyond expression and beyond thought! What
treatment, then, do those philosophers deserve, who would
deprive these noble and delightful scenes of all reality? How

should those Principles be entertained that lead us to think all the visible beauty of the creation a false imaginary glare? To be plain, can you expect this Scepticism of yours will not be thought extravagantly absurd by all men of sense?[82]

Later idealism, especially in the Hegelian form, has been generally sympathetic to the idea that good extends to all being. S. C. Pepper summarizes the Hegelian approach to value theory:

It is pertinent to observe that for the Hegelians value was always treated as a general theory. The core principle of coherence in their philosophy was intrinsically a universal value principle. Value for them permeated the universe.[83]

The empiricist Mill will have no traffic with either Aquinas or idealism. Yet I believe there is the hint of a reference to some good in all beings in the passage from *On Liberty* below. Whether Mill accepts the view he expounds here is doubtful; but at least we see his mind turning to the subject, and also an expression of how the view might be held.

Many persons, no doubt, sincerely think that human beings thus cramped and dwarfed are as their maker designed them to be, just as many have thought that trees are a much finer thing when clipped into pollards, or cut out into figures of animals, than as nature made them. But if it be any part of religion to believe that man was made by a good Being, it is more consistent with that faith to believe that this Being gave all human faculties that they might be cultivated and unfolded, not rooted out and consumed, and that he takes delight in every nearer approach made by his creatures to the ideal conception embodied in them, every increase in any of their capabilities of comprehension, of action, or of enjoyment.[84]

William James, a master at capturing human-interest content in memorable phrases, is no exception in this case, as he writes:

To anyone who has ever looked on the face of a dead child or parent the mere fact that matter could have taken for a time that precious form, ought to make matter sacred ever after.[85]

W. E. Hocking, far apart from James in philosophical perspective, converges—as we find so often in our present theme—on

what James might have called the sentiment of naturality. Writing
on science and religion, Hocking says:

> The physical universe is capable of evoking—not when we
> grasp it least, but when we grasp it most adequately—a re-
> sponse of almost personal devotion toward its majesty, its
> vastness, its beauty, its marvelous perfection, its unfathomed
> depths of intricate harmony, its stupendous rhythms and
> moving equilibria.[86]

Contemporary naturalism also converges in many instances. In
his *Reason in Religion* Santayana declares:

> There is . . . a philosophic piety which has the universe for
> its object. . . . Why should we not look on the universe with
> piety? Is it not our substance? Are we made of other clay?
> All our possibilities lie from eternity hidden in its bosom. It
> is the dispenser of all our joys.[87]

A similar sentiment is expressed by Lamprecht:

> A wholesome respect for nature and its potentialities is the
> beginning of civilization. It is therefore the end of philosophic
> wisdom. This respect is not to be confused with worship: we
> may worship the excellence and beauty which nature makes
> possible but we must respect the whole of nature, even that
> which brings evil and disaster in its train.[88]

Now to process philosophy, in which Whitehead has of course
been the great champion of a thorough going, nondualistic, metaphysical integration of fact and value throughout the universe of
actual entities. The first passage is from his well-known discussion
of the romantic movement in *Science and the Modern World:*

> Thus we gain from the poets the doctrine that a philosophy of
> of nature must concern itself at least with these six notions:
> change, value, eternal objects, endurance, organism, inter-
> fusion. . . .
>   Remembering the poetic rendering of our concrete experi-
> ence, we see at once that the element of value, of being valu-
> able, of having value, of being an end in itself, of being some-
> thing which is for its own sake, must not be omitted in any
> account of an event as the most concrete actual something.
> . . . Value is an element which permeates through and through
> the poetic view of nature. . . .
>   . . . The nature-poetry of the romantic revival was a protest

on behalf of the organic view of nature, and also a protest against the exclusion of value from the essence of matter of fact.[89]

The second quotation is more sentimental, from *Symbolism*:

> Now the love of the sheer geographical aspects of one's country, of its hills, its mountains, and its plains, of its trees, its flowers, its birds, and its whole nature-life, is no small element in that binding force which makes a nation.[90]

The panpsychism of Charles Hartshorne leads him to hold with Whitehead that there is felt value universally. But there is another sense also in which good is independent of man, according to this view. Hartshorne explains:

> Is the harmony of the moment, in fawn or human being, an imperishable contribution to some ultimate treasure . . .? I sometimes call the affirmative view "contributionism." . . . The fawn contributes itself, its own self-fulfillment, not merely the effects of its acts upon others.[91]

Neo-Thomist Jacques Maritain tells us that both beauty and goodness are universally applicable terms:

> So everything is beautiful as everything is good, at least in a certain relation. And as being is everywhere present and everywhere various, the beautiful likewise is scattered everywhere and everywhere various.[92]

A contemporary realist, Samuel Thompson, writing on the problem of evil, is our next example:

> The loss of any creature is an evil just in so far as the existence of that creature is a good. To say that nature requires such loss is not to deny the fact of the loss; it is only to acknowledge the necessity of evil. . . . When we fail to respect the dignity of existence, when we think we can manipulate the real world as we do our dream world, existence destroys the dream.[93]

We can even include a behaviorist within our circle of interested parties for the present purpose. C. A. Mace writes the following:

> The conception of an immaterial substance has acquired through history intense emotional significance. If then we came to the conclusion that material things are the only things

that exist, shock, to those who felt it, would be followed by
emotional adjustment. "If matter is all there is," they would
say, "what wonderful stuff it is!" And why not, indeed? If
material things can be literally beautiful, why should not the
behavior of material things, and dispositions of behavior, be
literally good?[94]

And now analytic philosophy. Though his successors would perhaps not generally agree with him, G. E. Moore held to the independence of beauty and therefore to the independence of at least
some portion of the good. A relevant passage from *Principia Ethica*
follows.

> "No one," says Prof. Sidgwick, "would consider it rational
> to aim at the production of beauty in external nature, apart
> from any possible contemplation of it by human beings."
> Well, I may say at once, that I, for one, do consider this ra-
> tional. . . . If in any imaginable case you do admit that the
> existence of a more beautiful thing is better in itself than
> that of one more ugly, quite apart from its effects on any
> human feeling, then Prof. Sidgwick's principle has broken
> down. Then we shall have to include in our ultimate end
> something beyond the limits of human existence.[95]

Existentialism appears ambivalent in its attitude toward nature.
Some spokesmen, such as Sartre, recoil from it as the epitome of
routine inferior being and dramatize the subjective instead. On the
other hand, Marcel, our original source here, has a different conception and can be counted in the fold we are shepherding in this
chapter.

> One thing now seems reasonably clear: being cannot, it is
> certain, be indifferent to value; it could only so be if one were
> to identify it as a crude datum considered as existing in its
> own right, and that we are not justified in doing; in fact we
> must resolutely reject the idea of the existence in its own
> right of such a crude datum.[96]

Likewise Helmut Kuhn, in a critique of atheistic existentialism,
refers to what he calls "the Ontological Affirmation, the premise
of all metaphysics which posits the ultimate identity of Being and
worth."[97] And here is a singular illustration of the same principle
in a commentary on the development of Heidegger's thought:

> Heidegger can now write about a house, a wine-jug, or a
> bridge as though they were holy objects, whose essence can

be grasped only by him who has profound piety for the simple things of life and a self-effacing humility when confronted with Nature's majesty. . . .

The attitude of piety recognizes that other beings than men have integrity, and must be allowed freedom to effect their own fulfillment and obey their own laws. . . .

The estimation of human possibilities and pride in them was for Aristotle not incompatible with humility toward the Nature whose regularity and constancy made her worthy of reverence. It is this sort of relation to Nature which appears so difficult for us to achieve today.[98]

My last example is from the always hard to classify Paul Weiss, also a vigorous defender of the coextensiveness of goodness and being. He declares:

Value is a natural phenomenon. Excellence of any kind, beauty, power, purity, comprehensiveness, and their negates are facts as hard as smell and shape, number and size. With thinkers of a century or so ago, it could of course be said that there were no values in nature. But since the world we daily confront is permeated with values, we should then have to say that the nature we daily know is an illusion, a man-infected, man-distorted nature. We should have to maintain that man had the fatal and unique gift of endowing what was in fact valueless with the appearance of value, and thus, alone of all beings, of self-deceptively hiding nature from himself.[99]

We have passed in review about a hundred expressions of a natural piety which sees a pervasive good in the natural cosmos. This is at least *prima facie* justification for taking the doctrine seriously. I shall have them in mind as primary supporting data as we go forward in the next chapters to a more formal account of the idea of nonhuman good.

9: Instrumental and Intrinsic Good

The Idea of Nonhuman Good

Two epistemological principles must underlie any philosophical investigation which can possibly hope to be impartial and comprehensive. The first is that all knowledge is derived from and is an interpretation of experience. The second is that such knowledge cannot *ipso facto* be assumed to refer solely to experience itself. Without experience, there would *a fortiori* be no knowledge; but only skepticism or arbitrary limitation could confine the import of that knowledge to the contents of experience alone. Our experience thus serves as a mediator to the intellect of what lies beyond our experience.

Modern philosophies, in their quest for knowledge about values, have rightly emphasized the first principle in preference to some older approaches which proceeded by *a priori* reasoning exclusively. But in doing so they have, on the whole, neglected the second principle and have become narrower and less universal than the older views. Specifically modern philosophies, in turning to conscious experience for the discovery of knowledge about values, have tacitly but arbitrarily assumed that such knowledge can have no bearing outside experience, or, in other words, that the good is the peculiar affair of human consciousness. A review of recent literature indicates that it is a commonplace to assume that the good is confined to human experience—except when, by way of courtesy, license is made for animal consciousness. The idea of nonhuman good, of good characterizing other beings besides conscious ones, and perhaps characterizing all being, sounds as antique to modern ears as the clash of knights in medieval armor. Part of the

reason for this banishment of nonhuman good is to be found in
the necessity of eliminating certain anthropomorphic conceptions
from an impartial investigation of nature—a legitimate reason in
itself. Part of the reason lies in the difficulty of understanding
what nonhuman good means—a doctrine which must be clarified
if it is to be maintained. And part of the reason is to be found
in man's adoption of himself as the hub of the universe and the
measure of all things—an unwarranted reason.

In any case, there can be little doubt of the fact that the banishment has taken place. However they may differ on other
topics, thinkers of all sorts, including many religious writers,
seem to take it for granted that good apart from conscious states
is a meaningless notion. The following illustration is only typical,
not exceptional.

> First, value may mean any conscious experience of liking,
> preferring, or enjoying. Let us call this a value claim. . . .
> Secondly, value may mean any conscious experience of
> liking or preferring which survives critical inquiry into facts,
> relations, and reasons. Such a value may be called . . . a
> true value or an ideal value as distinguished from an un-
> tested value claim. Both value claims and true values reside
> solely in conscious experience. Intrinsic value is no property
> of unconscious things or processes.[1]

We agree with the terminological use of "value" in this passage, but not with the further and main presumption that seems
intended.

Thus the steps in the banishment of nonhuman good are clear:
good is first of all defined in connection with some kind of conscious state, rather than in connection with the subject for whom
those states exist, and then, since enjoyings and likings and pre-
ferrings do not occur in the nonconscious realm, it is concluded
that all good resides in that segment of the universe which we
call "conscious experience," by which is usually meant human
experience.

Yet the choice of just this one area as the sole bearer of good
must be investigated. The conclusion follows from the identification of value and good, and then from the definition of value or
good as consisting in enjoying or liking, which, if it be offered as
a *real* and not simply as a stipulative definition, can readily be
questioned. Indeed, the fact that the writer (quoted above) distinguishes between "value claims" and "true values" indicates

that enjoyings and likings cannot themselves be the essential features constituting the nature of good. Some enjoyings and likings are admitted not to be "true values" at all, and hence some other factor must be appealed to which is more determinative of what value consists in and which is the deciding factor in discriminating which likings are "true values" and which are only claims to value. A truer account would find this other essential factor to be certain fulfillments, and particular values to consist in partial contributions to complete self-fulfillment or perfection. And if this be so, there is no reason, on such a view, to confine good to human or conscious states, for other things have a being which can be fulfilled and perfected as well. Human value can be subsumed under a wider conception of good.

An interesting exception to the customary modern approach just mentioned is that of G. von Wright. He says: "A being, of whose good it is meaningful to talk, is one who can meaningfully be said to be well or ill, to thrive, to flourish, be happy or miserable."[2] Except for the last phrase, "be happy or miserable," which seems to narrow and nullify the previous phrases, "to be well or ill, to thrive, to flourish," the general intention begins to move in the direction of the Aristotelian idea of fulfillment of potentiality. The definition is somewhat medical in tone, however, and hence the good is limited to living things.

> The question what kinds or species of being have a good is therefore broadly identical with the question what kind or species of being have a life. . . . Artefacts, such as cars and watches, have a life and therefore a good, only metaphorically.[3]

But what of the nonliving realm of nature other than artifacts? We shall explore whether there is a sense in which the good is universal in reference to being. Our approach will have more affinity to that of Henry Veatch, who explicitly relates the concept of good to the Aristotelian idea of actuality in relation to potentiality.[4]

Short of a universal view of the good, there are three ways of regarding the nonconscious realm in a theory which holds good to exist only in conscious states, such as enjoying. The first way is the one already mentioned, where the nonconscious realm is recognized as existing but is denied to have any worth except as an instrument to human devices. By suggesting that there is a more plausible alternative, I hope to show that this view is unduly limited in scope. The second way is that of the idealist, who denies the existence of nonconscious entities. If nothing exists except what is in conscious experience (human or divine), there would be no problem of interpreting the nonconscious realm with respect to good. Despite this metaphysical explanation, however, the realm of sticks and stones, mountains and molehills remains just as stubborn and "real"; and these things are quite different from conscious states such as enjoying. So the problem of relating the nonconscious realm, in respect to good, to conscious states would still remain. The third way is found in the theory which holds that there is a kind of consciousness which characterizes even this realm; this is the view of panpsychism, held by Leibniz and Whitehead. If all entities could be said to be in some sense conscious organisms, it could be maintained both that all good resides in conscious states and that the good characterizes all of reality. But, again, sooner or later it must be recognized that sticks and stones, mountains and molehills are different from human conscious states; so, in order to explain the kind of good which characterizes nonhuman entities, a theory is required which does not fall into the anthropomorphic conceptions involved in defining good as enjoying, liking, pleasure, etc. Even if these last two metaphysical theories —idealism and panpsychism—were correct, the problem would still remain of interpreting, from a valuational point of view, the relation between the realm which in common life is called the nonconscious and the realm of conscious experience.

Accordingly, there seem to be only two alternatives left; one of these is the first view mentioned, where the nonconscious is denied to have intrinsic good; the other view is the one we have suggested, which holds the opposite. If it could be made out that the first of these is arbitrary, we would apparently be required, as a matter of logic, to accept the second. But how can a doctrine of nonhuman good be made more specific?

The interpretation of nonhuman good is easiest in the case of animal consciousness, for here the analogy drawn from human experience is readily applicable. If human values consist in certain fulfillments—fulfillments of basic needs, on the one hand, and of certain creative faculties whose fulfillment gives rise to values over and above the satisfaction of needs, on the other hand—and have self-fulfillment as their ground, it is clear that values for animals can be explained in a similar manner, except that freedom, creativity, and inventiveness are apparently not present to such a marked degree. Nevertheless, there are some things which are "good for" them and contribute to the perfection of which they are capable and other things which hinder them and injure their fulfillment. Hence the same sort of analysis of value and disvalue as constituted by relational situations, which describes the nature of human values, is also applicable, *mutatis mutandis*, or by analogy, to animal experience.

The difficulty comes, however, in trying to understand the significance of good when we discuss the nonconscious realm. Perhaps the best introduction to this topic comes from considering a prominent instance of the relation between the human world, where everyone agrees value is present, and the nonconscious world, about which many people are in doubt as to its worth, except as a human instrument. Such a prominent instance of this relation is to be found in the work of manual labor, and I can do no better at this point than to quote from Paul Tillich's penetrating discussion of the mutuality involved in this relation of work:

> Personality and thing are united in the "work" in which the power of the thing is discovered and affirmed by the personality and in which the power of the personality is imprinted on the thing. This mutual reception of the personality by the thing and of the thing by the personality means the "fulfillment" of both of them. In creative work the actual freedom of personality and the potential nature of freedom are united. The personal power of self-determination and the determined power of things meet in the form of our work. This is the ethical justification of a full devotion to work, even if it implies the surrender of a fully developed cultural personality. But a sacrifice is also demanded of things: for the sake of a higher unity in which they are forced to enter, they must be restricted in their own natural power. This sacrifice laid upon things in every human dealing with them corresponds to the sacrifice laid upon the personality in every creative work. Both have to give up some of their potential power in order to reach a higher, actual power by entering a new creation. . . . What must be said generally about the relationship between personality and thing [is] that it is, in principle, a mutual service. The true work is a mutual fulfillment, the false work, a mutual violation of personality and thing.[5]

In work, therefore, not only are nonhuman things values for human fulfillment but human beings are values for the fulfillment of which these things are capable. How else can we interpret the significance of the patience with which the loving gardener tends each flower, the care which the scullery monk exercises in doing his dishes, the pride which the workingman takes in his "perfect" tools, or the submission which the artist undergoes to his materials, irrespective of publicity? Not only is value realized for these persons, and for the other persons served by the material "goods," but the things themselves more fully reach the achievement of their essential nature. And no arbitrary fiat can justify the declaration that there is no good in these entities or, in other words, that situations in which their being is more fully perfected have no worth' or significance apart from human designs. The good is not consciously apprehended, but it is the good of fulfillment and perfection of things and hence is analogous in kind to human value.

Goodness and Being—St. Thomas

In discussing the good as fulfillment of being, it may be helpful to begin with St. Thomas. According to St. Thomas, value or goodness means what is desirable, that is, what beings really desire by their very nature, as distinguished from particular wishes and passions which the term "desire" has come to signify. Now what every being desires is its own perfection. Hence goodness consists in perfection. "The essence of goodness consists in this, that it is in some way desirable. . . . Now it is clear that a thing is desirable only in so far as it is perfect, for all desire their own perfection."[6] But what does Thomas mean by "perfection"? He means simply actuality, the simple act of being, as distinguished from privation or nonbeing.

> Everything is perfect so far as it is actual. Therefore it is clear that a thing is perfect so far as it is being; for being is the actuality of every thing. . . . Hence it is clear that goodness and being are the same really. But goodness expresses the aspect of desirableness, which being does not express.[7]

Goodness means perfection; perfection means, simply, being; therefore goodness and being are one. *Omne ens qua ens est bonum.*

This is the classical doctrine of being and the good, where good, like being, is a transcendental, a universal characteristic. In Scholastic terminology this good, in the case of beings that are capable of development, can be differentiated into substantial good, that is, the perfection of the ontological essence, and a secondary good, for example, moral goodness in man, that in the technical sense is accidental since the substantial or ontological essence would still be in existence even if this further developmental good did not eventuate. In the terminology I proposed in chapter 1, the valuational essence covers both of these aspects of a being's nature, and since I wish to emphasize other distinctions I shall in what follows speak of the good in this inclusive sense, without denying the usefulness or soundness of a distinction between substantial and accidental being.

I now wish to give an independent analysis of the doctrine of the goodness of being, without implying that Thomists would agree or disagree with this analysis. Another quotation from Aquinas in which he defines the meaning of perfection in particular beings, will set us on our way.

> Now perfection in a thing is threefold: first, according to the constitution of its own being; secondly, in respect of any accidents being added as necessary for its perfect operation; thirdly, perfection consists in the attaining to something else as the end.[8]

These three aspects of perfection in a thing may be illustrated by a watch. First of all, a watch is perfect if it conforms to the essential nature of a watch—if in its structure it embodies the essence of "watchness." Second, if the watch runs smoothly and efficiently, it is perfect in respect of its operation. Third, the watch is perfect if it completely fulfills some other end for which it is designed, namely, in this case, the good of man.

Thus the two fundamental notions of goodness as the perfection of a thing are those of "good in itself" and "good for": intrinsic good and instrumental good. A watch may be "good in itself" either by fulfilling its type of watchness or by operating smoothly and efficiently. And it may be "good for" man by serving his needs.

The latter notion, of "good for" with respect to man, refers to a relational situation wherein the watch is a value through serving man's need. Such values come under the category of human value, which is not our concern here. We are interested, rather, in the notions of "good for" and "good in itself" with respect to nonhuman things themselves. Let us begin with instrumental good.

We first note that a thing does not reach its fulfillment through its own power alone. Hence the fulfillment or perfection of the thing cannot be said to reside solely in the being of the thing, taken in isolation, and its more unrelated actuality. A thing is what it is and can fulfill its nature only through and by virtue of other beings which sustain it. These are its *perficientia*. A watch can be a perfect watch, in structure and operation, only because of the watchmaker who made it and the jeweler who repairs it. Even when the watch is thus fashioned, its form and its running can be kept perfect only through the owner who cares for and winds it, through the natural surroundings which preserve rather than destroy it, through the persistency of each part, etc. Just as man cannot achieve self-fulfillment (cannot, for that matter, achieve the highest good on any theory) save through relations to the objective conditions of fulfillment, the nonconscious thing cannot become perfect and fulfill its being apart from the objective realities which sustain its being.

For this reason we shall have to conclude that if goodness has perfection or fulfillment as its ground, it will not be correct to say that a thing is "good in itself" (that is, good in and through itself). There is no goodness in the thing as a bare, isolated unity. It is not the mere act of being, the simple actuality of a thing, which constitutes goodness. Rather goodness arises only in relations of the thing to those other realities which sustain and fulfill the thing in question, its *perficientia*. Hence the fundamental notion here is that of "good for." Later we shall attempt to give some meaning to the concept of "good in itself." But as far as we are here concerned, we shall have to say that the only goodness which is to be found in the relational situations of fulfillment is to be located in the "good for-ness" which some objects have through sustaining and fulfilling other things. If those other things are "good in themselves," that will require another relational justification, as we shall see.

Thus an oak fulfills its potentialities, a knife becomes a perfect knife, a work of art is made unique only through the sustenance of the external realities which are "good for" them. And, in each case, good arises in the multiplicity of these relations of fulfillment. If a thing could exist all by itself, in undisturbed unity, and out of relation to anything else, then it would simply "be," and that is all that can be said. There would be no goodness involved. Such an entity could not even be perfect of its kind or conform to a type, for if that entity were the only thing which had being, there would be no type or essence apart from

itself to which it could conform. But if there were a separate type
or essence to which such an entity could conform, then immediately
a relation would be set up, so that the goodness in the situation
would consist not in the mere isolated actuality of the thing but in
the significance which the essence had for the entity through serving
it as a model.

Evidently, then, we can speak of good applying to the nonconscious realm in terms similar to those employed in describing human
value. The main point is that the perfection or fulfillment of a thing
does not characterize that thing if it is thought of as an isolated, abstract unity. Hence if ultimate perfection or fulfillment stands as
the ground for particular ascriptions of good, then goodness arises
only in the relations of a given entity to those other realities which
sustain and fulfill it. In these relations the sustaining realities are
"good for" the thing in question; they are its *perficientia*. Thus nonconscious things have their *perficientia*, just as do human beings.

Accordingly, we can accept the classical view that goodness has
perfection as its ground. But we must not think of this goodness as
consisting in the simple act of being, the mere actuality of a thing
thought of as an abstract, unrelated unity. It is not the simple being-
ness of a thing which makes it good. An undifferentiated, unrelated
being, even God, would only be a unity, with no goodness involved.
A thing is good only by virtue of relations to other beings which it
is "good for" or else by relation to that with reference to which it
may, through mediation, be said to be "good in itself," if that be
true.

Individuals and Types

This interpretation also allows us to overcome another difficulty
which is sometimes said to beset the classical theory of goodness.
This difficulty arises from its natural philosophy, which does not
account for the modification and evolution of types and species in
the natural world. It is assumed that there are fixed, immutable
types and species in nature to which individuals can conform. Thus
the goodness of a thing, for example, an oak, is said to consist in
its mere actuality, simply by virtue of the fact that it is a representative or embodiment of the type or species of oak. Individuals may
come and go, but there is no possibility in this conception for the
modification or alteration of fundamental types and species themselves. There are fixed orders of creation, and among them are
permanent created species. A thing is perfect in being, and hence

good, simply because it exists and is the embodiment of its immutable type or species. St. Thomas expounds this view as follows:

> Everything is said to be good so far as it is perfect; . . . Now a thing is said to be perfect if it lack nothing according to the mode of its perfection. But since everything is what it is by its form, . . . in order for a thing to be perfect and good it must have a form, together with all that precedes and follows upon that form. . . . But the form itself is signified by the species, for everything is placed in its species by its form. . . . Hence the essence of goodness, so far as it consists in perfection, consists also in limit, species, and order.[9]

Thus fixed, unchangeable species and immutable orders of creation seem to be presupposed. The individual, in acquiring form, takes its destined place in the species or type. And the individual is good by virtue of so doing, by virtue of conforming to the unchangeable type.

Yet there is nothing in a theory of goodness, as consisting in perfection or fulfillment, which requires that it be defined in terms of the conformity of a thing to permanent types or species and immutable orders of creation. And, conversely, if such a notion of immutable nature conflicts with scientific and metaphysical interpretations of evolution and process, as apparently it does, there is positive reason to define goodness otherwise.

We have defined perfection not as conformity to a static type or essence or species but as the fulfillment of a thing's essential being through relations to other beings which sustain and complete it. And by "essential being" we mean simply the necessary characteristics, powers, and tendencies of a thing which constitute its identity of being, without which it would not have its being and in the absence of which it would be destroyed rather than fulfilled in its identity and individuality. Thus perfection applies primarily to individuals rather than to types and species. Individuality is the primary locus of fulfillment. To be sure, part of what we mean by a thing's fulfillment is its full embodiment of its species.

For instance, a particular oak fulfills its essential being only by fully embodying the species of oak. But this relation of species to oak is only one factor that constitutes and maintains the particular oak's identity. The type has value for the oak as a model. But the oak also has many other relations to other things which determine and support its essential being and individuality—the acorn, the surrounding elements, the forester, etc. Goodness consists not

in the static conformity of the oak to its type but in all these things
which sustain and fulfill the being of the oak. Only through this
multiplicity of relations is the oak preserved and fulfilled in its essential being and individuality.

Thus species and orders can change with the changes of creativity.
Yet each new species and each individual which arises can have a
fulfillment which is peculiar to itself. No matter if species change,
no matter how temporal and fleeting a thing may be by its own nature, each thing has an excellence and fulfillment of which it is
capable. This is not to say that there are hidden and mysterious
entelechies in things which are striving and driving toward fixed
ends within those things. We are only challenging the arbitrary decision that good has no significance for the nonconscious realm but
is limited in significance and meaning to man. And we are doing so
by maintaining that the mere fact that a thing has being indicates
that there is a fulfillment of which it is capable and that there are
perficientia for it, namely, those realities which nourish, sustain,
and fulfill its being.

Evil

But at this point two difficulties seem to confront us. The first
is this: Goodness has been said to consist in relations between things
such that the one sustains and fulfills the other. For example, the
grass is "good for" the cow through contributing to its fulfillment.
But if goodness consists in that which sustains and fulfills, then
evil must be that which hinders and destroys a thing's being. So although the grass is a value for the cow, the cow in turn is a means
for destroying the being of the grass. Hence it would seem that our
view would force us to maintain that no good can be done without
a corresponding amount of evil. Good and evil are, then, always
equal. So instead of there being mutual fulfillment, as we said earlier,
there is always destruction, and every being must always return complete evil for the good done to it.

The resolution of this difficulty is to be found in the nature of
finite things. It cannot be the essential nature of a finite thing to
be eternal, to transcend itself continually to infinity, to dwell in its
own self-containment. It must be the essential nature of a finite
being either to lose its being or to be transformed. Therefore, while
the individuality of the grass is transformed in the cow, its essential
being is not destroyed, for its essential being is to be finite. When
the grass acquires its full nutritive powers and then enters into the

nourishment of the cow, the grass has achieved as much excellence and perfection as its essential finite nature allows it. The grass unites with the cow in a new creation and hence achieves the maximum fulfillment of which it is capable. If it did not do this, the grass would wither and die and so would fall short of what it could become through entering into the new production. The essence of a finite thing, therefore, must be defined in part by the potentialities it has for completing its finiteness through entering into and sustaining new creations. Thus the cow is also "good for" the grass in that it provides the means by which the grass can complete the limited kind of fulfillment which is possible to it by its finite nature.

It must be admitted, however, that this explanation of mutuality cannot be said to hold in all cases. For while the grass might achieve a higher fulfillment by entering into the nourishment of the cow instead of simply withering away, and while a brick might achieve a higher perfection by losing its individuality in the construction of a new edifice, we could hardly say, for instance, that a community reaches its highest fulfillment by contributing to the perfect functioning of an avalanche or that a missionary achieves his self-fulfillment by entering into the production of a well-developed cannibal. If we said that, it would amount to saying that every *de facto* relation between beings is *ipso facto* a reciprocal relation of good; and if this were true, there would be no problem of valuation and, furthermore, no evil.

The truth, however, is that, in addition to the mutual fulfillments we have suggested, there is in some relations of fulfillment a preponderance of evil for the contributory thing in question, and in other cases an equality of good and evil for it. Indeed, even in cases of mutual fulfillment there is probably a certain amount of evil which always accompanies it. The grass, in fulfilling its finite nature by entering into a more fully developed cow, also receives evil to the extent that it loses the perfection of its individual peculiarities and characteristics; the cow, in being slaughtered for man, may enter into a more important fulfillment, but it also receives evil to the extent that its individuality is sacrificed; etc. Nevertheless, the only point we were insisting upon in answering the difficulty above is that a being, in serving as a good for another, need not receive an equal or total amount of evil in return. There may be mutual fulfillment in the relation. And where evil does accompany mutual fulfillment, it need not be in preponderance over the good involved. Furthermore, it is precisely those situations where the returned evil is in preponderance, where the being that serves as a good finds

complete evil for itself in its mission, which are the situations we
seek to avoid in moral action. It is because, empirically, we do
not discover mutual fulfillment in such situations that we try to
eliminate and avoid them. Some of those situations, however,
are required because of the importance of the fulfillment of one
being—and here the necessity of sacrifice is involved. Other situations we simply do not have the power to prevent—and here the
reality of evil is involved.

But it was not our intention to deny either the necessity of
sacrifice or the reality of evil. Our only point has been that in
situations of fulfillment there need not be a total return of evil
for good, of destruction for fulfillment. There can be mutual
fulfillment. And where sacrifice is required, there can be mutual
sacrifice.

The second difficulty is this: The fulfillment of some beings is
not good but evil. Parasites, for instance, fulfill their individuality
only at the expense of destroying their prey and with no other
function in view except further destruction. To say that such fulfillments are good would be to call good what most people in
their right mind would call evil—a strange doctrine indeed. Goodness, therefore, cannot consist in fulfillment.

In reply it must be said, in the first place, that we do not intend to deny that there is natural evil just because we are affirming that there is natural good. The parasite is indeed evil and destructive to the beings on which it preys. It apparently does not
even unite, as does the grass, with other beings in the production
of higher creations.[10] Yet it must be remembered that we are thus
far considering only the nature of good for individual things. No
matter how destructive a parasite may be, therefore, its own fulfillment constitutes good for itself. The prey it eats is thus a good
for the parasite. The fact that the primary relation of the parasite
to the prey is one of destruction and evil does not prove that fulfillment is not the ground of individual good. Rather it indicates
that some fulfillments must be repressed when we consider the
ground of good for all beings taken together and when we decide
what kinds of action to adopt toward potential goods and evils.

Objectivity of Good?

So far we have been maintaining that, just as the ground for
human value is total self-fulfillment, so the good for nonconscious
things consists in their fulfillment. Such fulfillment, however, is

to be found not in the simple unrelated unity of the thing but
in the other beings and realities which sustain the thing and which
constitute *perficientia* for it. Thus goodness can be said to arise
only in situations which are relational in character. Goodness occurs in relations such that one being fulfills another. Evil occurs
in relations in which one thing hinders or destroys another. The
ground or warrant for saying whether the other realities are good
or bad is whether or not they contribute to the ultimate fulfillment and perfection of the essential being of the thing in question.

How do the terms "subjective," "objective," and "relational"
apply? In the first place, the good is always, from any perspective, relational. The relation may hold between two objects, so
that one sustains and fulfills the other as its *perficiens*. Or the
relation may be between an object and a person, so that in this
case the *personally* subjective element is a *perficiens* for the object, just as, with human values, objects are values for selves.

But in addition to being relational in character, these nonhuman goods are also objective. Two senses of "objective" are relevant here. In the first sense, "objective" means not constituted
by or modified by relation to any outside, judging subject. This
may be called "perspectival objectivity." In the second sense,
"objective" means existing independently of all consciousness.
This may be called "transphenomenal objectivity."[11] Now when
nonhuman goods are actually realized, they are realized, of
course, from the viewpoint of any outside human judge of them,
perspectivally objectively. Perspectival objectivity is, therefore, a
correct description in all cases, provided we understand that what
is objective is not a property but an entire relational situation.
The second sense of "objective" is also applicable, but in a somewhat more restricted way. That is, when both elements in the relation exist independently of consciousness, that value situation
is entirely transphenomenal and may be said to be totally objective in this second sense. However, when the *perficiens* for the
nonhuman object is a person, we can say that the good is only
partially transphenomenal and hence only partially objective in
this second sense. The idea of subjectivity, finally, cannot be
added as another description of nonhuman good except in a panpsychist theory.

Nonhuman good, in short, is both relational and objective in
the senses specified.

An implication of this view is that value judgments with respect
to nonconscious good are cognitive. Furthermore, they are both

descriptive and normative. They describe and prescribe that certain things do or do not, would or would not, fulfill the essential nature of another being. And the ground or warrant for the validity or invalidity of the judgments is the ultimate fulfillment or perfection of the being in question.

The Ground of Goodness

But the ultimate norm or ground of good cannot be given in terms solely of the good for individuals. Even though the warrant for discriminating good from evil for individual entities consists in their self-fulfillment, we must go beyond this in stating the norm for all goodness. For individuals are intimately related to each other: they limit each other, enhance each other, press upon each other, or complement each other. Hence the ground of good for the whole cannot be given as the sum of individual fulfillments. Just as in the case of human value a thing cannot be finally said to be good or evil by virtue of its conducement to one person's fulfillment alone, but must be referred to the harmonious perfecting of the community of selves; so in the case of all beings whatsoever, taken together, a thing cannot be finally said to be good or evil by reference to one entity alone, which it is good for, but must be reckoned in connection with the totality of interrelated beings. We are thus brought back to the idea of harmony among perfected beings, for surely when we judge something to be good or evil we presuppose that it will conduce to the harmony and integration of the related beings, rather than to their disharmony and disintegration. Harmonious perfecting, then—the ultimate situation in which each entity attains as much fulfillment as possible through its relations to the other realities which alone sustain and fulfill it, and is at the same time in harmony with all other beings—stands as the final ground or norm for the ascription of good to particular things. The goodness of each for all is the measure of its worth.

In this harmonious perfecting of all entities in their relations to each other, many beings must be restricted and limited in some of their possible expressions of potentiality. For the sake of a higher unity, a more embracing fulfillment, a new creation, each being must give of its fulfillment to the totality. A nonreligious world view, such as that of Schopenhauer, would see in this restriction and confinement an indication of the belief that the world is finally hostile to individual good, that it is a place of tragedy and despair, and that a cosmos in which such harmony must be the ground of goodness means that it is indifferent or evil to individual fulfillment. A religious world view, on the other hand, such as that of Aquinas, would see in this sacrifice and limitation the highest fulfillment of which a finite being is capable, in that its contribution is conserved in a purpose not to be identified with the particular purposes and aspirations of the finite entities themselves. But however it be interpreted, harmonious perfecting of all realities stands as the presupposed warrant for judging particular things good or evil.

Our account of the good has proceeded on two assumptions: first, that it is arbitrary and unjustifiable to maintain that nothing has goodness except as being good for human beings; second, that a being that exists in isolated unity, alone, without relations to anything else, would have no goodness. Good, then, exists in the relations between things, conscious or nonconscious, such that one is good for the other through completing and fulfilling the other. The ground for saying that this is good is, for the individual, self-fulfillment, and, for the totality of beings, the harmonious fulfillment of all. Thus the fundamental notion of goodness, so far considered, has been that of the "good for-ness" of something, of being contributory to some fulfillment or other.

As yet, we have not raised the question of the goodness of such fulfillment itself. Strictly speaking, we have confined ourselves to instrumental good. Yet it is clear that this final and ultimate question now looms large before us, namely: Is fulfillment itself good? And if it is good, how is it to be characterized?

From the point of view of much Western thought, the answer to this question would be simple enough: Self-fulfillment and the harmonious perfecting of all beings are intrinsic goods, goods for their own sake, and that is all that need be said. Such a reply has been the simple assumption of most traditional Western thought. Whether the good be said to consist in harmony of parts, *eudaimonia,* the beatific vision, moral virtue, pleasure, interest, survival, whatever, it has been held that their realization or fulfillment are *ipso facto* intrinsic goods, good in themselves. Whatever instrumental goods contribute to must, *a fortiori,* be intrinsically good when realized or actualized. Thus intrinsic good has always been thought to consist in some kind of realization or actualization or fulfillment, rather than the opposite.

Such an assumption, however, seemingly so self-evident for

Western thought, meets a direct antithesis in much Oriental thought, where it is not fulfillment but nonfulfillment, not affirmation of being but negation of being, which is thought to constitute intrinsic good. Yet the principal Western traditions—from Aristotle to Paul Weiss in one tradition and from Protagoras to Bertrand Russell in another, to mention only two—automatically assume that however the good be defined—whether as perfection of nature in the one case or as satisfaction of desire in the other—it must necessarily be some actualization or realization which makes for intrinsic good. The possibility of negation seldom enters our Western thinking. Yet to one Western tradition, much Oriental thought would reply that it is not self-fulfillment and perfection of being but nonfulfillment and negation of being which constitute intrinsic good; and to the other Western tradition it would reply that it is not the satisfaction of personal desire but the extinction of desire which is intrinsically good.

It is clear, therefore, that our task is not done. So far we have suggested that the ground for saying what is good for individuals is their fulfillment and perfection, peculiar to them, and for the totality of beings the ground is the perfecting of each so far as is compatible with harmony and integration. But if self-fulfillment and perfection of being are not themselves good, then negation will be the true ground of goodness, and our whole discussion will fall to the earth. Accordingly, there must be some kind of justification for saying that such fulfillment is itself good—is better than nonfulfillment. This is a point which has been too much neglected, especially by empirical and naturalistic writers. They simply assume that some kind of actualization constitutes intrinsic good and seldom even raise the question. The central question is this: By virtue of what can we say that fulfillment and realization are better than nonfulfillment and negation? In other words, what is the justification for holding that every being, when fulfilled through those things which are goods for it, is, when thus reaching self-fulfillment, itself good rather than not good? The justification cannot be less than metaphysical, for it goes far beyond what any empirical, phenomenological, or even ethical analysis (in the usual sense of the term) can give.

Two sorts of justification seem to be possible. The first is found in the idea of creativity and the second is found in the idea of God. The first involves a world view which maintains that the very nature of the world is affirmation and creativity. The second involves a world ground for which the fulfillment and perfection of things is intrinsically good. The two ideas may, of course, be combined; but historically they have not always been combined. Nietzsche, for instance, interpreted the world with creativity but with no God, while Spinoza interpreted the world with God but with no creativity. Let us, then, consider these three alternatives in turn: the two ideas and their combination.

(a) Thinkers as divergent as Nietzche and Bergson have maintained that the essential nature of the universe is creativity and dynamic development, so that the realization and fulfillment of new beings is its inevitable product. If, then, the very forces of the universe are driving toward growth and affirmation of new life and new things, a view which holds that intrinsic good consists in negation and nonfulfillment would run counter to the very nature of ourselves and the world at large. For such a view, it would be argued, would present us with a system of values which is impossible to carry out, since we are inevitably driven toward affirmation rather than negation. Thus for Nietzsche, since the governing forces in the world are dynamic and creative, intrinsic value consists in self-transcendence, in the unrestricted affirmation of the will to power.

The central weakness of such a position, however, is that which Schopenhauer had already pointed out. Just because the driving forces of the universe are dynamic and creative, it does not necessarily follow that intrinsic good consists in such affirmation rather than in negation. The driving forces, surging into novelty, may be indifferent and even ruthless to the products which they leave in their wake. Hence they may run counter to the true good of individuals, namely, extinction. Value cannot *ipso facto* be identified with the products of dynamism and growth, except through a question-begging definition which equates the two. Such an attack was in fact the view which Schopenhauer adopted. He recognized that the driving power in the universe is dynamic and affirming, namely, the will to live. But he also held that there is nothing in this which guarantees that the products of the will to live have value. Hence he concluded that the good consists in negation and nonfulfillment and he advocated the stopping of the will to live through effort and resignation. If this dynamic will to live could not be stopped, this would indicate that the universe is destructive and hostile to true good, not that goodness consists in affirmation and fulfillment. Mere creativity, then, mere dynamics making for the fulfillments of beings, cannot by itself justify the assertion that such fulfillments are intrinsically good, intrinsically better than nonfulfillment.

(b) The other justification for holding that fulfillment is better than nonfulfillment is found in the view which maintains that all things are intrinsically good through their relation to God, who is perfect. One such conception, which does not employ the principle of creativity, is that which identifies God with the whole of reality. This is the conception to be found in Spinoza and much of recent philosophical idealism. It holds that all fulfillments are good in that they are fragments of or embodiments within the "Absolute," whose total perfection endows each member with goodness by virtue of its harmony and integration into the whole. All fulfillments are intrinsically good because they are constituents within the single, perfect, infinite ego.

This view, however, is open to two serious objections. First, the theory holds that all finite individuals are not realities at all but only appearances. How, then, can the self-fulfillment of every individual being be said to have intrinsic worth if the very meaningfulness of individuals is denied? If individuals are only appearances, it is not self-fulfillment but extinction into the Absolute which has intrinsic value for them. Second, such a conception of God, as the all-embracing, all-inclusive reality, means that the universe is a monistic, undifferentiated unity. But such a being, existing alone in its own unity, unrelated to anything else, could involve neither good nor evil. It would simply "be," and that is all. This in fact is Spinoza's view. Such a God could no more serve as the ground for maintaining that fulfillment of individuals is intrinsically good than could, for instance, the Advaitin Brahman.

(c) Evidently, then, the two ideas, creativity and God, are both required. Mere dynamics alone can make possible the affirmation and fulfillment of individuals, but it cannot guarantee that such affirmation has goodness. A static conception of God can guarantee intrinsic value only through extinction of individuals. Both doctrines are untenable by themselves as justifications for the belief that self-fulfilled beings, existing in the relation of harmonious perfecting, have intrinsic worth. Creativity without God is blind; God without creativity is empty. Each doctrine, taken separately, could equally well justify the conclusion that intrinsic value consists in negation and nonfulfillment.

If, however, the creative principle and the value principle are one, that is if there is a being which at once allows for the affirmation and uniqueness of individuals and provides that such fulfillment is good rather than evil, we shall have a final justification for denying the doctrine of negation and for accepting the position outlined above. Self-fulfillment and harmonious perfecting, then, which we have seen to be presupposed as the ground of goodness for all beings, taken individually and collectively, can themselves be seen to presuppose the existence of a world ground through relation to which these beings, so perfected, can be said to have intrinsic value in themselves. Such a conception as it appears in Judeo-Christian thought and in some philosophers such as Whitehead—a conception in which the ultimate actualizing principle and the ultimate value principle are one—stands as the final ground for maintaining that realization, actualization, complete fulfillment of the essential nature of all things is itself a warranted ground for the values we have been discussing in the main. Through their concrete relation to God, who is at once the actualizing principle of being and the endowing principle of value, all beings become both fulfilled individuals and values in themselves, apart from their instrumental use. Being and goodness are one.

This is not to say that God creates and approves the evil in the world. Evil results from certain interactions and interrelations of beings which are in themselves good. The fact that they miscombine, misbehave, destroy and plunder each other, and deny each other fulfillment is not the result of arbitrary divine fiat. Evil is a problem for God as well as for man. It results partly from the waywardness and rigidity in the elements of the world itself and partly from the misbehavior of some of the world's members who have freedom. But this does not touch the fact that all beings are endowed with value through their relation to the cosmic spirit. The fact that God is the ground for saying that fulfillment and perfection are the legitimate ground for particular valuations does not entail the fact that there is no evil to be coped with, nor is it inconsistent with the fact of the existence of evil. Thus the essential nature of every being is good through relation to God, for whom it has value. The misuses of freedom, the unlimited expression of potentialities for evil, the waywardness in the relations between entities themselves do not alter the contention that fulfillment of the essential nature of each being has intrinsic goodness in itself.

We have suggested that most traditions of Western thought, no matter what they accept as the ground of value, whether it be self-fulfillment, the life of pleasure, a balance of interests, conformity to be categorical imperative, etc., have also presupposed that the highest good consists in realization and fulfillment. We blame these views not for maintaining this presupposition but for not carrying out what this presupposition presupposes. For fulfillment must be held to be better than nonfulfillment, contrary to much Oriental thought. And this can only be assumed through a being which is at once a creative principle and a value principle. For God, fulfillment is good, and through relations to him all entities have intrinsic worth.

An Objection

The foregoing, then, will constitute our reply to Mr. Urban's objection to the definition of good as fulfillment. He writes:

> I think there can be no doubt that this definition gets its meaning only from the assumption that fulfillment is better than non-fulfillment; and just as little doubt that this assumption can be questioned. In any case, value is assumed, the value relation "better than" being already assumed in the definition. ... The "value" notion is already imported into the relation —in the assumption that fulfillment is better than non-fulfillment. Without this the equating of the relation with "good" is meaningless.[12]

This assumption is indeed presupposed by us. If, however, fulfillment, rather than nonfulfillment, of beings can be said to be good through relation to the value-endowing power of God, there is sufficient warrant for the assumption. In any case, I wish to point out that such an assumption has been characteristic of Western thought, even though much of it has not been concerned with the implications or warrant. It is very interesting to note that, despite Urban's criticism, when he comes to giving his own theory of value he stays within the "great tradition" of Western thought and holds that it is some kind of realization or actualization, rather than the opposite, which constitutes intrinsic value. For him, "value" means "that a thing ought to be." But notice that the central contention is that a thing ought to "be" rather than that it ought to "not be." Thus fulfillment is assumed to be better than nonfulfillment. But why, after all, it might be asked, ought a thing "be" rather than "not be"? Why does "goodness" mean "ought to be" rather than "ought to not be"? Why should fulfillment be better than nonfulfillment?

Hence a similar justification would seem to be called for in Urban's view.

Modern thought would do well to ask itself this question with more earnestness: Why ought things to "be" rather than "not be"? Why is fulfillment better than nonfulfillment? The justification cannot be found, I think, short of some idea of God. And this is the position which has been adopted here.

But Urban offers another objection. He insists that value must be indefinable, for, if it could be defined, it would be reduced to some form of being and so would not be unique. "Value is a logically primitive concept, and cannot be deduced from, nor defined in terms of, anything else."[13] There are two points of truth in this contention. First, value must in some sense be intuited. That is, if there were no prior intuitive knowledge of what good and evil mean, no discussion of the topic could get under way. Philosophy must presuppose the original awareness in experience of goodness, badness, and duty. Understanding without experience is impossible. Second, value cannot be defined if its definition means to exhibit a complete characterization of value—its parts, relations, content, etc. That could be done only with complete knowledge and experience.

But "definition" has many senses, of which the most common is perhaps the characterization of things in terms of universals. In this sense, Urban has offered many things toward a definition of value. He apparently knows, for instance, that the essence of value is that it describes not "what" something is but "that it ought to be." He knows that it lies between "being and non-being," that it can be ranked and scaled, etc. Thus in defining "good" to consist in certain relations of fulfillment, we are not straying from what must be done in any rational inquiry, namely, defining in terms of universals. Furthermore, if goodness be characterized as some form of being, this does not necessarily mean that it is not unique. The kind of being which it has is different from the kind of being which other things have, empirical facts, for instance.

Conclusion

In this chapter we have been dealing with a problem which was central to the thought of the classical world but has received scant attention in modern philosophy, namely, the problem of the

the relation of goodness and being. In our present-day preoccupation with questions of epistemology and methodology, we have all but abandoned this most important and far-reaching of all ethical and metaphysical questions. Yet the problem cannot be solved by simply ignoring it or by tacitly assuming that human consciousness is the focal point of all good. If classical thought is to be improved upon, this cannot be done by ignoring its problems.

10: The Goodness of Things

In the previous chapter we dealt with an easily intelligible sense in which it is possible to speak about goodness in reference to nature. This is the sense in which one thing is good for another by contributing to its sustenance or development. Every *perficiens* is instrumentally good for its *perficiendum,* whether this relation occurs in the human realm or in the nonhuman domain of nature. We then raised the more problematic question of whether natural *perficienda* could themselves be said to be good, that is, intrinsically good, good in themselves. We suggested that to this question there can be no affirmative answer apart from a relation of nature to a cosmic source of good, but that, conversely, in such a relation there is an intelligible sense of intrinsic good in the world of things.

Two difficult problems now confront us. One is to expound in more specific detail the concept of intrinsic good in nature. The other is to treat of the goodness of God in a manner that is rationally explanatory of the concept of natural good and not simply a pious evasion of philosophical questions. We shall deal with the first problem in the present chapter and the second in the next chapter.

Datum and Theory

To say anything is intrinsically good is to say it is good by virtue of its inherent properties. We have seen that this means the integration of these properties so as to constitute such perfection as is possible to the entity in question. But "intrinsic good," like all submeanings of "good," bears the connotation of the most

general meaning of "good," namely, that of being reasonably
favored. To say that the things of nature are intrinsically good,
therefore, is to say that the perfections in nature are reasonably
favored in their existence just because of their inherent properties and not because of their human utility. If it could be established that there is such favor, our primary contention in this
part of the book would be made out.

Now in trying to establish that nonhuman perfections are
favored reasonably, it is well to keep in mind the difference between the datum of favor, that is, the fact of a pro-attitude in
this matter as it occurs in many people, and the theoretical attempt to justify that favor as reasonable. In chapter 8 we cited
many quotations which illustrate how amazingly widespread is
the elemental feeling about the goodness of things, a goodness
that is expressed more abstractly as the good in being as such.
This is not the only attitude people have toward the world of
things, to be sure, but it must be acknowledged as a prevalent
one. This datum puts our theoretical attempt in perspective. Our
theoretical discussion is not foisting a new and weird notion but
is only seeking whether there is a valid reason for an attitude
which exists quite apart from any stated reason justifying it. Attitudes may be bad and harmful, and in any case are not self-
vindicating as far as truth is concerned. But they may also be
cognitively relevant data if they are deeply native and are not
the obvious products of social disfiguration.

So impressive is the chorus of natural piety that one is tempted
to follow an attractive but naïve solution to the problem. If the
attitude of natural piety were to be extended—by promotion, by
persuasion, by instruction—so that there developed a well-nigh
universal appreciation of things in the world for their own sake,
would this not be the vindication sought? What more could be
required to affirm the reality of intrinsic goods in nature than
that people in fact find such an attitude of appreciation a reasonable one to have? In that case, the theoretical problem would
resolve itself into the practical one of education in natural piety,
and the outcome would depend on the possibility of getting universal consensus.

Such a solution is unsatisfactory for two reasons, even if universal consensus could be approached.

First, anything that is good, that is, reasonably favored, is so
because of its objective characteristics and not solely because of

subjective feelings toward it. No extension in subjective attitudes would justify our contention if the objective characteristics did not warrant the judgment of intrinsic good. Without the latter, the subjective attitudes might comprise not a reasonable but an unreasonable favor. Our attention must therefore be directed to the objective conditions that warrant natural piety.

Second, we do not experience intrinsic good in natural things in the same direct way that we do in human values. In human values that we may consider intrinsically good such as knowledge, freedom, or love, which are intrinsically good insofar as they are ingredient in man's self-fulfillment, we can have direct and immediate awareness of the goodness of such experiences because they are within and a part of our own consciousness. We cannot experience natural things in the same way. We remain outside them, as it were, even though we may have empathy or intuition in Bergson's sense. Hence any judgment of good involves an imputed attribution and not a directly felt experience of the kind we have of our own human values. It is clear, then, that some further account of intrinsic good in nature is necessary if our judgment is to be anything more than a very tenuous analogy.

This second reason is considered so weighty by many philosophers that they think we simply have no business speaking of good in reference to anything but felt experiences. Aside from felt experiences there are only neutral natural facts. There may be instances of properties forming what could be called natural perfections; but to call them good in a valuational sense is not meaningful, and no amount of appeal to natural piety will change the neutral facts.

Incidentally, this criticism would also devolve on our attempt to speak, as we did in the last chapter, of instrumental goods in nature other than those that contribute to human values. One thing may contribute to the sustenance or growth of another, but if the *perficiendum* is not itself intrinsically good, the *perficiens* will not be instrumentally good. It will be an instrumental agent, but not an instrumental good in the sense of being reasonably favored as contributory to an intrinsic good.

The Factor of Consciousness

Let us now face squarely the question of the relation between consciousness and the good; and first I want to do full justice to the common view that apart from consciousness there is no intrinsic good or bad whatever. "Everything is good merely *for* something except persons, or at least sentient beings, but these are good in themselves."[1] No philosopher can fail to recognize the core of plain truth in such a judgment. Our perfectivist theory of good does not proceed by repudiating it but rather by seeking to understand it, to explore it, to interpret it. Having affirmed it, however, we may properly ask what qualifications need to be made concerning the judgment in order to do justice both to it and to the datum of natural piety, which discovers a goodness in things. Even though we accept the judgment about the necessary presence of consciousness, we are unwilling to interpret the fact of natural piety as but a fanciful personification of a stark and valueless nature or as a more or less misleading way in which we get to feel good about what is not good.

One qualification would seem to be that while we do not speak of good and bad atoms or molecules, we can and do speak about good and bad trees, good and bad horses, good and bad cells, good and bad scenery. The fact that there is no meaning to perfectibility at one level of natural phenomena (if that is true) does not imply that this notion is entirely devoid of significance at all levels of nature. Wherever there is a possibility of development within an individual entity or within a nexus of entities there is the possibility of relative degrees of perfection. This means there is one ordinary sense of "good," namely, "good of its kind," or, more accurately, "good of development," which is quite applicable to natural phenomena whether they are conscious beings or not. This is a main component in intrinsic good. It is not the only component, for we also have to show, as pointed out above, that such good is reasonably favored. But it is an aspect of good that may be independent of consciousness.

Another qualification is suggested by an ambiguity in such expressions as "consciousness is necessary for there to be any good or bad." Such expressions may mean either (1) consciousness is necessary to *feel* the good or bad or (2) consciousness is necessary to *judge* the good or bad. The first interpretation specifically locates good and bad within conscious states, and so consciousness must be present to feel good or bad in order for there to be any good or bad. Panpsychism differs from other views of this sort only in extending the range of feeling states to include all entities. In the second interpretation, consciousness is necessary to judge of relative perfection, to apprehend good or bad, to confer or withhold reasonable favor; but what is thus judged and favored might be an independent perfection and not it-self a conscious state at all. Only with consciousness can there be any intrinsic good, because only consciousness can complete the partial conditions of goodness that is present in things through its bestowal of reasonable favor. But to be ac-curate, we shall have to speak of such good as being deter-mined as much by what is beyond consciousness as by the judgment of consciousness. We hold that the second interpre-tation may be held as an adequate exposition of the main contention about the necessary connection between conscious-ness and goodness.

A third qualification is the rather obvious one that when we say consciousness is necessary to have good or evil, the refer-ence need not be restricted to human consciousness. Many value theorists intend this restriction, though some allow that subhuman sentient responses may be good or evil. But the restriction to human consciousness cannot be the *meaning* of the judgment we are considering. If the restriction is made, it must be based on an argument that supports naturalistic humanism. If superhuman consciousness is a reality, goodness could be related to it quite independently of human conscious-ness. There would then be, from our point of view, an ob-jective good in the universe, not requiring our presence at all.

Now if the reference indeed includes superhuman as well as human consciousness, then the question of whether good is al-ways related to consciousness receives an axiomatic affirmative answer. Since God is regarded by theism as a factually neces-sary being, it would be ontologically impossible for any being, and hence any good, to exist somehow by itself, without rela-tionship to God. Unlike contingent human consciousness, which can come and go, allowing the question of independent good at least to arise for it, God has an existential relation to all goodness that is an ontologically necessary relation. This is the sense in which the judgment that consciousness is necessary for good and evil to exist is a tautology—an ontological tautology. We repeat, however, that our interpretation of this tautology is that such goodness as there is in the universe apart from man consists in objective perfections, favored by God as part of his cosmic pur-pose, and not merely in "feeling states" of sentient beings. An important implication of this kind of interpretation is that, though there could be no good apart from God's consciousness, nevertheless he wills the good because of the objective conditions of good and not merely from irrational fiat.

Only with these qualifications, I believe, can we synthesize the claim that good and evil are categories of consciousness and the voices of natural piety that find goodness in things. Evidently there is an ambivalence in our attitudes which is not easy to dispatch. On the one hand we feel that good and evil would not apply to anything apart from conscious awareness and judgment, and we are often impatient with speculations to the contrary. On the other hand we feel goodness has an objective vector and is real in the universe, quite apart from our feelings. Let us call this ambivalence the "antinomy of valuation."

The main line of our solution to the antinomy is now clear from the qualifications just explained. A further distinction will help to illuminate it.

Good-in-Itself and Good-for

The distinction is related to the familiar notions, discussed in the last chapter, of intrinsic and instrumental goods. More particularly, the distinction is a further analysis of the idea of instrumental good. Upon inspection we notice that there are two somewhat different ways in which something can be *good for* a conscious being, though this would not be so in the case of nonconscious beings. Illustrations of these two ways may be taken from our common experience.

If one cracks and devours a coconut, this action may satisfy an immediate biological need for food and drink. But if during the process one pauses to appreciate the features of the coconut just because of their engaging quality, from a sense of curious interest, there is a different kind of value experience. In both cases the coconut is an instrumental good for the experient, but not in the same way. It might be said that the latter experience is merely the satisfaction of an immediate esthetic need and is not different in kind from the former experience, both being satisfaction of an interest. Yet the concentration may be entirely on the biological aspects of the coconut and not particularly esthetic in character at all. One is simply admiring the coconut, and that is all. Here is an object of nature, the product of a life process, which seems worth admiring, that is, something to be admired in itself.

A cultural example is that of an artist creating a painting or poem. Here the performance of creating, including the muscular movements, the emotional responses, the whole psychic awareness, is *good for* the artist. It does him good to create, as popular speech might put it. But in what sense is the painting or poem, the art product, good for him? Not being completed as yet, it is not a good for him in the same way that the act of creating is. Moreover, when the work is completed, the esthetic need which was satisfied by the act of creating may be fulfilled, and the artist may have a rather detached attitude toward the finished product. Usually he will continue to admire it, as will other beholders (though some artists have turned against their previous works). His esthetic feelings may be rekindled by the work from time to time, as will those of other beholders. But the artist's impulse to create will move on to other creations. Thus both the act of creating and the eventual product of the creation are instrumental goods for the artist; but one is a good experienced as immediate fulfillment of need, the other is a good beheld in a mood of relative detachment.

Another example would be the difference between the experience of newly won political freedom to the people of a formerly downtrodden nation and the approval of that emergent freedom by democratically minded people in another country. The freedom situation is a value for both groups of people, but certainly of a different order for each.

Now in all such cases, when we are speaking of the human value of these experiences, we may call the values of the first type "values of immediate contribution" and the values of the second type "values of detached beholding." Or if we speak of the components or objects which are the instrumental goods in the situations, we shall call the one type "contributory goods" and the other type "beheld goods." The similarity between the two is that both are considered good, not in and of themselves (not in relation to anything else), but precisely in and because of their relation to something else which they are good *for*. There is always some *perficiendum* which in some way is fulfilled through the relation. This is the difference of both these goods from intrinsic goods, which are considered good just because of the inherent properties of that which is judged good.

The differences between the two types of instrumental goods may be summarized as follows.

1. Beheld goods can only be good for conscious beings, whereas

contributory goods, as we saw in the last chapter, may be related to any being whatever that can be a *perficiendum* since every such being has *perficientia* which sustain it.

2. Phenomenologically speaking, the contributory goods which enter human value are experienced with psychical closeness, whereas beheld goods in general are experienced with psychical distance.

3. Contributory goods fulfill some lack or some need, whereas beheld goods are valued over and above any specific service to needs or completion of lacks. This means that at the human level the two are correlated with the distinction made in chapter 3 between need values and variety values.

4. Contributory goods are valued because of the specific properties of the object that will satisfy the need in question. Beheld goods are valued because of some perfection or partial perfection which captures the disinterested attention and favor of the conscious agent.

Let us now employ this distinction in resolving the antinomy of valuation. The principal thesis is that the *perfections* in the natural cosmos—whose status as *intrinsic goods* has so far been problematical—plus the *contributory goods* that sustain these perfections are *beheld goods* for a *supreme valuing consciousness*. This thesis implies that (a) there are no goods in the universe that lack relation to some consciousness. In this way we accept the insistence of value theories which stress the necessary presence of consciousness for value or good. But the thesis also implies that (b) from a human point of view there are intrinsic goods in the cosmos that are independent of us, because such goodness consists in inherent properties and relations that are in no way dependent on us for their reality. In this way we accept the datum of natural piety that finds goodness in things.

To define "intrinsic good in nature" in this way seems to make instrumental good or "good for" prior to intrinsic good or "good in itself," and this may seem strange. Yet this is exactly the assertion that is made in the special case of goodness in nature. This does not mean, however, that there is no objective intrinsic goodness from a human perspective. All it means is that from God's perspective the intrinsic goodness of being is equivalent with beheld goodness. Such intrinsic goods may also become beheld goods for us, or even contributory goods; but these are additional relationships.

It is true that we do not experience the intrinsic goodness of things in the same intimate, personal way that we experience the intrinsic values of our own perfective development. But the logic of the judgments is the same, namely, that the perfection of being is good in itself, whether it be human perfection that is humanly felt or nonhuman perfection that is humanly beheld.

It might be objected that to define natural goodness by relation to God is a roundabout explanation which at most shows that nature has intrinsic goodness to God but does not show that it has it for man. The point to be emphasized in response is that the explanation of natural goodness here given is only the theoretical base, the ground, for judgments of good which occur beforehand; it is not intended as a proof of intrinsic goodness in nature. Insofar as there is any warrant for the belief, it must be found in the data of natural piety plus the reflective judgments of man that perfection is somehow good in itself, wherever it may occur. What we have been doing, then, is merely trying to investigate the presuppositions of these more original experiences of life and of nature.

The Extent of the Good

A further question to be considered is this: How extensive is the range of nonhuman good? This question somewhat anticipates the content of the following chapter, but it is relevant for the completion of our present theme.

Let us begin by surveying the logical possibilities in the case. If an entity is judged not to be intrinsically good, we shall consider the alternatives to be that it is either intrinsically evil or neutral with respect to good and evil. These are the three pure possibilities. A mixed possibility immediately suggests itself, namely, that an entity might be both good and evil with respect to its different inherent characteristics. I shall rule out, however, any further mixed possibility that might include neutrality as one component, since philosophers, when they judge entities to be neutral with respect to intrinsic good and evil, generally refer to entities as wholes and not just to parts of them. A further reason for this exclusion will appear shortly when we interpret evil in nature as a lack of good. Thus the possibilities we have for an individual entity are that it might be intrinsically good, intrinsically evil, partly good and partly evil, or totally neutral.

Working with these four possibilities for individual entities, we can ask what are the possibilities for a universe of entities. Here,

of course, we must consider the combinations of the four possibilities, since the various entities in a universe might exemplify
different possibilities, so that the total universe would be some
combination of the possibilities.[2] Surveying all the combinations,
we see that there are fifteen relevant combinations that a universe
might exhibit.[3] These can be set out conveniently by saying that
a universe might be composed of individual entities which are
  1. All intrinsically good;
  2. Some good, some evil;
  3. Some good, some good and evil;
  4. Some good, some neutral;
  5. Some good, some evil, some good and evil;
  6. Some good, some evil, some neutral;
  7. Some good, some good and evil, some neutral;
  8. Some good, some evil, some good and evil, some neutral;
  9. All evil;
  10. Some evil, some good and evil;
  11. Some evil, some neutral;
  12. Some evil, some good and evil, some neutral;
  13. All good and evil;
  14. Some good and evil, some neutral;
  15. All neutral.
Since all of these alternatives are combinations of the three basic
concepts of good, evil, and neutrality, it is with these concepts
that we must first be concerned in discussing the possibilities. The
thesis I wish to advance is that there are no purely evil or totally
neutral beings. This would eliminate as genuine options all the alternatives except 1, 3, and 13, for each of the other combinations
would include some evil or neutral entities.

That there are no totally neutral beings with respect to good
and evil is what we have been attempting to render plausible
throughout the sequence of thought in this part. We are expounding the view that it is both meaningful and reasonable to speak
of nonhuman good and evil. Our contention is that such a view
is the natural outgrowth of much of our primitive experience of
nature, and also that it is the fitting outcome of our reflection on
the cosmos. A further reason for this view would stem directly
from a theistic perspective, for if God is conceived of as the creator of finite beings, it is usually concluded that none of them is
created for complete waste or total exclusion from the ultimate
purpose he envisions in creating.

We must, however, make a rather significant qualification in this doctrine of nonneutrality. It is that intrinsic goodness is to be thought of as applying only to beings which display a distinctive character as entities in their own right, or to unified nexus of entities, and not merely to juxtaposed bits of matter or heaps of entities. We would not speak of perfection or imperfection characterizing a miscellaneous pile of leaves, though we might do so in the case of particular leaves, or at least the tree from which they fell.

But are there any criteria for designating an entity or nexus in this required sense, or does it all depend on the arbitrary whim of the beholder? I do not believe the matter is entirely arbitrary or that criteria are lacking. There are, in fact, two criteria implicit in natural piety. The first is that there must be a definite, inherent unity of organization within the entity or nexus of entities. This eliminates mere conglomerations, artificial conjunctions, disordered arrangements of heterogeneous content; it also implies that judgments of perfection may pertain to the whole of a being but not to its parts, since there might be a unified organization in the whole but not in the parts taken separately. A well-developed organism may illustrate a perfection in being; but we do not always speak of the anatomical components in the same way. The other criterion is that a being or nexus of beings be capable of exhibiting a natural perfection of its own which is not primarily and essentially a product of concurrent human intervention. Such capability of natural perfection can only be judged by conscious beings; but what is thus judged is not human feeling but natural fact. Human beings may inaugurate or modify these natural perfections, as in the development by hybridization of new living forms. Still, the capabilities for growth that result are objective and natural and are in fact the unfolding of potentialities already latent in nature.

On the basis of these criteria we can identify three classes of beings or nexuses of beings which are capable of exhibiting a distinctive perfection. One of these classes is the functionally subliving entities which constitute the physical world. Their perfection consists in the bare actualization of possibilities, with apparently no potential for growth within the sort of being, momentary or enduring, which they have. A second class comprises such physical and chemical syntheses of these entities as could be judged by conscious beings to possess an independent unity of organization or harmony of structure and to function at the level of observable objects. The third class is that of living organisms that are

capable of growth toward inherent or chosen ends. In this class
we have the capacity for developing fulfillment of potentiality.
We shall call these classes, respectively, "primordial entities,"
"perceptual harmonies," and "organic beings." The last includes
the union of organic beings into societies. It should be noted
that even if Whiteheadians are right in the theory of universal
organism, the above distinctions may still function since they
are valuational and not metaphysical distinctions.

These classes of being are the loci of natural perfections and
are therefore the objects of judgments of intrinsic good or evil.
All else in nature comes under the heading of external relations
among beings, and here of course there is much neutrality regarding good and evil. Such relations are instrumental relations wherein one entity might be good for, bad for, or simply indifferent to
the perfection of another. Thus the neutrality in nature can be
thought of as referring to relationships among beings and not to
beings themselves.

Can we go on and deny that there are beings which are totally
evil in character? Yes, with even more reason. To defend this assertion, let us consider the meaning of evil in this connection. If
intrinsic good is to be interpreted as the *reasonably favored perfection of inherent characteristics, that is, complete realization of
the essential potentialities of anything,* then evil must be defined
as failure to achieve such realization. We are thus able to use a
time-honored philosophical conception of evil, namely, evil as
the lack of some positive good.

I am far from saying that this is the only meaning of evil that
is relevant to the world; but it is the meaning of intrinsic evil. All
evil is frustration of good, but sometimes this is better thought
of not simply as a lack but as positive acts of destruction. Thus
we may speak of negative and positive evil. These positive acts
are the instrumental relations between beings whereby one of
them does injury to another, and the evil of such acts is instrumental evil. When such evil results from actions in nature, we
call it natural evil; when from human acts, moral evil. Instrumental evil produces some destruction of good, some failure to
perfect, some lack, that is, intrinsic evil. So while there is much
else in the world that we call evil—and this is often a greater focus of attention—we can nevertheless see that intrinsic evil, as the
lack of good, is the primary defining concept of evil.

Now when we consider evil in this sense of lack of good, we
must readily conclude that there can be no totally evil being; for

to be totally evil would be to lack all positive perfections, and this would be equivalent to not being. To be is to manifest some realization of inherent possibility, some positive perfection. Just to be is therefore already some distance toward complete intrinsic good. Thus we can affirm another classic teaching of philosophy, namely, that goodness and being are coterminous, or, in traditional language, that both good and being are transcendentals. If we believe, as we must, that finite beings generally do not display the full perfection of which their nature is capable, that they fail to realize all their essential possibilities, that they exhibit nonbeing as well as being, evil as well as good, this does not change the contention that insofar as they are anything definite, they realize part of their essential being and are to that degree good. Pure evil can be no being at all.

If these inferences hold up, we can return to the list of logically possible universes, confident that only 1, 3, and 13 are real possibilities. We must decide between these three.

Possibility 1 asserts that all beings are good intrinsically, with no admixture of evil. This view can be called "perfectological monism." It is attractive to all those who are impressed by the feeling that evil has the status of an appearance—an illusion—compared with the positive character of the good. It asserts, in a word, the unreality of evil.

To uphold this view would require a judgment that accords ill with our day-to-day experience and reflection. We would be required to maintain that there is no real failure of being, no real thwarting or stifling of what might be, no lack, incompleteness, or limited achievement, no real imperfection. This is more than we can conscionably say. Though evil is dependent upon the good, both definitionally and ontologically, it is not unreal for that reason. Of course, there is a paradox here which cannot be denied. Evil, as the lack of good, does not have the positive status of actuality that the good has, and it is therefore in this sense nonbeing. But the main point is that the creatures who suffer the lacks, the failures of fulfillment, the imperfections, the evil, are themselves real, and real in a form that is short of their essential possibilities. Their lacks are real and not imaginary. Seen from their perspective, evil cannot simply be an illusion: nonbeing is not nothingness. Paradox there is; but it is metaphysical not valuational. Valuationally, we cannot eliminate intrinsic evil as an aspect of reality.

Possibility 13 supposes a universe composed solely of beings

which are both good and evil, that is, imperfect beings. We shall
call this view "perfectological dualism." The view might be
thought of as applying to all finite beings, thus excluding God.
But if a metaphysics had the conception of a finite God, with a
surd element in his very nature, as part of the universe, then the
view might be all encompassing.

Dualism does not suffer from as radical a difficulty as monism,
for it acknowledges the reality of evil. Yet there seems no sufficient experiential reason for supposing that everything which
exists has some deficiency, some imperfection, some failure to
be what it might be. Aside from the idea of a finite God who
contains evil within himself, which seems repugnant to religious
experience, we may point out that the first class of beings mentioned earlier, the primordial entities, apparently have no potentiality for development or growth within their given nature and
therefore just *are* what their essense is. They just *are* the natural
perfection that is open to them, with no lack in relation to some
further end. The case might seem to be otherwise if the primordial entities are interpreted as Whiteheadian occasions with their
strata of subject, object, and superject; yet even here it would
seem that there must be accumulations and organizations of occasions before there can be significantly distinct beings with the
potentiality for continuing growth. As for the other two classes
of beings, there seems no reason to deny that some of these beings attain the limited possibilities their nature allows. There are
many thwartings, stuntings, imperfections; but there are also
many instances of what appears to be the full flowering of the
limited inherent potentiality with which something is endowed.
If this be so, we must conclude that complete dualism overstresses
the evil and imperfection in the world, just as monism understresses
it.

The upshot of our discussion is that we affirm possibility 3 to
be the most reasonable hypothesis. It asserts that the real universe
comprises a vast variety of perfections and imperfections, of beings
fulfilled or partly fulfilled in their natures. This view is "perfectological pluralism," and it accords best with our experiences of the
world we inhabit. The universe we know illustrates an admixture
of intrinsic good and evil. It is partly perfected and partly fallen,
partly manifesting its essential goodness and partly deprived of
that pinnacle.

The Perfectological Argument for God's Existence

The goodness of things suggests an argument for the existence of God. Its statement will form a transition from this chapter to the next. Another reason for including it here is that while God is important to the present value theory, his existence is nowhere else treated in this book. The value theory does not depend on this particular argument, and certainly the existence of God does not; but if the argument has any merit, we shall have a bonus dividend from our speculations. Whether the argument convinces more minds than other arguments have, or even as many, is of course extremely problematical. But I take it that this consideration does not affect the logic of the case if the argument turns out to have merit.

The argument can be stated as follows:[4]

1. Intrinsic good pertains to being as such and not only to sentient feeling states.

2. This good, both human and nonhuman, is most adequately interpreted by the concept of perfection, that is, the fulfillment of essential possibilities.

3. The full meaning of "good," which must include the general characteristic of reasonable favor, can be completed in the case of human good through man's approval in experiencing his own fulfillment; but this can be done in the case of nonhuman good only through reference to a transcendent consciousness that favors the nonhuman good in willing to create it.

4. Therefore, the real existence of God is a necessary presupposition of thought about the world's goodness, and though such a necessary presupposition does not absolutely justify the transition to real existence apart from thought, it creates a strong presumption in favor of this conclusion.[5]

This argument should not be confused with a spurious argument that could be formulated. We have suggested that reference to God completes the full meaning of nonhuman good. Now if this were taken to mean that the belief in God provides the only reason or evidence for asserting any goodness in the natural world, and if the goodness of the world, so defined, were taken to imply the existence of God, the argument would indeed be a bad case of circularity. It would be begging the question of God's existence even to state the premise about the goodness of the world. But our argument starts from the contention that there is independent ground for affirming goodness in the world, that ground being the sentiment of natural piety and attendant reflection. The goodness in the world is a valuational datum to start from, and it is in need of an explanation. The question is what is the most adequate explanation. Thus the argument moves from data in the world needing explanation to the existence of God.

It is instructive to compare the argument with the five arguments of St. Thomas. It has a similarity to each of them but it is not identical with any. It is similar to his first three arguments, the cosmological ones, in that it begins with some characteristic of the world and moves to God. It might be objected that causation and contingency are much more empirically obvious characteristics of the world than is the goodness of things. This represents a notable difference in the arguments. On the other hand, it can be pointed out that neither causation nor contingency nor goodness are empirical qualities like yellow or length. Hume in fact denied causation, and Spinoza contingency, though both knew the same empirical world that other philosophers know. Such characteristics, and also goodness, involve reflection besides simple impression, and this is a similarity they have. Our argument is similar to St. Thomas's fourth way in that it employs the concept of perfection. But our argument does not infer that because there are degrees of perfection in being there must be a most perfect being. There is a similarity to his fifth argument in that there is in both an appeal to conscious purpose beyond nature in order to account for some feature of nonconscious entities within nature. But the feature in question is not an inward teleological movement toward goals but the intrinsic good which is felt to characterize many things in the world.

Like any argument, this one can be attacked either on its formal validity or on the adequacy of its premises. The attack on premises is most significant, since most philosophical arguments can be stated or restated to meet the criterion of formal consistency.

Our first premise is based primarily on the fairly pervasive sentiment—in poets, nature lovers, contemplatives, and plain men—that goodness has a more extensive status than location in human feeling and that it somehow pertains to things in general. Another reason is that when we begin to think through the nature of human good, analogies with nonhuman things appear, so that it seems not altogether inappropriate to speak about the good of nonhuman things also.

In defense of our second premise we point out, as we did in chapter 2, that in the case of human value the perfection theory of good seems to be presupposed by those pursuits such as religion, psychotherapy, and law which are most involved practically in the actualization of value. The self-fulfillment of every individual is the moral ideal to which these pursuits aspire. As a further reason, we found that other theories are one-sided or incomplete in their selection of some one aspect of the total value situation. In the case of nonhuman entities, the perfection theory seems to be the only one that is plausible, since panpsychism, the only real alternative, requires a metaphysical extension of feeling that is too indefinite or too remote in meaning to explain a notion of universal good. Without such an extension, it is still meaningful to speak of reasonable favor assigned to the realization of each thing's possibilities, the perfection of its essential being.

The third premise says that though we have an intimation of nonhuman good, a good of being *qua* being, this is a semi-complete notion, a quasi-conception, unless such good can be seen as willed good, endowed good, the product of conscious favor and creativity. If this is so, there must be an appeal for completion either to finite beings or to a transcendent consciousness. Now finite beings such as man (and we can only assume that other finite beings are similar to man in relevant respects) do not, phenomenologically, feel themselves to be creators of the cosmos or of such good as they find in it. The appeal must then be to a transcendent consciousness, in whose will to create and perfect we find the completion of the idea of nonhuman good. The other options would be to stay with the quasi-conception of good without completing it, or to abandon the whole idea altogether. But the quasi-conception is indeed a halfway house, demanding some resolution, and the abandonment of any notion of nonhuman good does not account for that intimation of natural good which is independently sensed to pertain to being as such.

If these premises hold up, the conclusion would seem to follow, since it would be difficult to complete the theory with a nonexistent God who is only a mental construction. The conclusion does not follow as a rigorous demonstration but as the most reasonable outcome of the suggested premises. But the whole question of the status of such arguments is undergoing, among friends and foes alike, reconsideration. They may, in any case, belong to an uncharted subject to be called "philosophical eschatology."

11: The Goodness of God

Nonhuman good can be divided into two parts: the goodness of the world of things and the goodness of God. I omit any reference to other finite consciousnesses besides man because in general structure the analysis would probably be similar to that for man, and in specific content there is no evidence to go on. In this chapter we shall try to state an intelligible and nontautological conception of good in reference to God. Then, with this in mind, we can return and complete the discussion of natural good. That discussion, developed in the last two chapters, has not yet been concluded satisfactorily. Several questions may still persist.

Suppose it is true, as we have suggested, that the world of things can be said to have intrinsic goodness through its relation to divine consciousness; what, specifically, does this mean? If God, upon creating the world, sees that it is good, what does he see, that is, by virtue of what does he see it as good? What must be the characteristics of both God and the world for such an evaluation to be rendered?

Again, even if the world shows intrinsic goodness to a divine consciousness, why would this make it good from a human point of view? Why wouldn't it be just neutral for us, no matter what value it might have for other modes of consciousness? What is there about relating the world to God that renders it good in an intelligible sense from a human perspective?

Such is the business of this chapter—and a knotty business it is, although, we may hope, it is fit to be untied.

The Term "Good" in Reference to God

Some recent analytic philosophers have maintained that to speak of God as good is to speak tautologically or circularly and hence not informatively. One form of this charge has been the claim that the statement of God's goodness is always made in a convictional context by believers, who assert it not as a verifiable or falsifiable proposition but as a tenet of faith which they will not give up, no matter what. In fact, a test of faith is that it will *not* be given up despite counterevidence. Thus evidence against the statement is not admissible; so the statement must function not as an ordinary proposition but as an emotive utterance, or at least as a tautology that is true by stipulation.

This analysis of the statement seems, however, to be logically incorrect, even though in other respects it may depict the believer's religious attitude. The statement that God is good *is* intended by those who assert it to characterize a state of affairs as well as to express a conviction and, therefore, to be a proposition in some sense true or false. And it does not seem correct to say that believers will entertain no falsifying evidence—evil, for example—even if they do not consider such evidence convincing. It appears that this sort of analysis badly mixes the psychological state of the believer with the logic of the proposition he is asserting.[1]

Another charge is that theological talk is circular. The charge says that when God is spoken of as good, the understanding is that this goodness stands as an independent norm of good, a guide, model, or director for human values. But whence comes this conception of divine goodness, except by extrapolation from the notion of good already known and defined in our human framework? If it is something else entirely than human good, then it is irrelevant to us since we are limited to human conceptions. And if it is but an extension of our human term, then it is not an independent norm or meaning of good after all but simply a human concept, terrestrial in origin and logically circular when extended.[2]

This charge can be answered, I think, in the following manner. (1) It is true that the basic conception of good can be known, and is known, in a purely natural way, and this meaning with its submeanings, is reflected in man's rational discourse. (2) In addition, many people, through religious experience, are brought to the conclusion that there is an operative power of divine goodness which is not identical with human reality, and they believe that the source of this conception is not so much the ordinary modes of natural experience as the extraordinary moments of insight and revelation which are not invented but which, so to speak, come upon them. (3) It turns out that the two sorts of good, the two encounters with goodness, are not entirely opposed; rather they match up, link up, hook together in certain respects, so that one is convinced one is confronting not two equivocal meanings of good but a common intelligible meaning. (4) Yet the two kinds of good, though continuous, the extra-natural with the natural, are thought to be so different in some respects that it is necessary and proper to speak of a real difference between human and divine good.

Thus the intention is to assert of the divine good both a continuity with the meaning of human good and yet a difference due to the objective reference of the divine good—a reference from which, it is believed, the concept of divine goodness is in part formulated. This seems to be a perfectly plausible, non-circular use of language, and it would seem therefore that the opponent's real task is not to attack at the level of linguistic usage but to examine the belief in the reality of God. And that is quite a different matter from the charge we started with.

So much for negative rebuttal. What is the positive way in which the term "good" legitimately applies to God?

If the reader will consult our outline of the senses of "good" at the end of chapter 1 (p. 17), he will see the range of senses from which we draw. Of these, there are perhaps three that are central: reasonable favor, intrinsic good (and with this the idea of perfection), and divine good.

First of all, in speaking of divine goodness one must certainly have in mind the most general meaning of "good," namely, that which is reasonably favored. Otherwise he would not be entitled to use the term "good" at all, or else he would be using it in a totally equivocal sense. So the minimum we mean in saying that God is good is that his nature reasonably elicits an approval or favor from man. Incidentally, this can be true of nonbelievers as well as believers, since what nonbelievers object to is not the *idea* of divine goodness (they must employ it themselves) but the belief that there is any *reality* with that description.

There is an oddity in the expression that God is reasonably favored by man, because it sounds as if God must pass muster before us and as if we then bestow a quality of goodness upon

him by our favor. In one sense, of course, everything that is
judged to be good must be tested by us, for we can hardly be
expected to hold something good which offends every trace of
decency and reasonableness within us. Still, the oddity remains
in the expression as I have put it.

The oddity is removed, however, if we notice two points. The
term "reasonable favor," in the first place, is merely an analytical
phrase that indicates the lowest common denominator in many
expressions and is not designed as an adequate description for
other purposes. We are much more inclined to speak of God's
being as eliciting devotion, praise, love, conviction, or to speak
of him as being worshiped, cherished, glorified. The oddity dis-
appears in these more usual phrases. But philosophically, they
all involve the minimal meaning of reasonable favor or approval.

The other point to notice is that, as I have insisted, the term
"reasonable favor" is not a bestowal phrase but a recognition
phrase. That is, we reasonably favor something (consider it good)
not because we endow it with a quality but because we find in
it some trait or harmony of traits which elicits our response.
Thus we do not make God good by projecting our favor; rather
his very being elicits our favor in the first place. The judgment
of good would not apply without the reasonable favor; but the
reasonable favor is not self-generating and is not the whole explanation of what is good. The *reason* in the reasonable favor
lies in the object favored.

This brings us to the other two relevant senses of "good."
God is certainly favored (cherished) by man in virtue of intrinsic characteristics: God is intrinsically good. And our interpretation of intrinsic good, to repeat, has been in terms of another
meaning of "good," namely, perfection, so that in our scheme
these senses collapse. The intrinsic goodness of God, therefore,
means, as with all entities, the perfection of his nature. This
general categorization is not altered by the belief that God's perfection is viewed as a unique instance, that is, that his being
manifests the supreme actualization of all those attributes that
are characteristic of his nature (unity, power, knowledge, love,
and so forth), whereas this is not the case with other beings.

The other sense of "good" that is most applicable to God is
what we would call in a human context moral good. But though
the kind of attribute involved here is continuous in meaning with
moral good in our mundane sense, so that there is no breach in
intended meaning, still the quality of moral goodness God repre-

sents to us is considered so exalted, compared with man's am-
biguous attainments in this regard, that it seems wise, in keeping
with much actual usage, to refer to God's goodness of this kind
simply as divine good, and to reserve the term "moral goodness"
for a description of human character. In any case, what is intended here is the attribute of God wherein he is supreme love,
willing and seeking the perfection of all things, acting to har-
monize all conflicts, holding all creatures in endless and limitless
concern.

These senses of "good" can be brought together in this summary statement: The goodness of God signifies the intrinsic perfection of his nature, especially his supreme love, which elicits
reasonable favor, or even rapturous response, from creatures who
behold it. Thus defined, this conception seems to me both continuous with and distinct from the human good, so that we are
in no trouble on linguistic grounds.

Incidentally, we might also hold that God represents the supreme case of instrumental good. If he is indeed the creator and
sustainer of the world, then it is his existence which above all
else is "good for" other beings. But I have chosen not to stress
this in the main definition because, for one thing, this instrumental good is entirely rooted in the intrinsic perfection of God, and,
for another, those who think about the matter disinterestedly
judge the goodness of God to consist not in what they can obtain from him instrumentally but in his intrinsically worshipful
and holy nature.

Valuational Characteristics of God

I propose the term "axiogenesis" for the process whereby the
appreciation of goodness emerges into prominence within consciousness. Our concern here is with the ontological aspects of
this process of axiogenesis. The phenomenon of axiogenesis can
be divided into two parts: human axiogenesis and natural axiogenesis. Human axiogenesis is the province of value theory in the
ordinary sense, and it is the subject of discussion whenever the
attempt is made to analyze the origin or composition of man's
value experience. We dealt with this subject in part 2. Natural
axiogenesis indicates the process whereby the things of nature
become viewed as independently good, as "beheld goods" in our
terminology. I say we are concerned here with ontological as-

pects in order to differentiate our concern with chronological interests. No doubt there was a point in the human past when human values, on the one hand, and natural goods, on the other, were first appreciated intrinsically, and no doubt the hereditary and environmental factors involved in this emergence could be analyzed. But our concern here is more Kantian, the concern with presuppositions, with categorial ingredients rather than chronological antecedents. We want to know the ontological conditions needed for natural axiogenesis to have occurred.

It is not that men have no immediate and direct experience of good in nature apart from this ontological speculation. Quite the contrary, they have; and the sentiment of natural piety might seem to be enough vindication without further analysis. But natural piety is purely phenomenological and of itself carries no ontological justification. Without an adequate ontological explanation of natural good, the sentiment of natural piety might be said to be' an illusion, a distortion, a poetic cover-up of a barren world.

In the previous two chapters we have vied for the contention that a divine consciousness, creating the world and endowing it with good, through that very act of creating is necessary for the maintenance of a doctrine of objectivity of natural good. Now we are to analyze that contention further, asking what are the valuational characteristics of God and the natural characteristics of the world that make such objective goodness a possibility and a reality.

First, what are the valuational attributes of God that make for the independent goodness of things? The answer to this question will comprise a selection of characteristics from the total nature or perfection of God. And what do we mean by the total nature or perfection of God (which constitutes his own intrinsic goodness, metaphysically considered)? Traditionally it has been held, with good reason, that the full nature of God cannot be known; but, within partial knowledge, it has been widely held that the perfection of God would include the perfection of the following attributes or aspects of his nature.

1. Capacity for self-existence
2. Self-sufficiency of being
3. Unity of being
4. Transcendence and immanence
5. Eternity and temporal grasp
6. Power to act

7. Freedom and creativity
8. Knowledge of all possibility and actuality
9. Love and responsiveness to creatures
10. Joy or happiness[3]

Now how do such characteristics lead us to our intended conclusion? The primary valuational characteristic of God is perfect love, that is, the unqualified capacity to desire and seek the good of creatures. From this capacity the creation of things is effected for no ulterior self-glorification or mastery but in order to actualize in the world independent perfections. These things all reflect traces of the divine perfection and in that sense glorify their creator; but this cannot be thought of on the analogy of a potentate granting privileges in order to be flattered and to provide objects for manipulation. Love rules out such motives. And they are also ruled out by a further characteristic, namely, the self-sufficiency of God in his own being. He does not need—in the ordinary sense of need—other beings to fulfill his incompleteness, to take up his lacks, to perfect his being by meeting some deficiency. His nature is of the sort Plato spoke in the *Philebus*, when he said that "the being who possesses good always everywhere and in all things has the most perfect sufficiency, and is never in need of anything else."[4] This means that with pure purpose and consistency he can project finite perfections, that is, goods, into actuality. Of course it is possible to speak in a special sense of God's need to create. Perfect love overflows in a need to create and share the goods that would otherwise be possibilities only. This combination of perfect love and self-sufficiency entails a universe of independent goods. Two quotations from Teilhard de Chardin will help to illuminate these two primary valuational characteristics in the divine nature.

> In the beginning was *Power*, intelligent, loving, energizing. In the beginning was the *Word*, supremely capable of mastering and moulding whatever might come into being in the world of matter. In the beginning there were not coldness and darkness: there was the *Fire*.[5]

> Were creation's dust, which is vitalized by a halo of energy and glory, to be swept away, the substantial Reality wherein every perfection is incorruptibly contained and possessed would remain intact.[6]

Other characteristics, however, are also involved in the emergence of natural good. One of them is God's complete noetic

vision, his knowledge of all actualities as good and of all possibilities createable as good. If the good must in the end be defined by reference to consciousness, there could be no such good
in nature without this knowledge of actuality, and there could
be no creation without selection from known possibilities. The
realm of all possibilities, therefore, and the realm of all actualities are present in the divine knowledge.

Charles Hartshorne has taken this topic as the frontier for a
breach with what he calls the classical idea of God. He insists
that the classical idea has no place for this notion of possibility
which I have stated. In "The Logic of Perfection" he says:

> The classical view was, in effect, that it is all one to the
> deity whether His world be this or that; the unactualized
> possibilities for worlds were not conceived as unactualized
> divine potentialities. God could, it was thought, be con-
> ceived to have acted differently, or at least with different
> results, but not to have been different.[7]

If the unactualized possibilities in God's knowledge *are* interpreted as divine potentialities, then God's nature has potentiality
for becoming as well as changeless actuality, and hence the shift
to the neoclassical idea of God.

> Let us then try the other tack, and say that unactualized
> possibilities increase, rather than decrease, with the rank of
> a being, and that, accordingly, perfection does not mean a
> zero, but a maximum, of potentiality, of unactualized power
> to be, as well as to produce beings in others. To define this
> maximum in purely a priori terms, we have only to say that
> the divine power-to-be is absolutely infinite, or is all power
> to be. . . . The absolute infinity of the divine potentiality
> might also be called its *coincidence with possibility as such.*[8]

One wonders, however, whether a reconciliation between the
two views might not be effected by employing another classical
notion, the distinction between essence and accident, that is, between God's essential nature and his concomitant contingent relationships to the world. One could then say that God's essential
nature does not change but remains ever actually what it is,
whereas his contingent relations to the world undergo modification, thus accounting for what is implicit in the notion of potentiality or becoming.

One difficulty in speaking about divine potentiality is that it conjures up an image of the entire divine nature caught up in a process of evolution, an upheaval which in time may produce a different divine nature from that which is now encountered. Such a notion is unthinkable in connection with God, and in fact that is not Hartshorne's meaning at all. It turns out that the only things he means by divine potentiality can be included in two categories: (a) the capacity for coming to know as actual those things which are now only possible and (b) the power to create such actualities from possibilities. This restriction of meaning is evident in his exposition of the idea of God.

> Item for item, everything actual is accounted for in His actual knowing, as everything possible is in His potential knowing. Thus we may define perfection as *modal coincidence,* and we may interpret this under the analogy of infallible knowledge. . . .
> One may put the matter a little differently. If God is conceived as Creator, this means, "whatever world actually exists, God is thought of as having created it; and whatever world might exist, God is thought of as capable of creating it." Thus the actual is what God is or is the maker of; and the possible is what God could be, or be the maker of. Again we have modal coincidence.[9]

Thus divine potentiality means simply, for Hartshorne, the potentiality for knowing and for creating. But one wonders why these two notions cannot be incorporated into a classical idea of God (at least an idea not foreign to all of classical thought) by means of the distinction mentioned above. Thus the *essential nature* of the divine knowing includes a total noetic grasp of all being, and this, as complete, does not change. This knowing includes the actual and the possible. To be sure, God does not know as actual those things which are not yet actual, but he knows their natures and their potentialities. What is added when possibilities become actual is not a change in the *essential nature* of the divine knowing but rather an *existential relation* between knower and created things which did not obtain before. The essential nature of God's knowing does not change, but his concomitant contingent relations to the world, experienced as an existential difference between the possible and the actual, do change.

Also, the power to create need not be thought of as a potentiality in the ordinary sense of that word, that is, as the latent

capacity to become something else than what one now is, like
the capacity of a child to become a man. (I presume we are not
dealing here with a little godling gradually becoming greater and
greater, till he finally passes into a different sort of being.) God's
power to create is simply his actual power, the power he possesses
in fact, though apparently it is not exercised to make everything
actual that is possible. The *essential nature* of his power remains
ever the same, though its use in relation to the world is contingent and progressive.

One further aspect of the divine knowledge is crucial for our
theory and must be emphasized. Since we have frequently spoken
of the fulfillment of potentiality, the perfection of a being's essence, reaching the supreme limits of a being's attainment, and
the like, the question arises as to the ontological basis of such
terms. Now we can emphasize the view that such ideal limits
have the status of elements in the divine envisionment of the natures of all possible beings. That is to say, God's total knowledge
of possibilities comprises the essence, the potential accidents, the
limits of attainment, and the range of possible deflections for
every possibility of being. Some ontological reference such as this
is necessary for valuational talk about the nature of something or
the fulfillment of a being, and I see no other solution to the problem of status than to say that we have here an ontological ultimate—the possibilities in the divine knowledge.

Now we must shift from the notion of the actual and the possible in God to the notion of time. If we say that the actual
comes from the possible in some literal sense, if God knows as
actual goods things that were once only possible goods, we are
employing the notion of temporal change in modes of being: the
possibly good becomes the actually good. It seems, therefore,
that we must say God is no stranger to time, not totally devoid
of temporal experience, though we may again add that this in no
way affects his essential nature.

There has been, as we know, a sharp controversy between those
who hold that God is purely eternal, timeless, beyond time altogether and those who maintain he is a thoroughly temporal being
like all other beings. One wonders whether there is not a false
dichotomy here also, which could be reconciled by exploring the
idea that God's essential nature is eternal in the sense of not
being affected by time, and yet that he experiences the reality of
all times there can be.

Oscar Cullmann has pioneered another reconciling notion,

namely, that there may be far different and more comprehensive modes of time than what we conceive of as time. We tend to think of time in a uniform linear way, based on our days and years. But beyond our time there may be other dimensions of time within divine experience. From this point of view,

> eternity . . . does not signify cessation of time or timelessness. It means rather endless time and therefore an ongoing of time which is incomprehensible to men; or, as it may be still better expressed, it means the linking of an unlimited series of limited world periods, whose succession only God is able to survey.[10]

Cullmann also insists that the idea of pure timeless eternity comes more from Greek philosophical thought than from Hebraic-Christian religious belief. He declares unequivocally:

> The terminology of the New Testament teaches us that, according to the Primitive Christian conception, time in its unending extension as well as in its individual periods and moments is given by God and ruled by him. Therefore *all* his acting is so inevitably bound up with time that time is not felt to be a problem. It is rather the natural presupposition of all that God causes to occur.[11]

And again:

> Primitive Christianity knows nothing of a timeless God. The "eternal" God is he who was in the beginning, is now, and will be in all the future, "who is, who was, and who will be" (Rev. 1:4). Accordingly, his eternity can and must be expressed in this "naive" way, in terms of endless time. This time quality is not in its essence something human, which first emerged in the fall and creation. It is, moreover, not bound to the creation.[12]

The final characteristic we need to emphasize for our purpose is the intensity of the divine consciousness, described in human terms by such words as happiness or joy. For there to be natural goods, they must be favored, cherished, enjoyed, and this is how we may look upon God's relation to created things. To this extent we can agree with Hartshorne when he asks and answers:

> How is the divine inclusion of all values, actual and possible, to be conceived? Thus: God must Himself value all things; for nothing possesses actual value but an actually-enjoying

subject, while the potential possession of value can only
be the potential enjoyment of a subject.[13]

But I must insist, as Hartshorne does not, that the good in this
situation is not exhausted in, or fully explained by the enjoying.
It is the objective perfection which, as a beheld good, is enjoyed.
The enjoying is a value, but it is the enjoying *of something,* of
a beheld good, whose goodness is partly independent, even though
the whole relation would be only potential without the divine consciousness. There are many human analogies for this interpretation.
A father takes delight in his child's accomplishment: the father's
delight is a value for him, but the child's accomplishment has the
good of a perfection even without the father's delight. An artist
enjoys his completed painting: his enjoyment is a value for him,
but it is the enjoyment *of* an objective perfection now independently real.

Requirements for Natural Axiogenesis

One feature of the universe, then, which makes for natural
good is the valuational nature of God, accounting for the creation
and enjoyment of beheld goods. But the world of things also must
exhibit characteristics of a valuational sort, or else our judgment
would be an illusion. We must now identify these characteristics.
What is required *in the world* for our judgment of natural good
to hold up?

The general requirement must be that natural things be able to
exhibit, in a sense not altogether equivocal, the traits that are
characteristic of intrinsic goodness in general, or, as we have interpreted this notion, perfection. In chapter 1 we identified what
appear to be the two bases for judging the perfection of an individual being, namely, structure and function, and we went on to
specify structural perfection as involving the criteria of purity, harmony, and richness of content and functional perfection as involving the criteria of proficiency and economy. By these criteria we
judge whether an individual being is fulfilling the nature possessed
by that being. Now it seems clear that these aspects of perfection
can be applied to natural things as well as to human beings, so
that judgments of relative perfection or imperfection are meaningful here. It is true that there is little richness of content, little opportunity for development, in the most natural things, though if we

take seriously Teilhard's thesis that there is a "radial energy," a psychic "within,"[14] in every element of matter, we would have to admit some minimum development, some movement toward perfection, in each thing or element that exists. Suffice it to say that we can speak of individual perfections in nature, individual fulfillments of structure and function, as the objects of conscious enjoyment.

What must be added now, if we assume that divine consciousness is related to the world, is the attempt to see the perfection of individual beings as functionally related to the wider framework of the cosmos as a whole. That is, besides their individualized immanent structure and function, what is the connection of of individual things with the divine purview of the world, which makes them objects of good in a wider purposive sense? If they fit into a wider whole, it would perhaps be granted that their goodness would be enhanced. And this need not be thought of as instrumental good only, certainly not instrumental good for man. It is the cosmic function of things that we are asking about, which would comprise an element of their good from the divine perspective. But how do things fit into a cosmic whole?

It is at this point that the thought of Teilhard de Chardin is most relevant for our purpose. Without commenting on the adequacy of his entire synthesis, I wish to select three features of the world which he elaborates in many ways in various places. These features are the unity of the cosmos, purposive direction, and support of spiritual fulfillment. Accordingly, we may view the valuational function of natural things under these three headings. Our contention would be that if each thing could be said to illustrate this threefold cosmic functioning, this would constitute an effective reason for affirming that the good of each thing is enhanced. It is not easy to establish these features against certain difficulties which we shall have to consider. But first I wish to quote some statements to give more content to these categories of interpretation.

First, cosmic unity implies that no existing thing is totally irrelevant to or outside the overall system of good reflected by and purposed in the cosmos. No matter how simple or trifling a thing may seem, it enters into the web of sustaining interrelationships whereby the cosmos has its being and moves in its course. Teilhard calls this feature "global unity," and writes:

This we may have come across already—first in primordial

matter, then on the early earth, then in the genesis of the first
cells. . . . Though the proliferations of living matter are vast
and manifold, they never lose their *solidarity.* . . .

I repeat this same thing like a refrain on every rung of the
ladder that leads to man; for, if this thing is forgotten, nothing
can be understood.

To see life properly we must never lose sight of the unity
of the biosphere that lies beyond the plurality and essential
rivalry of individual beings. This unity was still diffuse in the
early stages—a unity in origin, framework and dispersed impe-
tus rather than in ordered grouping; yet a unity which, together with life's ascent, was to grow ever sharper in outline,
to fold in upon itself, and, finally, to centre itself under our
eyes.[15]

In referring to the discoveries that accumulated since the nineteenth century, he concludes that the net result has been that of

revealing the *irreversible coherence* of all that exists. First the
concatenations of life and, soon after, those of matter. The
least molecule is, in nature and in position, a function of the
whole sidereal process, and the least of the protozoa is structurally so knit into the web of life that, such is the hypothesis,
its existence cannot be annihilated without *ipso facto* undoing
the whole network of the biosphere. The *distribution, succes-
sion and solidarity of objects are born from their concrescence
in a common genesis.* Time and space are organically joined
again so as to weave, together, the stuff of the universe. That
is the point we have reached and how we perceive things today.[16]

Thus we find it maintained on scientific grounds, let alone theistic grounds, that there is a unity of the cosmos. And it is held that
this is not only a reasonable hypothesis for our thought about the
cosmos and our investigation of it but a hypothesis that is empirically supported. Our further philosophical claim is that this makes
it possible for us to maintain that each thing has a functional role,
as entering into such good as is manifest in the cosmos as a whole.

Teilhard also thinks it possible to defend on scientific grounds our
second thesis, namely, that there is a direction in the cosmic process.

Leaving aside all anthropocentrism and anthropomorphism,
I believe I can see a direction and a line of progress for life, a

line and a direction which are in fact so well marked that I am
convinced their reality will be universally admitted by the
science of tomorrow.[17]

Teilhard finds the empirically observable mark of direction in the
ever more complex nervous system, making possible the conscious
experience of reflection and spiritual life.

Among the infinite modalities in which the complication of
life is dispersed, the differentiation of nervous tissue stands out,
as theory would lead us to expect, as a significant transformation. *It provides a direction;* and by its consequences *it proves
that evolution has a direction.*[18]

Teilhard's term for this sphere of reflective spiritual life, which
culminates the emergence of the physical spheres and the sphere of
life, is "noosphere," so that his final conclusion is this:

The greatest revelation open to science today is to perceive
that everything precious, active, and progressive originally
contained in that cosmic fragment from which our world
emerged, is now concentrated in and crowned by the noosphere.[19]

Now whether or not the belief in purposive direction in the universe can be established by science, we may take as a moot question
at this time. The answer depends partly on the meaning of "science."
It may be that no hypothesis about purposive direction can be entertained without the use of valuational categories. Those who would
rigorously exclude them from science will have no traffic with the
hypothesis as a scientific one. Those who, like Teilhard, seek a synthesizing conception of science will consider the hypothesis relevant.

Certainly my purpose is not to suggest that quoting Teilhard is
sufficient to settle this matter. My purpose is quite different. We
are exploring not a question in science but a question in theistic
metaphysics, namely, universal good. And, given the theistic framework, Teilhard has expounded a very plausible account of how each
thing can be seen to have a cosmic role, namely, by having some
share, no matter how humble, in carrying the cosmos forward to
its purposed goal.

In this connection, the topic that needs to be explored further
in our day is the possible development of many other biospheres
and noospheres in the total cosmogenesis, of which we have as yet
fragmentary knowledge. Teilhard clearly recognized this possibility,

though he did not deal much with it. In principle, there seems no inconsistency in holding that the noosphere, as we know it, is the culmination of our region of the cosmos, and yet that this is but one focus of a much wider divine purpose, namely, the creation of all good possible.

If purposive direction is a real aspect of the cosmos, then the third feature follows as a further explication of it. That is, every existing thing leads to or supports, chronologically and ontologically, the spiritual life that is possible in the universe. In the words of William Temple:

> Matter exists in full reality but at a secondary level. It is created by spirit—the Divine Spirit—to be the vehicle of spirit and the sphere of spirit's self-realization in and through the activity of controlling it.[20]

This role of the material world is an instrumental function, but it is not prohibited on this account from also being intrinsically good, any more than a bodyguard of the United States president is prevented from having intrinsic worth because he serves the wider function of vitally supporting the president. In fact, in our interpretation intrinsic good in nature *means* beheld instrumental good, so that in the divine perspective this wider function can be viewed as adding to the beheld goodness of things.

Under these three headings we have stressed the cosmic function of entities rather than structural factors in the world, for function relates the world more immediately to purposive worth than does structure, which often seems random and inexplicable. In this connection I quote from a letter of Teilhard in which this idea is clearly expressed, though in a Christian rather than a philosophical phraseology.

> You should note the following point carefully: I do not attribute any definitive or absolute value to the varied constructions of nature. What I like about them is not their particular form, but their function, which is to build up mysteriously, first what can be divinised, and then, through the grace of Christ coming upon our endeavors, what is divine.[21]

Difficulties in Natural Axiogenesis

The problems in maintaining this point of view, however, are for many minds stupendous. If there is directed purpose in the natural world, they ask, if there is a divine stamp of approval on all things as good, both in themselves and as contributory to emergent spiritual worth, why do we experience some of the features of the cosmos that we do? In particular, why does the universe, and life, seem to exhibit so much waste, profusion, and unassimilated detail? Why do they seem to be so unconcerned with the individual unit of matter and of life, which gets lost in the mass but which is supposed to be the locus of intrinsic good? Why does there appear to be so much randomness and chance in cosmogenesis and biogenesis, instead of easily identifiable purposive trends throughout the cosmos?

These are not easy questions to answer. And in fact the first thing we must admit is that we cannot answer them adequately. We do not know why God chose the particular cosmos we experience, with its peculiar strains of movement and patterns of relationship. We do not see in detail how each thing fits into the whole as divinely intended or permitted. We are truly involved here in what Marcel calls a mystery rather than a problem. The most we can hope for is what I shall call "principles of reduction," that is, considerations that will reduce the antitheistic and antiteleological drift of the questions and enable us to uphold the universal goodness of being despite the mystery of it.

One such principle is a point that Hartshorne insists upon frequently, namely, that the very implication of modal coincidence in God, and the lack of it in us finite creatures, is that God alone is able to know fully every specific entity and enjoy its worth, both for itself and for its function in the whole. Man's range of specific sympathies is extremely limited; beyond them he has available only a kind of general categorial sympathy. But God, we may presume—not from our piety but because of his nature—has an intimate consciousness of the whole in all its detail. We cannot expect such a purview.

Another principle is that we must apparently acknowledge a certain amount of delegated spontaneity and creativity in nature, which allows for a measure of free play, of side effects, in the ascent to spiritual fulfillment. If creativity is one of the great marks of spiritual life, it seems reasonable to suppose that a degree of it was delegated from the very beginning—chronological and ontological—of finite being. We know of its presence in man, discern it somewhat in animals, and may infer some semblance of it throughout the cosmos of beings. If this is so, there might be a certain "planned randomness" in the scheme, which

would make it unreasonable to ask specifically of each detail why
it is there and how it fits into the whole, for it is simply part of
the creative act, leading to the perfected whole. We do not ask of
a Chopin composition why it is in D flat instead of E flat, why
it has 96 bars instead of 104, why its grace notes and trills are
just where they are; these are asides, and yet at the same time
integral, in the creative thrust toward formed beauty.

Another principle is that which bids us view nature in terms
of a cumulative and aggregate generic teleology. Thus individual
units which may seem superfluous in isolation may be seen as
minute sustainers, or at least as interconnected by-products, of
the main course of the process toward purposed ends. Why this
mode of teleology was chosen may remain a mystery; but at least
it permits us to hold that seemingly irrelevant entities have a role
in the cosmic process. Here again it is most appropriate to quote
some reflections of Teilhard on the problems of wasted profusion
and disregard for the individual. Concerning the profusion of nature he says:

> Life advances by mass effects, by dint of multitudes flung
> into action without apparent plan. Milliards of germs and
> millions of adult growths jostling, shoving, and devouring
> one another, fight for elbow room and for the best and lar-
> gest living space. Despite all the waste and ferocity, all the
> mystery and scandal it involves, there is, as we must be fair
> and admit, a great deal of biological efficiency in the *struggle
> for life.* . . . This groping strangely combines the blind fan-
> tasy of large numbers with the precise orientation of a spe-
> cific target. It would be a mistake to see it as mere chance.
> Groping is *directed chance.* It means pervading everything
> so as to try everything, and trying everything so as to find
> everything. Surely in the last resort it is precisely to develop
> this procedure (always increasing in size and cost in propor-
> tion as it spreads) that nature has had recourse to profusion.[22]

Thus, from this point of view, though we may see but dimly or
not at all the good of the individual unit (particle, cell, organism,
physical object) when taken in isolation, this good is more evident
when taken in relation to the ongoing process. "What matter the
millions of years and milliards of beings that have gone before if
those countless drops form a current that carries us along?"[23]
Perhaps in the cosmos, as in human life, entities find themselves
by losing themselves.

> By the phenomenon of association, the living particle is
> wrenched from itself. Caught up in an aggregate greater
> than itself, it becomes to some extent its slave. It no longer
> belongs to itself.[24]

As for the randomness and chance in the world, Teilhard views
this as giving a one-sided picture of things if we concentrate too
exclusively on the external, physical aspect of the world—what he
calls "tangential energy." Seeing the process from within, from
the angle of what he calls "radial energy," gives us a different perspective.

> It is thus entirely by its tangential envelope that the world
> goes on dissipating itself in a chance way into matter. By
> its radial nucleus it finds its shape and its natural consistency
> in gravitating against the tide of probability towards a divine
> focus of mind which draws it onward.
>   Thus something in the cosmos escapes from entropy, and
> does so more and more.[25]

All this does not eliminate the mystery. In a brief and remark-
able passage Teilhard focuses on both the empirical reality of
chance in relation to purpose and the mystery of it, to which in
the end we must submit.

> But does not everyday experience teach us that in every or-
> der of Nature, and at every level, nothing succeeds except
> at the cost of prodigious waste and fantastic hazards? A mon-
> strously fragile conjunction of chances normally dictates the
> birth of the most precious and essential beings. We can only
> bow before this universal law whereby, so strangely to our
> minds, the play of large numbers is mingled and confounded
> with a final purpose.[26]

Man, God, and the Good

But what does this theistic interpretation have to do with our
human evaluations? Suppose it is true that in theistic metaphysics
the natural world can be said to be good from God's perspective,
and that he can enjoy its very details. Does it follow that there is
any intrinsic goodness there for us? Does not the natural world
have the same "neutral tones" for us, despite the way in which
it might appear to other beings in the universe?
    In reply we may say that the relevance of our ontological ex-

ploration comes at two points. They correspond to the two ways
in which men come to the appreciation of good in nature: directly
through their immediate response to nature (natural piety) and
indirectly through their religious belief in God (theocentric piety).

The relevance of the first approach, that of immediate natural
piety, is that we can offer these ontological remarks, or something
like them, as a vindication that natural piety is not illusory in
what it feels so spontaneously. Of course this vindication is not
needed in order to have the feeling of natural piety, and it may
even be resented by those who are inclined to rely on direct feeling in these matters. But, then, our remarks were never intended
as an aid to natural piety but rather as a part of philosophical
argumentation. And within this philosophical context we suggest
that here at least is one point of view which, if valid, will justify
the intimation that our spontaneous awareness of a goodness in
things is indeed grounded in the nature of things and is not merely
a desperate, deluded lunge toward what is not and can never be.
The relevance at this point, then, is something like that between
philosophical ethics and immediate moral insight. And, as Kant
pointed out, though immediacy in such matters is a wonderful
thing, if it is not philosophically grounded it may be deceived or
weakened.

The relevance of the other approach comes when we observe
that many men do not have much sense of natural piety and
therefore arrive at an interpretation of nature only through their
religion. Apart from this, they have little thought that there is
any intrinsic good in nature, and they might be of the same mind
as the independent philosophical neutralist. But their belief in God
leads them to various conceptions that are not otherwise natural
to them. For this camp, if our conception of natural good in terms
of theistic metaphysics is justified, that would constitute a good
reason for such persons to affirm the intrinsic goodness of things.
This is so because people who believe that God is the ultimate
explanation of the world believe also that what is true as a consequence of their belief in God is true *as such* and therefore true
for men. Thus if, through God, the world of things can be said
to have perfective possibilities, cosmic unity, directed purpose,
and therefore beheld goodness, that is a proposition for man to
accept and to make relevant, where possible, to his obligations
and attitudes. Nature is read, in short, through the concept of
God.

God from this perspective is the great conserver, the pre-
server of all values, the lover of all good, the harmonizer
of all conflicts, the being in whom all things find their
place and are perfectly adapted to one another.[27]

The religious person seeks to share as he is able in that perspective. God is the perfect good and therefore the paradigm on
which all other good is modeled.

Fortunately, we do not have to evaluate or choose between
these two approaches. They reflect different types of persons.
All the same, they are not incompatible. A third type of person
may very well begin from a native, spontaneous responsiveness
to the great and awesome world of nature and find his sentiment
sanctioned and supported by his theistic belief.

As our discussion of nonhuman good comes to a close, we
must admit that our overall interpretation does not amount to
any kind of rigorous proof for the reader. What we claim, instead, is the delineation of a plausible alternative to neutralism,
a live option which has a coherence and in which some of the
major difficulties have been partly attenuated. Perhaps this is all
that philosophy can do; at least it is all that I have aimed for.
In any case, the presentation of a live alternative in a coherent
way, whether I have achieved it or not, is one requisite, and an
important one, for its acceptance.

PART FOUR

Rebuttal

12: Objections Overruled

In this concluding chapter it is my intention to carry out an obligation commonly felt among philosophers, namely, to anticipate and answer the objections of critics. One danger in such undertakings is that the protagonist may not anticipate those objections which an opponent might consider the most serious, or at least may not state adequately those he anticipates. The only antidote would seem to be—besides just being aware of this danger—to make use of actual formulations of charges by critics and to rethink one's anticipations for comprehensiveness. Some of the objections, raised and dealt with below, have been raised and discussed in particular contexts in previous chapters. But here we shall try to bring all the major objections together in a block in order to make a final scrutiny of the approach to value taken in this book. A preliminary list of the charges to be considered can be given in a unifying introductory statement.

The objections hold, in turn, that to interpret *good* in the normative sense as *perfection* is to employ a concept which is

1. Trivial
2. A case of misplaced meaning
3. A case of the naturalistic fallacy
4. A case of begging the question
5. Morally unsatisfactory
6. Psychologically abnormal
7. Sociologically irrelevant
8. Anthropomorphic
9. Uselessly vague
10. A denial of individuality
11. Theologically inadequate
12. Static

In referring to particular writers, I do not imply that they necessarily had the perfection theory of value in mind when they
wrote. Some did and some did not. It is rather that what they
have said has relevance for us, whether intended or not, as possible criticism.

The Charge of Triviality

I first wish to quote some words from Mr. Charles Hartshorne
about the term "perfection":

> It must in all this discussion be understood that certain
> doubtful or trivial meanings of "perfect" or "unsurpassable"
> are excluded (merely to save time and energy), such as that
> a squirrel is perfect if it has all that is demanded by the
> concept (whose concept?) of a squirrel, or that a nail is as
> good as any other could be if it holds the building together
> as long and as well as is wanted. Such merely subjective or
> merely instrumental perfection is not what is meant.[1]

Obviously, a generalized perfection theory of the good cannot
begin if its fundamental notion is too trivial to bother with. But
is "perfection" in the sense of "good of its kind" or "fulfillment
of essence" a trivial notion? The grounds for saying so in the
passage quoted are that the idea is either subjective or is limited
to merely instrumental good.

I deny that the characterization of classes of things as having
certain definite traits is purely subjective. If it were, we could,
through the manipulations of thought, make squirrels have the
properties of nails and nails the traits of squirrels. This is absurd.
Any realistic epistemology or metaphysics must hold that there
are entities that are independent of private thought, and must
hold also that these entities have definite features that constitute
what they are, or else there would be no discriminable objects as
distinct independent entities. The fact that we do not always
know what these essential characteristics are in given cases, or
that there is often wide room for subjective emphasis based on
interest, has nothing to do with whether things have definite
traits that constitute their being. As a matter of fact, we have
much knowledge, through classificatory science and common experience, of the natures of things, and we cannot simply mix
them any-which-way at will. This being the case, it is not merely

subjective to say that something has a certain perfection when it exhibits its characteristic traits to the fullest extent that its being permits.

Nor is the concept of perfection in our sense a case of instrumental good. We hold, on the contrary, that it defines intrinsic good. We should not speak of instrumental good as a perfection at all. The reason is that perfection is a qualitative category, the fulfillment of potentiality, whereas instrumental good is a relationship between two things wherein one thing contributes to the perfection of the other. An instrumental good is simply a *perficiendum*, helping to unfold the perfection of the *perficiens*. Of course, it should be added that it is often the internal perfection of the *perficiendum* itself which makes it into a possible candidate for instrumental good. For example, it is because a nail is what it is and has a certain perfection that it can be an instrumental good; otherwise it might be thrown out. But perfection and instrumental good are not the same in meaning: one is a quality, the other a relation. Now if perfection refers to intrinsic good, it is not a trivial notion.

The Charge of Misplaced Meaning

The criticism which continues to be most crucial for any theory which suggests that there is good in the nonhuman realm is that the term "good" is meaningless when so applied. This charge has been with us all along in part 3, but I want to hear it again explicitly in order to give a summarizing statement regarding it. Its expressions are plentiful, but perhaps the directness of Walter Lippmann, as a nonprofessional philosopher will serve:

> The categories of good and evil would not apply if there were no sentient beings to experience good and evil. In such a world no object would be any better or any worse than any other object; nobody talks about good and bad electrons.[2]

Our first reaction to this contention must be, I think, that in the ordinary, popular sense of its meaning it is correct. This ordinary, popular sense is that we cannot speak of nonconscious things as being, *without qualification*, simply good or bad intrinsically. But two qualifications entitle us to speak of in-

trinsic good or bad in a derivative sense in reference to such
beings.

The first qualification is that there can be a perfection of being
in things apart from consciousness, and this is at least the formal
aspect involved in intrinsic goodness. However, the additional
characteristic of being reasonably favored, which is also necessary,
involves a relation to consciousness. So our conclusion must reflect a synthesis of conscious and objective factors rather than a
blanket banishment of the term "good" to the subjective realm.
As far as least physical particles (electrons?) are concerned, theirs
is a perfection of a truncated, almost trivial sort, since they apparently just are what they momentarily are, with little or no
process of perfecting or sustained development of individual potentialities. Even so, however, it is well to remember the Whiteheadian claim, or that of Teilhard de Chardin, that there is some
emergence through process in every least particle or occasion; so
we should not rule out a nontrivial meaning of perfection even
at this level.

The second qualification is that we can consider natural things
as good if we take into account the factor of detachment, that
is, that factor in the axiogenetic process whereby what is not
ontologically independent of all consciouness nevertheless becomes phenomenologically independent for us. Thus I agree that,
ontologically, natural entities cannot be considered good in and
by themselves, apart from any relation to consciousness whatsoever. But this relation can be interpreted to be a relation to divine consciousness, quite apart from man. The intrinsic goodness
of these entities, comprising both their internal perfection and
their contribution to cosmic unity and purpose, is grounded in
that relation. Phenomenologically, then, *for us*, they can and
often appear to have an independent intrinsic goodness in a derived, detached sense.

The Naturalistic Fallacy

The next two criticisms have been so effectively stated in correspondence that I shall quote from it instead of from a published work. The first criticism runs as follows.

> First, how do you avoid the taint of the naturalistic fal-
> lacy, the challenge of the "open question", or whatever else
> you may call it—i.e. the charge that while you may have

defined or offered primary evidence for the "good" in its
uniquely valuational meaning? What, in short, is there about
your view that will lead a person that agrees with you to
thereby take perfection as his goal in life, as his good; what
is there to prevent him—as I myself feel inclined to do at
times—from saying "Metaphysical perfection may not be
very good after all, indeed may be simply built into the
natural structure of things and reflect nothing about the
goodness or value of existence—so understood—as such"?
If it is bad or indifferent that nature exists, it is probably
bad or indifferent that there is or is not perfection within
it.[3]

The criticism to be dealt with is that perfection may be one
thing but good another. A rigorous application of the naturalistic
fallacy would insist that the two must necessarily be distinct,
since we can always ask of any natural state, such as perfection,
whether it is good, thereby showing that the good is a distinct
quality from the natural state. It is clear that we must defend
the synthetic connection that I believe to obtain between these
two notions.

I agree that perfection and intrinsic goodness are not equivalent concepts. What I hold, instead, is that perfection is the
major, objective, defining component in intrinsic goodness (the
other components being reasonable favor in all cases and, in the
case of human values, experience of perfecting).

Though the two concepts are not equivalent, however, which
denies naturalism, that does not mean we can accept the idea of
good as a nonnatural quality that pervades natural facts but is
not identifiable with them. I also deny nonnaturalism. Rather,
the two concepts are distinct but synthetically connected.

Thus the perfection theory of good cuts across the naturalism-
nonnaturalism controversy and suggests a third position which
avoids both the naturalistic fallacy and nonnatural properties.
Judgments of intrinsic goodness, and of moral ought-ness, are
judgments of would-be situations, that is, what would be actual
occurrence if the perfection of a being, or the perfection of
voluntary conduct, were realized fully. Such judgments refer
primarily to the ideal limits of what perfection in reality would
be if realized, and secondarily to partial realizations of such perfection. In the full actualization there is a coalescence of factual
occurrence and normative ideal. Yet short of full actualization
there is not such coalescence, so that value judgments do not

simply *mean* factual statements that are open to empirical verification, as in naturalism. Value judgments, in short, are not equivalent with factual judgments, and neither do they point to nonnatural properties. Rather they specify what would be factual states of affairs if full perfection were realized. Value properties are neither simple facts nor nonnatural qualities but the supreme limits of attainment of anything, or, more often, partial realizations of that attainment.

This way of viewing the matter requires, as the criticism rightly demands, that primary evidence be given for taking perfection as the key notion to define the intrinsic good, since the two are not synonyms. As far as the human good is concerned, the primary evidence for the perfection theory can be found, I suggest, in ordinary language, in the concerns of psychology, social effort, and religion, and in a certain demand of logic.

In ordinary life, it seems to me that perfectivist language predominates in value talk, though a more thorough study of this aspect of the subject is necessary. We speak of being one's real self, of developing oneself, of becoming what we can become, of achieving our goals, of perfecting our abilities, of being mature human beings; and such expressions seem to be more inclusive, more revealing, more valuationally normative than the similarly prevalent speech about satisfying particular desires, promoting particular interests, and the like, and certainly more indicative than such remote talk as that about synthesizing values, balancing pleasures and pains, and the like.

If it be argued that this very reference to ordinary ways of speaking merely confirms the charge of the naturalistic fallacy on the ground that only *sometimes* do we talk perfectively whereas *always* we speak of the good, thus showing a difference in usage between "good" and "perfection"—which is enough to commit the naturalistic fallacy—there is a ready reply. In ordinary practical life we often use the term "good" as the most convenient shorthand word for what we intend, without giving or even understanding the full content of it, that is, without doing philosophy in the process. The very business of philosophy is to explicate these convenient concepts. Furthermore, many nonperfective phrases, such as "pleasure as good" or "preference as good," often indicate particular features that are includable within, or incomplete approaches to, the wider ideal of perfection of self-fulfillment. Finally, we do not expect from ordinary speech, considered sociologically apart from analysis, to have the needed consistency or to be the unexceptionable standard of philosophical truth. Ordinary language can afford evidence and directional trends, but not finality of judgment.

Secondly, in discussions of mental health, social opportunity, and religious aspiration we find that ideals are expressed in terms of the unfolding of the self, the integration of the person, growth into full human maturity, the right to self-development, the realization of the unique individual, and so forth. Such expressions of ideals seem implicitly to reflect a perfectivist understanding of value.

Finally, the plain demand of logic in value theory is that there must be some unifying category which explains why we judge the various intrinsic values as we do. Separate intuitions with no common form will not do as an explanation. What unites them as intrinsic values? Why are they all called such? To suggest pleasure or satisfaction as the common form goes part way but is too superficial. What makes them satisfying? Why are some valuable, with little or no pleasure associated? The only reasonable unifying concept, and the one that is linguistically most natural and experientially most obvious, is employed when we say that these values are all integral aspects of the self's maturing, of human fulfillment, of the perfection of the individual. What we seek in the end is not just balances of conscious states but the blossoming into full fruition of sacred, dignified human individuals.

As far as nonhuman good is concerned, the reason for adopting the idea of perfection is to be found in the logic of analogy. It is obvious how we speak of full growth, maturing, or perfection in plants and animals as the main component that elicits reasonable favor when we consider the actualization of their possibilities. Stunted development means the loss of a potentiality; full maturity means its attainment. So if intrinsic good is a possibility here at all, perfection would be basic in it. And the reason for extending the notion universally is that there is no plausible ground for asserting a break—for example, between the living and nonliving—at which to stop and declare that on one side perfection is relevant but on the other side it is not. Every entity exhibits some perfection of some possibility, and the inexorable logic of analogy forces us to conclude that, assuming the meaningfulness of nonhuman good, all being is good by virtue of its perfection.

I may add, in reference to the last sentence of the quoted criticism, that we must certainly agree that *if* it is bad or indifferent that nature exists, *then* it is bad or indifferent that there are perfections in it. But, of course, in the theistic metaphysics we have explored it is not bad or indifferent that nature exists. Hence we are not obliged to draw the conclusion. In fact, we may claim the best reason for drawing the opposite conclusion.

A Dilemma about Essence and Value

Another fundamental criticism is stated as follows.

> Second, how do you avoid the charge that the distinction between essential and accidental elements in the nature of a being—a distinction upon which everything rests—is not already the importing into metaphysics of prior valuational standards? How do you determine the essence of a being, in fact? Other than a purely anatomical or zoological classification, what is there to lead one to prefer man "the worshipping animal" to man "the tool using animal" or man "the laughing animal" to man "the economic animal" and so on? What is there, except a covert sensitivity to what is important in human life that says to you—"Whoa, worshipping is somehow more deeply significant or valuable and *hence* more essential to man's nature"?
>
> The dilemma is this: if you can determine the essence of a being independently of value considerations, then you still require independent value judgment to establish it as "good" to realize. If you cannot determine it independently of value considerations, then valuational judgment remains autonomous and the notion of essence is in a sense irrelevant (or at best subservient).[4]

I accept the first horn of the dilemma and admit that the determination of the essence of a being is not analytically equivalent to the determination of its intrinsic goodness. An independent value judgment *is* required to establish it as "good" to realize. I have no intention of denying the distinction between value judgments and factual statements. But my contention is that the requisite value judgment lies ready to hand and is quite justifiable. That the perfection of man's essence is good to realize is grounded in the direct awareness of value that we experience in self-fulfillment or in partial realizations thereof, and is further supported by the

kinds of evidence cited in answering the previous criticism. That
the perfection of nonhuman essences is good to realize is grounded
in theistic axiogenesis, resulting in independent beheld goods, and
is further supported by the logic of analogy, as mentioned before.

But there is more to say in the case of human good—though
this point will not apply to nonhuman good. We have agreed that
the determination of an essence is not identical with a judgment
of intrinsic good. That is, it is one judgment to say that man's essence includes certain biological tendencies, rationality, free choice,
and so forth, and another judgment to say that their actualization
is intrinsically good. But this does not mean that judgments of
value are irrelevant to the understanding of man's essence. We
know in general that valuational activity would have to be included in any formal definition of man's essence, and perhaps
this could be considered a metaphysical or a psychological judgment. But to know, specifically, what fulfills man's essence and
what does not, we must know about the nature of values. We
cannot know in what ways valuational activity fulfills man's being
without knowing about the content of value, any more than we
can know how his rationality perfects him without knowing about
the rules of evidence and logic. Thus judgments of value lead us
to a more specific knowledge of man's essential nature and how
it is to be perfected.

This point means that we can also accept the antecedent of
the second horn of the dilemma, but deny the consequent. We
cannot determine essence in all respects apart from value; but it
is not the case that essence is therefore irrelevant. Rather, knowledge of value is one aspect of our knowledge of essence. In knowing value we know more completely what the perfection of our
essence is or would be.

We must distinguish, then, between (1) factual judgments about
what man's nature includes, (2) judgments about particular values
which help us to understand more specifically what fulfills our
nature and what does not, and (3) the judgment that man's perfection of nature is intrinsically good and ought to be realized.
Point 3 means that we take the first horn of the dilemma and turn
aside its thrust, and point 2 means that we do the same with the
second horn.

As a further general comment on the objection, I must add
that I think it proceeds on a false assumption. The assumption
is that the perfection theory is attempting to set forth a factual
account of essence or perfection in order to be able to know

automatically, or at least by simple derivation, the nature of the good. I admit that this has been the attempt of many philosophers, who seek some simple empirical key to unlock all the knowledge about value. Opponents then attack such attempts in order to protect the autonomy of value judgments. But our attempt, I must say emphatically, has been nothing of the sort. In fact, it has been somewhat the reverse.

We start from the fact that we have some autonomous awareness of values and of intrinsic goodness, and then, in thinking through these concepts, we find that they lead us into the notions of essence and perfection as the most adequate interpretation. Our thought moves from value to perfection, from awareness to explanation. The connection, however, is not purely analytical, and a defense is needed, as we have seen, for employing the idea of perfection rather than some other. Also, we say in the end not only that perfection of essence defines intrinsic good but that all perfected beings are intrinsically good and ought, barring greater evil, to be actualized. This judgment, too, is synthetic and needs justification, which we find in a theistic metaphysic.

The Inadequacy of Self-realizationism

The previous two criticisms have been very serious ones and difficult to meet, and before going on to more of this type I want to dispose of two or three that I do not consider so serious, because they rest on confusions of concepts. One of them is the often repeated charge against self-realizationist ethics, to which a theory like perfectivism is subject. Our dissociation from self-realizationism in ethics should already be clear, but for emphasis I want to dispose of any such charge. The charge runs as follows.

> . . . The formula of self-realization leaves out of consideration the central problem of ethics—that of the relation between self and others. In the end, it is not any form of self-fulfillment that is desirable, but only that which is compatible with the fulfillment of others. Clearly such an end goes far beyond what any particular individuals actually desire, and it may require them to abandon or sacrifice a good deal of what they so desire.[5]

I fully endorse the main point in the criticism of self-realizationist ethics but deny altogether that such a criticism applies to

our theory. Any thought that it does apply is simply a confusion.
The reason why the criticism does not apply is that, while we use
the notion of self-fulfillment or perfection to define the good of
the individual, we do not use it as the basis for the theory of right
action. We derive the meaning of rightness autonomously from the
ideal of perfection in voluntary conduct and not from self-realization. And perfection in voluntary conduct, we know, involves disinterested good will, which may require sacrifice. On this matter
we are in agreement with Kant, who states the relationship by
saying that

> perfection in man . . . is the possession by man of the powers,
> capacities and skill requisite for the achievement of whatever
> ends he sets before himself and is not synonymous with moral
> goodness. . . . Moral goodness thus lies in the perfection not
> of the faculties, but of the will.[6]

It is obvious, therefore, that our theory is no self-realizationism
of the Hegel-Bradley type, or of the Nietzsche type, or even of the
Frommian type or Aristotelian type, even though we make use of
the Aristotelian idea of perfection of potentiality.

Perfectivism, Not Perfectionism

The term "perfection" has currency in other realms of discourse,
such that, if the meanings there were confused with our more Aristotelian usage, misdirected charges could result. The meanings I have
in mind suggest a lack of psychological realism. To forestall such
charges, the equivocations will be mentioned.

Karen Horney uses the term "perfection" in describing neurosis.
The neurotic person, she says, sets up an idealized image of himself which he thinks he has achieved or should achieve. In this
image, perfection is a tyrannical albeit unrealistic demand.

> Among the drives toward actualizing the idealized self *the
> need for perfection* is the most radical one. . . . Like Pygmalion
> in Bernard Shaw's version, the neurotic aims not only at re-
> touching but at remodeling himself into his special kind of
> perfection prescribed by the specific features of his idealized
> image.[7]

But since this extreme demand for perfection does not coincide with
reasonable expectation or actual attainment, inner conflict and dis-
turbance prevail.

> With all his strenuous efforts toward perfection and with
> all his belief in perfection attained, the neurotic does not
> gain what he most desperately needs: self-confidence and
> self-respect.[8]

Obviously, to aspire to perfection in this sense is to seek
something psychologically abnormal and to be caught up in a
flight from reality. Just as obviously, this meaning is not our
usage. We are not using "perfection" in reference to a mental
image but in reference to a metaphysical aspect of being.

The term "perfection" is also used in connection with the
notion of "moral perfectionism," which, though vague in meaning, apparently signifies an ideal or command to be saintly and
holy in one's moral goodness. Such a usage seems often to have
the connotation of a lack of realism about the limits of one's
capabilities and about the evil in human nature, and hence to
designate a hypocritical preoccupation.

Again, "perfection" may suggest to some a concentration on
perfecting oneself to the exclusion of concern with the need
for public action. Perfecting saintly virtues within oneself, this
usage suggests, will solve social ills. And meanwhile, as the per-
fectionists cultivate their private perfection, rascals dominate
the public arena.[9]

Such usages are equally foreign to our theory, both in meaning and in spirit. All of these uses of "perfection" and "perfectionism," and others which could be mentioned, imply psychological or moral inadequacies of some kind and should be dissociated
from the intention of our usage.

Natural Piety and Modern Life

A pertinent criticism against one part of our theory stems from
the peculiar conditions of modern life. It can be made against any
outlook which stresses a good in nature and the values associated
with natural piety. The criticism is that such an outlook is simply
outmoded and has become sociologically impossible and irrelevant.
I shall again quote some powerful sentences from that shrewd
critic of modern society, Walter Lippmann.

> The modern man . . . has replaced natural piety with a
> grudging endurance of a series of unsanctified compulsions.
> . . .
>   They have seen through the religion of nature to which

the early romantics turned for consolation. They have
heard too much about the brutality of natural selection to
feel, as Wordsworth did, that pleasant landscapes are divine.
They have seen through the religion of beauty because, for
one thing, they are too much oppressed by the ugliness of
Main Street. . . .

The city is an acid that dissolves this piety. . . . It is not
natural to form reverent attachments to an apartment on
a two-year lease, and an imitation mahogany desk on the
thirty-second floor of an office building. In such an environment piety becomes absurd, a butt for the facetious, and
the pious man looks like a picturesque yokel or a stuffy
fool.[10]

Have natural piety and the idea of goodness in things indeed become irrelvant and ridiculous for modern man? Let it be pointed
out, first, that even if they have, this would not affect the validity
of the perfection theory of good when limited to the human level.
We would have a truncated version of perfectivism; but its essen-
tials could still remain as the most adequate interpretation of human value.

But the most direct frontal attack on the charge is this: If natural piety as a source of insight and value has been lost to modern
man, so much the worse for modern man. Must we change our
value theory to suit the more unfortunate and despicable tendencies in modern society? Are they the controllers of our thinking,
the measure of our aspirations, the lord of our values? Are we to
abandon ideal value possibilities for the sake of subordinating ourselves to the age of appliances? Are we to give up what might be
for what, prefabricatedly, is?

The truth is that the situation to which Lippmann calls attention is a practical problem and not a theoretical difficulty. There
is good reason to think that it has grown worse since he wrote the
above lines, and that it will get still worse before it gets better.
But the crucial point is that the values associated with natural piety
have not been stamped out altogether. Nature lovers are not ex-
tinct; home gardening continues; poets still write about geese and
otters (even though they may be in zoos); legislators fight for restricted domains to preserve natural surroundings and natural
beauty; camping, in order to be out with nature, is an ever-increas-
ing pastime; et cetera. This point is crucial theoretically because it
means we have not reached the place where we are violating the
elementary ethical consideration that "ought" implies "can."
We are not yet speaking of a good which is so inaccessible that

some kind of existential contradiction is involved in advocating it. And the point is crucial practically because it suggests that sociological trends may possibly be reversed with effort.

But how can there be a reversal? How can the modern man of Lippmann's description ever find any goodness in things except through incidental escapes from his stifling city life? One way would be to make such times less incidental, and another would be to make them less of an escape. The first may be accomplished as a by-product of shorter working hours, whose main purpose is the creation of more jobs. The second way is not so clear; it requires a rebeautifying of the environment around people and a reorientation toward things that can't be beautified. Neither is easy. Both can be worked at. Both require the recognition that artificial constructions share at least one affinity with natural surroundings, namely, they are configurations of the same world-stuff which it has been seen fit for man to inhabit and to utilize in working out his own perfecting.

Anthropomorphism

A more serious charge from a theoretical standpoint is that the very notion of good in nature is a crude anthropomorphism. It reminds some of old medievalisms, of talk about hidden powers in things and about entelechies moving mysteriously toward innate goals. To them, the notion appears antiquated, quaint, peculiar. It is too much like a personalization of things, too fearfully close to the attitude in which one supposes "that a fig tree wept when it was plucked, and that the mother-tree shed milky tears."[11] They are afraid it will bring us to the brink of the occult in an age of science.

The surface objection, as I have stated it, does not seem to me very serious, but there is a further implied objection which is. The surface objection of out-and-out anthropomorphism can simply be denied. We have not personalized things internally at all, though we have seen some similarities between things and persons. We have not even defined the intrinsic good in nature by reference to physical feelings (prehensions) or inward strivings but, instead, have employed the notion of perfections favored by higher modes of consciousness. Further, the theory of panpsychism, which is much more subject to anthropomorphism, is not a part of our theory of valuation, though it may have much to commend it on strictly metaphysical grounds. There is no basis, therefore, for this charge, taken in its surface sense.

But I think there is a further underlying charge that is implicit. It is that this concern with nonhuman good is not really significant. What difference could it make to focus on so remote and lowly a topic? With the questions of human value so central and so pressing, what is the point of this phase of the theory?[12] Of course the conception of nonhuman good is not the only part of our theory of value, nor is it the major part. Something should be said, however, on why it is important.

One reason is the interest that arises from various theistic statements. The best example is the scriptural assertion that God made the world and saw that it was very good. Now from a philosophical standpoint, as distinguished from a religious mood, there is considerable curiosity about the meaning of such a statement. What, upon analysis, does it mean? So one important reason for our topic is speculative curiosity in the philosophy of religion. This reason, to be sure, will be of more interest for a theistic outlook, though I should think nontheists might also be interested in interpretations of items which they reject.

Aside from satisfying curiosity, theological or philosophical, I shall suggest several ways in which the concern with nonhuman good might redound indirectly upon human value.

First, nonhuman things can enhance the joy in appreciation. We already have models for this in well-known paradigm situations: esthetic contemplation of nature, gardening, craftsmanship in wood or stone, the tea ceremony, the everyday treasuring of favorite objects. Why would anyone want such value situations diminished rather than extended?

In the cultivation of this appreciation perhaps there is much to learn from the play and imagination of children among things. Of course, as adults we like to think we know better than children; we know, after all, that things are just things—lifeless, passionless, brutish bulks—though we admit there is potential here for tools, instruments, contrivances, gadgets, even toys. But I am speaking not of toys but imagination. Children have imaginative dramatizations with objects in themselves, and this quality of feeling may not be entirely unwholesome even when we have left childish anthropomorphisms behind. Call it a knowing, smiling, deliberate, jovial anthropomorphism, if you like; it is the feeling of appreciation, rather than anything propositional, that is important for value.[13] After all, we must live with things in any event.

Second, to know an object in Bergson's intuitional sense is to increase noetic awareness of the good. In our previous terminology, it can be said that such knowing, being a knowing of the perfection of things, would, when suffused with conscious favor, increase the beheld goods in the world. It would, in short, actualize more good in the universe, and this is to be encouraged by the principle of universal piety. Mr. Paul Weiss once asked quizzically, "If I know an apple, is it not ennobled in some way?" In the sense defined in chapter 10, this would be true from our point of view; that is, the inherent perfection of the apple would have one aspect of its potentiality for intrinsic goodness actualized through the noetic act, namely, its potentiality for becoming a beheld good for man through a relation to our conscious appreciation. We hold that things would have intrinsic goodness, apart from us, by being beheld goods to the divine consciousness; but they become intrinsically good for us only by entering into our conscious appreciation.

Lastly, while we should quite properly insist (a) that there is no independent warrant for focusing on nonhuman good, with complete disregard for problems of human life, and (b) that a concern with nonhuman good cannot solve the problems of human life, it may nevertheless be the case (c) that there is no ultimate solution to the problems of human life apart from some correlative value response to being as such. That is, there may be a relationship of valuational entailment between the human and the nonhuman, such that some affirmative response to the latter is a necessary, though not a sufficient, factor in the solution of man's distress and imperfection. I take it that this is what most of the religions of the world, and some of the philosophical systems, have been saying in widely different forms. Of course there is a latent danger of other worldly mysticism here if such an entailment is taken to apply directly to short-run situations or to suggest that social problems are not really social problems in the literal sense. But when we realize that the entailment points to a dimension of all experience and is not a specific solution to any specific problem, and that it is an ontological and not a technological consideration, the proposition seems well worth contemplating. It means that the response of the whole self to the whole of reality is relevant to every detail and that ultimate fulfillment requires such a response.

The Charge of Vagueness

Now we come to the charge that is perhaps the most difficult
to deal with. It says that perfection is simply too vague and indefinite a notion to be of any service in value theory, either theoretically or practically. Thomas Hill states this objection master-
fully when he surveys possible meanings of "human nature," the
perfection of which is supposed to define value, and finds them
all inadequate. I quote his analysis at length.

> While the definition of value of the natural law theories
> manages to avoid the error of attempting to reduce the mean-
> ing of good beyond the warrant of the data, it falls into
> the opposite error of excessive indefiniteness and even ob-
> scurity. What do these theories intend by that human nature
> in conformity to which they find the meaning of value?
> They never tell us clearly, and in any case the possible in-
> terpretations are not very promising for the discovery of a
> reasonably precise definition of value. Do they intend all
> that lies within man's nature wherever it is found? This
> would be of little help, for humanity includes moral mon-
> strosities as well as saints. Do they then mean what is *nor-
> mal* in human nature? If so, they still fail to furnish any
> even remotely satisfactory criterion of normality and, even
> if they did, this criterion, and not human nature as such,
> would then be determinative for ethics. Do they then mean
> that which ordinarily would be regarded as normal human
> nature? Such nature involves even upon its surface what im-
> partial common sense would recognize to be serious moral
> deficiencies and contains besides, as we have seen in study-
> ing psychological and sociological forms of ethical skepti-
> cism, grave submerged disorders both in thought and in
> deed that clearly preclude its representing a satisfactory
> ethical standard. Do our theories then intend by human na-
> ture such nature at its best? If they do, the whole question
> is still before them what *best* means. Or, if they define the
> human as the rational they have still to indicate the ends
> to which rationality is directed. Do they, finally, mean the
> metaphysical being of man apart from his special character-
> istics? If so, they intend something which cannot be
> defined at all, for what man is apart from his particular

characteristics it is clearly impossible to say. In any case, the
fact that something *is,* as we have had occasion to see, gives
it no special claim to value or to rightness.[14]

He concludes:

> Human nature is, to be sure, the primary medium in and
> through which values come into existence, and for this rea-
> son the attempt to attain them apart from knowledge of it
> is foolish; but human nature is not therefore the meaning
> of value any more than the sea is the meaning of the fish
> that swim in it and live by its products. We do not live in
> order to be human beings. Rather, already human beings,
> we live to obtain and share such enjoyable and worth-while
> experiences as human life may afford; and while knowledge
> of human nature can point out our capacities and limita-
> tions and help us to obtain values, provided we already
> know what they are, it cannot as such reveal values to us
> or inform us as to what they mean.[15]

I shall begin the reply to this criticism with a prefatory point.
There seems to be, in all the above analysis, a methodological in-
version attributed to natural law theories—with which our theory
has an affinity—that is not, however, accurate to the theories, or
at least to our approach. We do not set out to define "human
nature" *a priori* and then derive deductively a definition of "value"
and the principal values themselves from that starting point. Rather
we learn about the content of value and about human nature in-
ductively, experientially, just as Mr. Hill implies that we do. We
then go on, however, as he does not, to suggest that there is a
unifying connection, and that this connection is best expressed
by the generalization that human value is what fulfills man's
essential nature, his essential potentialities, that is, what actualizes
fully developed selves. From this point of view there is perhaps
not as much difference as might first appear between perfectivism
and other value theories of the type Hill supports. These theories
stress disparate intuited values, with no unifying thread except
that they are said to be intuited as intrinsically good. We stress,
on the other hand, a unifying, capstone category which is missing
from the related theories stressing isolated values. We want to
know what all these disparate values have in common, why they
are all in the picture, what they all lead to in the end, and we

find the answer in a modernized Aristotelian notion: the perfection of personality, the bringing to fruition of our true selves.

It is still incumbent on us, however, to indicate, in the wake of the criticism, what conception of human nature we are employing, in relation to which perfection is conceived. The answer is that Mr. Hill's last suggestion, about "metaphysical being," gives the best clue, though it is badly stated by him. Of course "metaphysical being" is an empty notion if it is defined apart from "particular characteristics," when these are taken to comprise the sum total of man's dispositions, activities, etc. But we have in mind the much more common, traditional idea of the essence of man, assuming a meaningful distinction between essential and accidental characteristics. We think the same distinction can apply to individuals, however, and not just to the species. For example, one who is born with considerable musical talent has that trait far more essentially in his being than a person who cannot carry a tune. We insist that essential and accidental characteristics of man are discovered through experience. For example, it seems clear, on this test, that reasoning is essential to man's nature while thumb-twiddling is accidental. We say, then, that the good of the individual consists in the perfection of essential capacities, plus such accidental characteristics as are compatible with this and are of interest to the individual as variety values.

One implication of this conception is that we do not know all about the essence of human nature as yet. We discover it progressively, or at least we have done so in part, though it is hardly inevitable that we shall continue and come to know all. Hill's criticism is quite right, therefore, in saying that we have not given a complete and exact definition of human nature in order to allow value deductions to be made from it.

I believe that this situation, even though it is not what we might wish from the standpoint of general human knowledge, is actually a strength in our theory because it is recognized frankly. It means we must have an openness to further insight about human nature and therefore about values. It is the intuitionist theories, it seems, that are virtually committed to a more closed position, since they seem to claim a once-for-all knowledge about values through self-evident intuitions. I, on the other hand, am not at all sure that when we know much more about human nature, and therefore more about the best life for man—or, if you like, the blessed life—this best life will correspond to our present

images. I am convinced, like the intuitionists, that some fulfilling values are permanently assured by our experience—reverence, appreciation, love, knowledge—else there would not be
partial knowledge but simply skepticism. But I allow for and
anticipate emerging insight about many phases of "the best
life for man."

Thus I have to say, in the end, that "human nature" refers to
the understanding of man's essence that would be had by an intelligent inquirer, if complete knowledge of man were attained.
Of course, in a theistic metaphysics it is believed that such knowledge is already present in the mind of God, although that specific
reference is not needed in a formal definition such as the one just
given. For us, then, the "perfection of man" must also have this
projective, suppositional status: it is what would be the case if
full human realization occurred.

The second quotation from Hill involves a rather elementary ambiguity. Certainly, as he says, "we do not live in order to be human
beings" if "to be human beings" means simply the factual matter
of "being living people, members of the human race," for of course
we are this already just by being born. But we *do* live in order to
be human beings if "to be human beings" has the normative meaning of "being fully what perfected human beings can be, instead of
just surviving as members of the species." Mr. Hill blatantly con-
fuses these two senses and attributes the wrong one to the natural
law theories.

There is a subsidiary criticism, which we should take note of,
based on the charge of vagueness and indefiniteness. It is that
evil tendencies become justifiable as much as good ones. That is,
not only is "human nature" too vague to be of any positive help,
but, being indefinite, it permits one to say that anything which
comes out of human nature, bad as well as good, is justified as
long as human nature is the criterion.

> To say that we should aim at becoming what we potentially
> are is not illuminating, since we are potentially evil as well
> as good and what we need is a criterion for distinguishing
> between them. The appeal to the "real" or "true" self is
> purely verbal, since the real self is not the self as it is but
> as it ought to be.[16]

I have dealt with this criticism at length, and in my opinion
sufficiently, in chapter 4[17]; so only two summary points will be
appended.

First, our position is that though many things may come out

of human nature, not all will perfect it. Rather, some will destroy it, and experience is a guide to this. All things may be possible, but not all are helpful. Moreover, to perfect one's nature one needs to exercise the capacity for choosing between good and evil, but one does not have to choose evil in order to do this. And if choosing evil helps to destroy oneself and others, that is a good reason for saying it is not justified. There is a serious confusion between saying (a) man may choose either good or evil and (b) evil tendencies are as essential to man's nature as good tendencies. Our theory requires only the former and specifically denies the latter.

Second, I believe there is a third logical intension, besides the two mentioned in the quotation, namely, "the self as it is" and the self "as it ought to be." This third intension is "the self as it *would be* in actuality if *essential* potentialities were realized." Thus the terms "real self" and "true self," which are normative and not simply descriptive concepts, refer not to any and all aspects of the person as he happens to display himself at present, nor exclusively to what ought to be in an independent moral sense (though that is true also), but to what would actually be the manifested self under specified conditions, namely, the realization of essential potentialities. Moreover, that self, we maintain, is what would be judged to be the person's true self by an impartial and fully knowing observer.

Individuality

The next criticism I shall consider would be extremely weighty indeed if it were to hold up. It is that any idea of perfection of man loses the individual, the very center of value, by submerging him under the general essence or type of man. This is the existentialist critique, and I present an incisive statement of it by Karl Jaspers.

> All ideals of man are impossible, because man's potentialities are infinite. There can be no perfect man. This has important philosophical consequences.
>
> (1) The true value of man lies not in the species or type that he approximates, but in the historical individual, for whom no substitute or replacement is possible. The value of each individual man can be regarded as unassailable only when men cease to be regarded as expendable material, to

be stamped by a universal. The social and professional types
that we approximate have bearing only on our role in the
world.[18]

I agree thoroughly with the emphasis in this passage upon the
value of the individual and on the location of value within the
individual. So strongly do I share this sentiment that if it could
not be incorporated into a perfectivist theory, I would consider
such an eventuality a good reason for modifying the theory and
not the sentiment. I could also agree that "there can be no perfect man," if this refers to what is actually possible under present
life conditions for ordinary mortals. But Jaspers seems to intend
this assertion to be the declaration of a logical impossibility
based on his understanding of man. Whether such a categorical
assertion can hold up depends on the essential nature of man and
on what is meant by "perfection."

This brings us back to the all-important and key first sentence
in the quotation, which claims that "all ideals of man are impossible, because man's potentialities are infinite." I take this assertion to mean that with infinite potentialities there are infinite
combinations of traits that make for individuality, and that therefore no notion of an ideal type or perfection is meaningful since
that would involve some uniform pattern instead of individuality.

Jaspers' statement, as given, forms an enthymeme, and we may
supply the missing premise to show the following syllogism:

All ideals of creatures with infinite potentialities are impossible
notions. (supplied premise)

All ideals of man are ideals of creatures with infinite potentialities. (immediate inference, by added determinants, from the
given premise)

Therefore, all ideals of man are impossible notions. (given conclusion)

Looking at the argument in this form, we may easily and
justifiably deny both premises.

To consider the second premise first, I see no reason to say,
and in fact do not know what it means to say, that man has infinite potentialities. Such a view certainly does not square with
any common understanding of man, since the awareness of abundant limitations is so obviously evident. Moreover, such a claim
seems to conflict with much psychotherapy, in which it is held
that to understand and deal with limitation is of paramount importance to man. Now in some respects, notably in creativity

and imagination, man has unknown and unforeseeable possibilities for expansion and novelty. But there is no ground for converting the understandable proposition that man has seemingly unending and indefinitely variable opportunities for development in some capacities into the totally mystifying proposition that man has infinite potentialities.

As for the first premise, I see no reason to think that, even if beings *did* have infinite potentialities, ideals that are common to them would be impossible notions. If men, for instance, had infinite potentialities, this would not deny that they would have much in common with all other men, and it certainly would not be a good reason by itself for saying that the best thing men could do would be to try to be as totally different from all other men as they possibly could. "Self-realization does not exclusively, or even primarily, aim at developing one's special gifts. The center of the process is the evolution of one's potentialities as a human being."[19] Though I would like to rephrase this sentence, I believe it has merit. If this is so, if we are to be normatively human, we need not be hindered by existentialist outbursts from holding that there are good metaphysical and ethical reasons for the belief that there are some common elements in the meaning of perfection of individual human beings.

We have not held, however, that this common meaning, applicable to all men and affording common ideals, absorbs the individual and eliminates individuality. Perfection pertains to individual potentialities and not only to the common human essence. There is plenty of potentiality in man for individualized achievements *of* the common ideals and for individual variety values *beyond* the common ideals.

I conclude that the contrasts involving the type and the individual, the universal and the particular, are not contradictory and should not be surrendered to existentialist overstatement.

A Theological Criticism

I now take note of a charge that might be forthcoming from a theological quarter, to the effect that "perfection," as I use it, is a metaphysical concept, originating in Greek rationalism, and, as such, completely misses the point of the religious norm for man. As Alan Richardson puts it: "The saint of New Testament theology is not a perfected being but a forgiven sinner."[20]

The answer to this is that "perfection," in our usage, is not intended to refer to, or suggest a substitute for, the ideal of religious aspiration. It refers not to the right or to virtue primarily at all, but to the good, the good for any being. Therefore the alleged opposition does not exist. There is no reason why a saint could not also be a perfected being in our sense. In fact, from a religious standpoint, one would think that saintliness would be a condition, not a replacement, for perfection.

Perfection and Time

The last criticism to be considered is that perfection is a static notion, suggesting an ideal of stoppage, of completion, of quiescent conclusion, an ideal which does not correspond to the temporal nature of existence. In the words of Whitehead: "The foundation of all understanding of sociological theory—that is to say, of all understanding of human life—is that no static maintenance of perfection is possible."[21] Now the question is whether anything we have said contradicts that "foundation . . . of all understanding of human life," which, we may add, is also the foundation of the nonhuman natural realm.

It seems to be no more than a historical coincidence that the idea of perfection became associated and then identified with the idea of timeless, motionless being, that is, with Plato's forms and Aristotle's unmoved mover. But the two ideas are not identical: "perfection" is defined as the fulfillment of potentialities and not as permanent immobility. And what if we suppose that "fulfillment of potentialities" includes the capacity to cope with all change constructively, to transcend the dormant and the static with brighter activity, to see ever new possibilities for joy and love and beauty? If this capacity were in the divine consciousness, as well as being the model for men to emulate, the idea of perfection would be freed from notions of stoppage and catatonic quiet. Such an idea of perfection, in fact, seems more consistent with the God and world we feel.

But the perfections we know most immediately are finite ones that have their day; that is what Whitehead is telling us in the quotation. So in one reading of the quotation he is saying not that perfection should not be our goal but that we cannot remain satisfied with finite perfections because there is something more ultimate than them, namely, the creative process. From this point of view, there is of course no inconsistency between perfection and time. Perfections may well be conceived as the immanent goal of the world process and our efforts, so long as we recognize that the process of creation moves always beyond these finite achievements and that we, in our thinking and our ideals, must do so as well.

At the same time we may believe that, even as the creative process moves forward, as ever new possibilities are envisioned and striven for by God and by those creatures who are themselves capable of creative endeavor, the whole is preserved in the supreme ideation and feeling with which God enfolds all possibilities and actualities. And we may believe that this is a supreme perfection, an awareness of which is adumbrated distantly and imaginatively in the experience of infinite piety in which such mysteries are held, even as they hold us spellbound.

Notes

Chapter 1: A Perfection Theory of the Good

1. Charles Hartshorne, *Man's Vision of God* (New York: Willett, Clark, 1941), app. to chap. 1.
2. Ibid., p. 7.
3. Ibid., p. 55.
4. In traditional language: "The individual, determined essence or the substantial core of the existence in its concrete individualization is meant, . . . since the universal as such cannot exist." *Philosophical Dictionary*, ed. Walter Brugger and Kenneth Baker (Spokane: Gonzaga University Press, 1972), p. 115.
5. Karen Horney, *Neurosis and Human Growth* (New York: W. W. Norton, 1950), *passim*.
6. Terence Parsons, "Essentialism and Quantified Modal Logic," in *Reference and Modality*, ed. Leonard Linsky (London: Oxford University Press, 1971), pp. 73–74.
7. Cf. Paul Weiss, *Man's Freedom* (New Haven: Yale University Press, 1950), pp. 197f.
8. See Erich Fromm, *Man for Himself* (New York: Holt, Rinehart and Winston, 1947).
9. William K. Frankena, *Ethics* (2d ed.; Englewood Cliffs, N.J.: Prentice-Hall, 1973), p. 91.
10. This definition is from A. C. Garnett and is discussed and qualified in chap. 5, below.
11. See chap. 10 and 11, below.

Chapter 2: Piety, Value, and Culture

1. The term "anthropocentric piety" is perhaps a more exact term, but I use the more familiar term "moral," employing it not in the strict sense of obligation but in the larger sense in which we might say, for example, that the values of human relatedness constitute the moral sphere of life.
2. Joseph L. Blau, *The Story of Jewish Philosophy* (New York: Random House, 1962), p. 288.

Notes to Pages 27-44

3. Huston C. Smith, *Religions of Man* (New York: Harper & Row, 1958), p. 251.

4. St. Bonaventure, *The Life of St. Francis*, chap. VIII, 1, trans. E. Gurney Salter and printed with *The Little Flowers of St. Francis* and *The Mirror of Perfection* (New York: E. P. Dutton, 1951), p. 461.

5. *Mundaka Upanishad*, in *A Sourcebook in Indian Philosophy*, ed. Sarvapalli Radhakrishnan and Charles A. Moore (Princeton, N.J.: Princeton University Press, 1957), p. 53.

6. Smith, *Religions of Man*, p. 168.

7. *Analects*, 1:2, in *A Sourcebook in Chinese Philosophy*, ed Wing-tsit Chan (Princeton, N.J.: Princeton University Press, 1963), pp. 19–20.

8. Epictetus, *Discourses*, book 2, 14, trans. P. E. Matheson, in *The Stoic and Epicurean Philosophers*, ed. Whitney J. Oates (New York: Random House, 1940), p. 308.

9. Marcus Aurelius, *Meditations*, book 2, 9, trans. George Long (Chicago: Gateway, 1956), p. 13.

10. Ibid., book 4, 23, p. 34.

11. Alvin Plantinga, *The Nature of Necessity* (London: Oxford University Press, 1974), p. 214.

12. Austin Fagothey, S.J., *Right and Reason: Ethics in Theory and Practice* (6th ed.; St. Louis: C. B. Mosby, 1976), p. 104.

Chapter 3: The Nature of Value

1. Wolfgang Köhler, *The Place of Value in a World of Facts* (New York: Liveright, 1938), p. vii.

2. John Rawls, *A Theory of Justice* (Cambridge, Mass.: Harvard University Press, 1971), p. 426.

3. Ibid., p. 427.

4. The term, in its general use, does not seem to antedate the nineteenth century.

5. This reduction to the biological seems to be Dewey's position, despite his commendable insistence on turning to the sources of valuation in order to discover the nature of value. See his *Theory of Valuation* (Chicago: University of Chicago Press, 1939).

6. I am aware of the criticism that might be made of this notion of theological need from the point of view of those interpreting Dietrich Bonhoeffer, namely, that modern man, "come of age," can get along very well in the world without God and has no need of him. God may remain an ever-present possibility for free choice but not a need. See Dietrich Bonhoeffer, *Prisoner for God: Letters and Papers from Prison*, trans. Reginald H. Fuller (New York: Macmillan, 1954), p. 122f.

It seems perfectly reasonable, however, to distinguish between sociopsychological and ontological needs and then to agree with the criticism, if the first sense is intended but not the latter. I think that what is really being objected to is the use of religion and "God" for problems that more appropriately call for human effort as a solution. A crutch is not needed when sturdy legs will do better. But this has nothing to do with whether man is ontologically unfinished without communion with God. It is in this latter sense that we speak here of theological need.

7. I am glad to enlist the support of Erich Fromm in the notion of universal needs as the basis of value. He says that "the concept of mental health follows from the very conditions of human existence, and it is the same for man in all ages and all cultures" (*The Sane Society* [New York: Holt, Rinehart and Winston, 1955], p. 69). He differs, however, in his classification of needs, for which see chap. 3 in the same work.

8. William E. Hocking, *Human Nature and Its Remaking* (rev. ed.; New Haven: Yale University Press, 1923), p. x (Italics in Hocking).

9. Incidentally, these examples afford good illustrations of both the conjunction of and the difference between the two sources of valuation. Although the coat, the wind, and the apple have properties that may serve needs, the properties of blueness, fragrance, and sweetness may be valued not because they are needed but because they please our sensuous or esthetic appreciation, i.e., our variety capacities.

10. Ralph Barton Perry, *General Theory of Value* (New York: Longmans, Green, 1926), p. 115.

11. A. C. Ewing, *The Definition of Good* (New York: Macmillan, 1947), p. 98.

12. W. R. Sorley, *Moral Values and the Idea of God* (Aberdeen: Aberdeen University Press, 1918), pp. 74–75.

13. Nicholas Rescher, *Introduction to Value Theory* (Englewood Cliffs, N.J.: Prentice-Hall, 1969), p. 56.

14. Ibid., p. 52.

Chapter 4: The Ground of Value Judgments

1. Nicolai Hartmann, *Ethics* (New York: Macmillan, 1932), 1:207.

2. Bertram Jessup, *Relational Value Meanings* (Eugene: University of Oregon Press, 1943), pp. 44, 47 (Italics in Jessup). .

3. See pp. 7–8.

4. The remaining paragraphs of this chapter are adapted from my article "Why Should I Be Moral?—A Reconsideration," *Review of Metaphysics*, 12, no. 4 (June 1959): 584–86.

Chapter 5: A Theory of Ethics

1. Arthur Campbell Garnett, *Ethics, a Critical Introduction* (New York: Ronald Press, 1960). Page references to this work are embodied in the text.

2. This does not involve metaphysical naturalism as a world view.

3. This is the most general meaning of "good," as explained in step 2, below.

4. A. Campbell Garnett, "Good Reasons in Ethics: A Revised Conception of Natural Law," *Mind*, 69, no. 275 (July, 1960):353.

5. Ibid., p. 355.

6. Ibid.

7. Ibid., p. 360.

8. Benevolence in this sense seems to me to be the typical virtue reflecting the spirit of utilitarianism, although I do not deny that *agape* may be compatible with utilitarianism.

9. John Rawls, *A Theory of Justice* (Cambridge, Mass.: Harvard University Press, 1971), p. 3.

10. Ibid.

11. Of the thinkers with whom Garnett associates his theory—Plato, Aristotle, Bradley, Fromm, and Dewey—I believe that the first three appeal in the end to enlightened self-interest. The matter is uncertain to me in Fromm because of his great emphasis on self-love. Dewey alone avoids this tendency, but only because of a pragmatism which does not allow him to take any principle as having permanent priority.

Chapter 6: The Classification and Choosing of Values

1. For a fine exposition of an Aristotelian conception of good, see Henry B. Veatch, *Rational Man: A Modern Interpretation of Aristotelian Ethics* (Bloomington: Indiana University Press, 1962), chap. 2.

2. For an effort to interpret the Kantian *summum bonum* along classical Aristotelian lines, see my article "Kant's Conception of Nonmoral Good," *Southwestern Journal of Philosophy*, 3, no. 3 (1972):7-19.

3. See W. D. Ross, *The Right and the Good* (Oxford: Clarendon Press, 1930), chap. 5.

4. See John Dewey, *Reconstruction in Philosophy* (New York: New American Library, 1948), p. 141.

5. "Reason can perceive the inner dynamism of the human being, his abilities and capacities craving fulfillment, and the suitability of certain acts and objects to contribute to the human being's fulfillment of his being." Austin Fagothey, *Right and Reason: Ethics in Theory and Practice* (6th ed.; St. Louis: C. B. Mosby, 1976), p. 102.

6. Immanuel Kant, *Lectures on Ethics,* trans. Louis Infield (New York: Harper & Row, 1963), p. 121.

7. See Rudolf Otto, *The Idea of the Holy*, trans. John W. Harvey (New York: Oxford University Press, 1958), chap. 8.

8. William Wordsworth, from "Lines Composed a Few Miles above Tintern Abbey."

9. Nicholas Rescher, *Introduction to Value Theory* (Englewood Cliffs, N.J.: Prentice-Hall, 1969), chap. 2.

10. A helpful alternative classification of principal values is given by William Frankena in his *Ethics* (2d ed.; Englewood Cliffs, N.J.: Prentice-Hall, 1973), pp. 87-88.

11. Peter A Bertocci and Richard M. Millard, *Personality and the Good* (New York: David McKay, 1963), in the title of chap. 15.

12. "The essence of a finite existent, because it is finite, lacks the fullness of existence; it includes only a small part of the possibilities of existence while the essence of God embraces the infinite fullness of existence." *Philosophical Dictionary*, ed. Walter Brugger and Kenneth Baker (Spokane, Wash.: Gonzaga University Press, 1972), p. 115.

13. See Josiah Royce, *The Problem of Christianity* (New York: Macmillan, 1913), vol. 2.

Chapter 7: Esthetic and Religious Value

1. The use of this Wittgensteinian notion outside the theory of meaning was first suggested to me by Abraham Kaplan, who employs it in his discussion of world philosophies in *The New World of Philosophy* (New York: Random House, 1961), pp. 7f.
2. John Hall Wheelock, *What Is Poetry?* (New York: Scribner's, 1963), pp. 21–22.
3. Gerardus Van der Leeuw, *Religion in Essence and Manifestation*, trans. J. E. Turner (New York: Harper & Row, 1963), 2:600.
4. Ibid., p. 636.
5. Ibid., 1:48 (Italics in Van der Leeuw).
6. Paul Weiss, *The God We Seek* (Carbondale: Southern Illinois University Press, 1964), p. 79.
7. Theodore Meyer Greene, *Moral, Aesthetic, and Religious Insight* (New Brunswick, N.J.: Rutgers University Press, 1957), p. 83.
8. Van der Leeuw, *Sacred and Profane Beauty*, trans. David E. Green (New York: Holt, Rinehart and Winston, 1963), pp. 285–86.
9. Alfred North Whitehead, *Adventures of Ideas* (New York: Macmillan, 1933), p. 348.
10. Van der Leeuw, *Sacred and Profane Beauty*, p. 284.

Chapter 8: Voices of Natural Piety

1. From "Pied Beauty," by Gerard Manley Hopkins.
2. From "In the Field," by Charlotte Mew.
3. From "The Invitation," by Percy Bysshe Shelley.
4. From "The Nightingale," by Samuel Taylor Coleridge.
5. From 'A Summer Day," by Alexander Hume.
6. From "Childe Harold," by Lord Byron.
7. "Finis," by Walter Savage Landor.
8. From "Answer to a Child's Question," by Samuel Taylor Coleridge.
9. From "Song of Myself" (30–31), by Walt Whitman.
10. From "To Blossoms," by Robert Herrick.
11. From "Song: Rarely, Rarely, Comest Thou," by Percy Bysshe Shelley.
12. From "May," by Edward Thurlow.
13. From "Blow, Blow, Thou Winter Wind," by William Shakespeare.
14. From "The Tables Turned," by William Wordsworth.
15. From "Lines Composed a Few Miles above Tintern Abbey," by William Wordsworth.
16. From "The Tables Turned," by William Wordsworth.
17. From "Influence of Natural Objects in Calling Forth and Strengthening the Imagination in Boyhood and Early Youth," by William Wordsworth.
18. From "Lines Composed a Few Miles above Tintern Abbey," by William Wordsworth.

19. Ibid.

20. From "The Tiger," by William Blake.

21. From "Christ and the Universe," by Alice Meynell.

22. From "The Darkling Thrush," by Thomas Hardy.

23. "World-Strangeness," by William Watson. This poem and the quatrain by Landor are the only poems quoted in their entirety. It is recognized, of course, that partial quotation does not do justice to the poetry; but our purpose in this chapter is philosophical and not poetic, so we beg forgiveness.

24. From "The Sea and the Skylark," by Gerard Manley Hopkins.

25. From "There Is No Natural Religion," by William Blake.

26. From "Ah! Sun-flower," by William Blake.

27. From "An Essay on Man," by Alexander Pope.

28. From "The World-Soul," by Ralph Waldo Emerson.

29. From "My Delight and Thy Delight," by Robert Bridges.

30. From "The Grandeur of God," by Gerard Manley Hopkins.

31. Huston C. Smith, *The Religions of Man* (New York: Harper & Row, 1958), pp. 231–32.

32. Wisdom of Solomon, 11:24. This and the other biblical quotations are from the R.S.V.

33. *The Song of God: Bhagavad-Gita,* trans. Swamy Prabhavananda and Christopher Isherwood (New York: Harper & Row, 1944), p. 145.

34. Muni Kirti Vijay, *Jainism in Nutshell* (2d rev. ed.; Bombay, 1957), pp. 4–5.

35. Kakuzo Okakura, *The Book of Tea* (Tokyo: Kenkyusha, 1962), pp. 1, 14, 80.

36. Smith, *The Religions of Man,* p. 185, and "Accents of the World's Philosophies," *Philosophy East and West,* 8, nos. 1–2 (April–July 1957):11.

37. John A. Hutchison and James A. Martin, *Ways of Faith* (2d ed.; New York: Ronald Press, 1960), p. 215.

38. Moses Maimonides, *The Guide for the Perplexed,* trans. M. Friedländer (New York: Dover, 1956), p. 274.

39. Martin Buber, *I and Thou,* trans. Ronald Gregor Smith (Edinburgh: T. and T. Clark, 1937), pp. 7–8.

40. St. Augustine, *City of God,* book 11, chap. 16, in *Basic Writings of St. Augustine,* ed. Whitney J. Oates (New York: Random House, 1948), 2: 158.

41. Ibid., book 12, chap. 5, 2:182.

42. Ibid., book 14, chap. 5, 2:244.

43. Boethius, "How Substances Can Be Good in Virtue of Their Existence without Being Absolute Goods," in *The Theological Tractates,* printed with *The Consolation of Philosophy* in Loeb Classical Library, trans. H. F. Stewart and E. K. Rand (Cambridge, Mass.: Harvard University Press, 1918), pp. 43–45.

44. Leo of Assisi, *The Mirror of Perfection,* 118, trans. Robert Steele, printed with *The Little Flowers of St. Francis* and *The Life of St. Francis* (New York: E. P. Dutton, 1951), p. 386.

45. Ibid., 120, pp. 387–89.

46. Meister Eckhart, "Being Is More than Life," in *Meister Eckhart,* trans. Robert Bernard Blakney (New York: Harper & Row, 1957), pp. 171–72.

47. Francis de Sales, *Introduction to a Devout Life,* pt. 2, XIII, ed. Thomas S. Kepler (Cleveland and New York: World, 1952), p. 115.

48. Blaise Pascal, *Pensées*, VIII, 579, trans. W. F. Trotter (New York: E. P. Dutton, 1908), p. 161.

49. Ibid., VII, 457, p. 128.

50. Henry Drummond, *The Greatest Thing in the World* (New York: Grosset & Dunlap, n.d.), pp. 18–19.

51. Robert L. Calhoun, *God and the Day's Work* (New York: Association Press, 1957), p. 105.

52. C. S. Lewis, *Letters to Malcolm: Chiefly on Prayer* (New York: Harcourt, Brace & World, 1963–64), p. 25.

53. Ibid., p. 55.

54. William Temple, *Nature, Man, and God* (London: Macmillan 1934), pp. 443–44. The first three quoted phrases within this passage are footnoted by Temple to Blake, Browning, and Genesis, respectively.

55. Fyodor Dostoyevsky, *The Brothers Karamazov*, trans. Constance Garnett (New York: Modern Library, n.d.), p. 351.

56. Thomas Hardy, *Tess of the d'Urbervilles* (New York: Harper & Row, 1891), pp. 152–53.

57. Herman Melville, *Benito Cereno*, in *The Works of Herman Melville*, vol. 10: *The Piazza Tales* (New York: Russell & Russell, 1963), pp. 168–69.

58. George Santayana, *The Last Puritan* (New York: Scribner's, 1936), p. 278.

59. Ralph Waldo Emerson, "History," in *The Complete Essays and Other Writings of Ralph Waldo Emerson* (New York: Random House, 1950), p. 128.

60. Emerson, "Character," in ibid., p. 372.

61. Nathan A. Scott, "The Meaning of the Incarnation for Modern Literature," *Christianity and Crisis*, 18, no. 211 (Dec. 8, 1958):174.

62. Miguel de Unamuno, *Tragic Sense of Life*, trans. J. E. Crawford Flitch (New York: Dover, 1954), p. 138.

63. Loren Eiseley, *The Firmament of Time* (New York: Atheneum, 1960), p. 8.

64. Thomas Traherne, meditation 341 in *Centuries of Meditations*, quoted in C. A. Coulson, *Science and Christian Belief* (Chapel Hill: University of North Carolina Press, 1955), p. 117.

65. James Jeans, *The Growth of Physical Science* (Greenwich, Conn.: Fawcett, 1958), p. 48.

66. George W. D. Symonds in an interview on the radio program *Viewpoint* (Jan. 7, 1964).

67. Harold K. Schilling, "Toward a Wholistic Ethic," in *Earth Might Be Fair*, ed. Ian Barbour (Englewood Cliffs, N.J.: Prentice-Hall, 1972), pp. 108–9.

68. Ian Barbour, "Attitudes toward Nature and Technology," in ibid., p. 151.

69. Jane Addams, *Twenty Years at Hull-House* (New York: Macmillan, 1910), p. 17.

70. These quotes are, respectively, from Marilyn Firth, Judith Pommer, Robert Hansen, Paul Anderson, and Martin Thomas.

71. John Dewey, *The Quest for Certainty* (New York: Minton, Blach, 1929), pp. 44, 267.

72. Bertrand Russell, "A Free Man's Worship," in *Selected Papers of Bertrand Russell* (New York: Modern Library, 1927), pp. 5, 14.

73. Archibald MacLeish, as quoted in *Time,* Dec. 22, 1958, p. 56.

74. Bertrand Russell, *The Scientific Outlook,* quoted in *The Examined Life,* ed. Troy Wilson Organ (Boston: Houghton Mifflin, 1956), pp. 178–79.

75. John Dewey, *A Common Faith* (New Haven: Yale University Press, 1934), pp. 25–26.

76. William Henry Hudson, quoted in John Dewey, *Art as Experience* (New York: Minton, Balch, 1934), p. 28.

77. In Pierre Teilhard de Chardin, *Hymn of the Universe,* trans. Simon Bartholomew (New York: Harper & Row, 1965), pp. 68–71.

78. Teilhard de Chardin, "The Spiritual Power of Matter," in ibid., p. 64.

79. Aristotle, *Nicomachean Ethics,* book 1, 9, in *The Ethics of Aristotle,* trans. J. A. K. Thomson (Baltimore: Penguin, 1955), p. 44.

80. Frederick Copleston, *Aquinas* (Baltimore: Penguin, 1955), p. 94.

81. Etienne Gilson, *The Philosophy of St. Thomas Aquinas* (Cambridge: W. Heffer, 1929), pp. 202, 205.

82. George Berkeley, *Dialogues between Hylas and Philonous,* in *The Works of George Berkeley,* ed. A. C. Fraser (Oxford: Clarendon Press, 1901), 1:422–24.

83. Stephen C. Pepper, "A Brief History of General Theory of Value," in *A History of Philosophical Systems,* ed. Vergilius Ferm (New York: Philosophical Library, 1950), p. 495.

84. John Stuart Mill, *On Liberty* (New York: Liberal Arts Press, 1956), pp. 75–76.

85. William James, *Pragmatism* (New York: Longmans, Green, 1907), p. 95.

86. William E. Hocking, *Science and the Idea of God* (Chapel Hill: University of North Carolina Press, 1944), pp. 17–18.

87. George Santayana, *Reason in Religion* (New York: Scribner's, 1905), pp. 190–91.

88. Sterling P. Lamprecht, "Man's Place in Nature," *American Scholar,* 7 (Winter 1938):77.

89. Alfred North Whitehead, *Science and the Modern World* (New York: New American Library, 1948), pp. 89, 95, 96.

90. Alfred North Whitehead, *Symbolism* (New York: Macmillan, 1927), p. 68.

91. Charles Hartshorne, "Science, Insecurity, and the Abiding Treasure," *Journal of Religion,* 38, no. 3 (July 1958):172–73.

92. Jacques Maritain, *Art and Scholasticism,* quoted in *The Problems of Aesthetics,* ed. Eliseo Vivas and Murray Krieger (New York: Holt, Rinehart and Winston, 1953), p. 67.

93. Samuel Thompson, *A Modern Philosophy of Religion* (Chicago: Henry Regnery, 1955), pp. 493–94.

94. C. A. Mace, "Some Implications of Analytical Behaviorism," in *Contemporary Philosophic Problems,* ed. Yervant H. Krikorian and Abraham Edel (New York: Macmillan, 1959), pp. 422–23.

95. George Edward Moore, *Principia Ethica* (Cambridge: Cambridge University Press, 1903), pp. 83–84.

96. Gabriel Marcel, *The Mystery of Being,* vol. 2: *Faith and Reality,* trans. René Hague (Chicago: Henry Regnery, 1951), p. 44.

97. Helmut Kuhn, *Encounter with Nothingness* (Chicago: Henry Regnery, 1949), p. 120.

98. J. Glenn Gray, "Heidegger's Course: From Human Existence to Nature," *Journal of Philosophy*, 54, no. 8 (April 11, 1957):202, 204, 206.

99. Paul Weiss, *Man's Freedom* (New Haven: Yale University Press, 1950), p. 105.

Chapter 9: Instrumental and Intrinsic Good

1. Edgar S. Brightman, "Freedom, Purpose, and Values," in *Freedom: Its Meaning*, ed. Ruth Anshen (Englewood Cliffs, N.J.: Prentice-Hall, 1940), p. 488.

22. Georg Henrik von Wright, *Varieties of Goodness* (London: Routledge & Kegan Paul, 1968), p. 50.

3. Ibid.

4. See Henry B. Veatch, *For an Ontology of Morals* (Evanston, Ill.: Northwestern University Press, 1971), pp. 105–20. For an argument that Aristotle's view of being and value is confused because it wavers between subjective and objective accounts of the good, see Whitney J. Oates, *Aristotle and the Problem of Value* (Princeton, N.J.: Princeton University Press, 1963).

5. Paul Tillich, *The Protestant Era* (Chicago: University of Chicago Press, 1948), p. 124. This passage illustrates both the affirmation of self-fulfillment as the ground of individual value and the denial of self-realizationist ethics in many of its forms. Since sacrifice of self is sometimes required, self-realization cannot be the only ethical principle of action, even though self-fulfillment is the individual ideal.

6. St. Thomas Aquinas, *Summa Theologica*, I, Q. V, A. 1, in *Basic Writings of St. Thomas Aquinas*, ed. Anton C. Pegis (New York: Random House, 1945), 1:42.

7. Ibid.

8. Ibid., I, Q. VI, A. 3, p. 53.

9. Ibid., I, Q. V, A. 5, pp. 48–49.

10. It must be remarked, however, that as knowledge increases, many things once thought inherently evil may be discovered to be good, as in the discovery of antitoxins. Perhaps many of our attributions of evil are the result of our lack of understanding.

11. This term is Köhler's. See Wolfgang Köhler, *The Place of Value in a World of Facts* (New York: Liveright, 1938).

12. W. M. Urban, *The Intelligible World* (New York: Macmillan, 1929), pp. 138–39. These quotations in their original context refer to a different theory of value from that presented above, but they are pertinent here as well.

13. Ibid., p. 139.

Chapter 10: The Goodness of Things

1. Charles Hartshorne, *Man's Vision of God* (New York: Willett, Clark, 1941), p. 11.

2. This statement holds on the assumption that the universe is composed of real individuals. If the universe were interpreted to be but a single individual,

as in extreme monism, the possibilities would of course be the same as they are for an individual entity as we have outlined them. I think the assumption is the most reasonable one to make; but I also recognize that dialectical defense of it would be necessary within the context of metaphysics.

3. Omitting, of course, the sixteenth possibility, namely, that something is neither good, nor evil, nor good and evil, nor neutral; for that would be tantamount to characterizing a nonentity, whereas we are concerned with actualities.

4. I proceed here with great trepidation in view of J. J. C. Smart's lines: "One very noteworthy feature which must strike anyone who first looks at the usual arguments for the existence of God is the extreme brevity of these arguments. They range from a few lines to a few pages. . . . Would it not be rather extraordinary if such a great conclusion should be got so easily?" "The Existence of God" in *New Essays in Philosophical Theology*, ed. Antony Flew and Alasdair McIntyre (New York: Macmillan, 1955), p. 29.

It would be extraordinary indeed. I can't help thinking, however, that it would be equally extraordinary if all the thought that philosophers have put into this subject should come to nothing because of an elementary logical puzzle that was mentioned in a few minutes on a quiet Sunday afternoon in Australia by Mr. Smart. Isn't it the case, really, that logical validity is not a matter of temporal or spatial extension? A syllogism is not invalid because it can be put on three printed lines, or even one. As for Smart's particular puzzle, I consider that subsequent discussion of the distinction between logical necessity and factual necessity takes care of it, though it doesn't of course establish any positive argument.

5. I have discussed this argument more fully and more formally in an article, "The Perfectological Argument," in *The Thomist*, 36, no. 3 (July 1972): 394-419.

Chapter 11: The Goodness of God

1. For an extended discussion of this problem, see the papers on "Theology and Falsification" by Antony Flew et al. in *New Essays in Philosophical Theology*, ed. Antony Flew and Alasdair McIntyre (New York: Macmillan, 1955), pp. 96-130.

2. For another statement of this problem and a line of solution, see John Hick, *Philosophy of Religion* (Englewood Cliffs, N.J.: Prentice-Hall, 1963), pp. 11-12.

3. Some of these characteristics are discussed from a historical perspective by Frederick Sontag in *Divine Perfection* (New York: Harper & Row, 1962).

4. Plato, *Philebus*, 60, in *The Dialogues of Plato*, trans. B. Jowett (New York: Random House, 1937), 2:396.

5. Pierre Teilhard de Chardin, "Mass on the World," in *Hymn of the Universe*, trans. Simon Bartholomew (New York: Harper & Row, 1965), p. 21 (Italics in Teilhard).

6. Teilhard de Chardin, "Christ in the World of Matter," in ibid., p. 54.

7. Charles Hartshorne, *The Logic of Perfection and Other Essays in Neoclassical Metaphysics* (La Salle, Ill.: Open Court, 1962), p. 36.

8. Ibid., pp. 37-38.

9. Ibid., pp. 38-39.

10. Oscar Cullmann, *Christ and Time*, trans. Floyd V. Filson (rev. ed.; Philadelphia: Westminster Press, 1964), p. 46.

11. Ibid., pp. 49-50.

12. Ibid., p. 63.

13. Hartshorne, *The Logic of Perfection and Other Essays*, p. 43.

14. See Pierre Teilhard de Chardin, *The Phenomenon of Man*, trans. Bernard Wall (New York: Harper & Row, 1962), book 1, chap. 2.

15. Ibid., p. 112.

16. Ibid., p. 217.

17. Ibid., p. 142.

18. Ibid., p. 146 (Italics in Teilhard).

19. Ibid., p. 183.

20. William Temple, *Nature, Man, and God* (London: Macmillan, 1934), p. 493.

21. Pierre Teilhard de Chardin, *The Divine Milieu*, trans. Bernard Wall (New York: Harper & Row, 1960), p. 67.

22. Teilhard de Chardin, *The Phenomenon of Man*, pp. 109-10 (Italics in Teilhard).

23. Ibid., p. 227.

24. Ibid., p. 111.

25. Ibid., p. 271.

26. Pierre Teilhard de Chardin, *The Future of Man*, trans. Norman Denny (New York: Harper & Row, 1964), p. 110.

27. Paul Weiss, *The God We Seek* (Carbondale: Southern Illinois University Press, 1964), p. 81.

Chapter 12: Objections Overruled

1. Charles Hartshorne, *Man's Vision of God* (New York: Willett, Clark, 1941), p. 11.

2. Walter Lippmann, *A Preface to Morals* (New York: Macmillan, 1929), p. 168.

3. John Compton in a letter dated Sept. 25, 1958.

4. Ibid.

5. Morris Ginsberg, "Psychoanalysis and Ethics," in *In Quest of Value*, ed. San Jose State College Associates in Philosophy (San Francisco: Chandler, 1963), p. 302.

6. Immanuel Kant, *Lectures on Ethics*, trans. Louis Infield (New York: Harper & Row, 1963), p. 26.

7. Karen Horney, *Neurosis and Human Growth* (New York: W. W. Norton, 1950), pp. 24-25.

8. Ibid., p. 86.

9. See Reinhold Niebuhr, *An Interpretation of Christian Ethics* (New York: Harper & Row, 1935), e.g., pp. 185f.

10. Lippmann, *A Preface to Morals*, pp. 10, 18, 62-63.

11. St. Augustine, *Confessions*, book 3, chap. 10, in *Basic Writings of St. Augustine*, ed. Whitney J. Oates (New York: Random House, 1948), 1:39.

12.   Roll on, thou ball, roll on!
          Through pathless realms of Space
                    Roll on!

What though I'm in a sorry case?
What though I cannot meet my bills?
What though I suffer toothache's ills?
What though I swallow countless pills?
             Never *you* mind!
                 Roll on!

—William Gilbert, from "To the Terrestrial Globe (by a miserable wretch)."

13. A poem which in my opinion expresses this spirit admirably, though I am puzzled by the ending, is "Everything" by Harold Monro.

14. Thomas E. Hill, *Contemporary Ethical Theories* (New York: Macmillan, 1950), pp. 254–55.

15. Ibid., p. 255.

16. Ginsberg, "Psychoanalysis and Ethics," p. 302.

17. See pp. 59–66.

18. Karl Jaspers, *The Perennial Scope of Philosophy*, trans. Ralph Mannheim (London: Routledge & Kegan Paul, 1950), p. 70.

19. Horney, *Neurosis and Human Growth*, p. 308.

20. Alan Richardson, *An Introduction to the Theology of the New Testament* (New York: Harper & Row, 1958), p. 237.

21. Alfred North Whitehead, *Adventures of Ideas* (New York: Macmillan, 1933), pp. 353–54.

Index